Only Good Comes to Me

Only Good Comes to Me

■ ■ ■

Introducing the LEP Frequency Tool

Ana Harvey

Waterside Productions

If you wish to contact the author please email lep@lepeducation.com or visit www.lepeducation.com for more information or a seminar schedule in your area. We love to hear from our readers!

Additional books by Dr. Harvey:
LEP Teaching Methods, Kendall Hunt Publishing, 2017
LEP Memory Hacks, Kendall Hunt Publishing, 2018

Cover credit 123RF.com

Little Flower Image credit @Shutterstock, Inc.

Printed in the United States of America

First Printing, 2021

ISBN-13: 978-1-951805-82-1 print edition
ISBN-13: 978-1-951805-83-8 ebook edition

Waterside Productions
2055 Oxford Ave
Cardiff, CA 92007
www.waterside.com

Acknowledgments

This book could not be possible without the help of my spiritual teachers and masters, who have patiently guided me in each page of the book. My love and gratitude to these incredible spiritual energies is difficult to be conveyed in just words. First and foremost, thank you, Jesus, for without you in my life, my heart could not experience the pure energy of joy, peace, love and service. Thank you, St. Germain, (through Godfre Ray King and Elizabeth Claire Prophet) for edifying the power of the Violet Flame, and allowing me to share it with the world, so that "all" may reap the benefit of Its use. Much gratitude is extended to Dr. Michael Newton, Edgar Cayce, Rosalind McNight, and Dr. David Hawkins, along with all my Angelic and Native American spiritual family, and the countless Helpers from beyond our physical realms, who have made this book possible. You will forever serve as my enlightenment, and encouragement. And lastly, to my spiritual mentors, Dr. Wayne Dyer, and Louise Hay, whom I tremendously respect and learned from, thank you for your ever-present guidance throughout the writing of this book. You have changed me as a person and redirected my life. You are my inspiration and my heart in the service of the light, and in the effort to raise the vibration of the world through expanding its consciousness. May I always be blessed with the presence of 'all' these loving energies in all my future work and my life as I complete my mission on earth. Namaste, I honor you, and 'see you on the other side.'

Additionally, I would like to once again acknowledge and thank all the writers I have quoted, those already listed, and all others within the pages of this book. An exhaustive search was done to determine whether previously published material included in the book needed permission to reprint. If there has been an error a correction will made in subsequent editions.

Dedication

This book is dedicated to my two sons, Adam and Jason Harvey, and all my animal companions who are the loves of my life, help me grow spiritually, and bring me joy beyond compare.

Table of Contents

PART 1
PREPARATION

The Big Picture

Even if at this moment you do not believe that energy work can transform your life, ACT as if you do! Follow the instructions in this book and soon your life will transform and you will live not only the life you desire but the future you want to face!

Dr. Ana Harvey

Why Shift into Higher Vibrational Frequencies?

You experience your reality by the speed of moving energy particles. Energy vibrates at many different frequencies. Each frequency field determines the form in which the energy appears in the physical world, which includes anything and everything and YOU. Thus, the frequency of your personal consciousness will determine your lived experiences. If you wish to change your lived experiences and create the life you wish to live and face, or eliminate any discordant energy in your life, you must first learn how to raise your vibrational frequencies to match that of your desire. In short, you must understand how to manage, direct and focus energy.

There is no magic involved. This is not fiction. This is not a trick, or a gimmick. This is science. This is the active law of physics, the *Law of Vibration, the Law of Polarity*, and the *Law of Attraction* at work. Miracles will be everyday occurrences because through the **LEP** (Lived Experience Phenomenon) **Frequency Tool,** which has the capability to expand your consciousness levels, you will have learned how to raise your vibrational frequency and direct energy to wherever you wish it to go. You will learn how to prepare for the journey ahead, send the right signals, and work with your authentic *'intention'* to raise your personal vibrational frequencies to create desires, heal and/or eliminate any discord in your life. In addition, it will give you an opportunity to balance your karma harmoniously outside of karmic cycles.

Karma is really just the **cause** and **effect** of energy. Generated karma is the sum of our deeds from all our past lives including the current life. Free will is caught in the events of cause and effect (Newton, 2009, p. 226). King (2012) clarified that the transmuting of karma through vibrational frequencies is a reordering of the balancing of the atomic activity. The electronic activity is always permanently balanced within itself. Discordant karma is the loss of balance of a particular element or atom. It is only when the electron becomes clothed in a low vibrational frequency that discord is possible and negative karma is generated. This book will instruct readers how to transmute negative karmic energy and offer them the opportunity to begin living from a clean slate.

Energy cannot be destroyed. Energy can only be transmuted through vibrational frequencies. This means you can change its shape and convert it to produce different outcomes, but you can never destroy it. You cannot destroy energy because the First Law of Thermodynamics (Conservation) clearly states that energy is always conserved, meaning that it cannot be destroyed. When you raise or decrease your personal vibrational frequencies you are, in essence, experiencing different aspects of your own being from different perspectives perceived in your consciousness in the current human earth time. Anytime you raise or decrease your personal vibrational frequency your life experiences change the aspects of the energy (your experience) based on the new frequency in your physical realm. Thus you either increase or decrease your power to use energy to create desires, eliminate discord or heal.

In divine reality there is no beginning and no end, as there is no time and space. There is no before or after. These are confining concepts created on the earth plane to create the illusions of time (McNight, 2013). That which we see and touch, including our human loved ones and all our experiences vibrates in an earth time and space level of consciousness (McNight, 2013). For example, on earth you think of death in terms of time, but from the timeless dimension death is just a change in the rate of vibration of the self's movement into a new existence, into a new consciousness (McNight, 2013), hence in death you are essentially still alive but your energy is now in a different form living in a different vibrational field. Death is nothing more than the movement of the molecules of the level of consciousness of the being experiencing it (McNight, 2013). Remember energy cannot be destroyed, it can only change form. Thus, the higher you rise in your vibrational frequencies in your current existence, the more rewarding and enriching your life will be in this physical time and space, and the higher your placement in the timeless spiritual realm once you leave this embodiment and change form from a physical body to a spiritual being.

This book offers you an indispensable life tool that can ensure that *only good comes to you*, and that in the physical realm of which you now exist you can shift and function on the highest level of your existence. The **LEP Frequency Tool,** if used properly, assures that new positive experiences will abound full of well-being, love, peace, joy, and prosperity. It will provide you every opportunity to not only live the life that you want in the here and now, but **live the future you want to face!**

The **LEP Frequency Tool** is a tool of consciousness. LEP Frequency Tool received its name because it deals with life phenomena of human being and has the ability to swiftly raise consciousness levels through vibrational frequencies in all who appropriately use the instrument. Once you master the use of the **LEP Frequency Tool** the energy around you will change. People will begin to respond positively to you. This includes individuals with whom you may have had trouble with in the past. Doors of opportunity will open, and your life will take on a different look, and feel. New uplifting thought and behavior patterns will emerge within you because you will live in a higher vibration which attracts higher prospects that are much more aligned with who you are, and will lead to more positivity and existence in a new reality where all things are not only possible, but probable.

The **LEP Frequency Tool** is a tool of consciousness and includes 3 key components: (1) the **Prep**; (2) the **Means** and; (3) the **Mechanisms**. The **Prep** prepares the readers for the shift into incoming higher energies. The **Means** identifies current personal vibrational frequencies, so that through the vehicle of the **Mechanisms** of *mental, emotional, physical/sensory* and *spiritual* energy they can be elevated to create whatever is desired in the readers' consciousness, and manifested it into their own physical reality. At the heart of the **LEP Frequency Tool** lie the divine energies of the **'I AM'** presence within the persons' causal body, and the **violet light**, which is the highest form of energy in the spectrum because it is the purest. The violet energy has the shortest wave length meaning that it is the closest to the Source Consciousness. The **violet energy**, also known as the **Violet Flame,** or the **violet light**, as depicted by St Germain, is known as the universal solvent or heavenly alchemy because it is of the highest vibrational frequency which makes it the most powerful in healing, creating of desires and releasing karma outside of karmic cycles. This means it clears the debt completely outside of the individual's' regular karmic activity.

Nothing is impossible for you. When you learn to listen, be in-tune and use these energies regularly there is no end to the powers to create your life that you will tap into. All readers are capable and have the ability to achieve what they desire in this lifetime through the use of the **LEP Frequency Tool** because regardless of your personal beliefs, societal outlooks, religious teachings, opinions and so on, science unequivocally concedes that that everything and everyone is 100% energy and that energy is available for your use. The **LEP Frequency Tool** will teach you how to focus, manage, and direct this energy in your daily life to sculp a new world for you to live in and experience. A world in which you will find joy, prosperity and a sense of an overall well-being. Sadness, unfulfillment, hopelessness, and frustrations will be a thing of the past because you will have learned how to tap into the energy of the Source Consciousness.

Max Planck, a German physicist, whose discovery of the 'energy quanta,' which won him the Nobel Prize in Physics in 1918, and earned him the universal regard and title of "father of quantum physics," and who was a hard-core atheist until his discovery, shared that "as a man who has devoted his whole life to the most clear-headed science, to the study of matter, I can tell you as a result of my research about atoms this much: There is no matter as such. All matter originates and exists only by virtue of a force which brings the particle of an atom to vibration and holds this most minute solar system of the atom together." This means that matter, of which all that is in the universe, including us, is energy that comes from a Source Consciousness/God from whom we all originate, and whom the Source Consciousness also Is and uses to create, is the same energy that we can command to create any constructive desire in our life. No exceptions.

Essentially, Planck validated that the *characteristics of everything* actually change at the molecular level because since everything is energy it can be directed and focused. Form of people and everything in the universe is determined by the speed of vibrations, meaning, how you look like and what shows up in our life. Essentially, your human form appears as so because of the energy waves within your vibrational patterns of alignment and the characteristics of everything that we draw to us is in response to, and of the same frequency in which it was sent. If the energy we send is in higher vibration it must return to us in our physical experience in that same frequency, as energy must obey the **Law of Vibration, and Law of Attraction**. These laws of physics are the most powerful systems human beings can use when working with energy for manifestation purposes, and are integral in bringing intentions from the consciousness into physical realities simply by aligning with its frequency. It is quite simple, you attract to you,

Only Good Comes to Me

who and what you are. What you think about you become and achieve since thoughts are the energy that activate vibrations.

Energy is all there was, is, and ever will be. Since human beings are 100% energy, they have full use of its power. Your personal vibration determines the level of power available for your use, which in turn effects the miracles that you can create in your life. Human beings vibrate at a certain frequency and experience life within that frequency through the **mental, emotional, physical/sensory** and **spiritual** consciousness vibrations.

In order to create and experience a better life you have to move up in vibration in all **4** of the **consciousness frequencies.** This is because all 4 mental, emotional, physical/sensory and spiritual consciousness domains are needed to activate peak vibrational frequencies that are required to create from the conscious mind into physical realities. A high vibration in one area, such as the **mental consciousness** but a low vibration in the **emotional consciousness** identifies that you are vibrating higher in your thoughts, but are unable to maintain that high vibration in your feelings. Meaning that even though you may be able to logically think things through, you may still cycle in emotional immaturity. This is a misalignment of energy and results in lower overall personal vibrational frequency, and causes a decrease in the power of manifestation because in order to manifest thoughts, and images in the mind must be supported by strong feelings.

Feelings are crucial in the manifestation process of bringing ideas from the consciousness into your physical reality because they **activate** the **Law of Attraction**. Thus, mental and emotional consciousness fields must be aligned to produce quick and tangible results. Strong, supportive feelings must always align with thoughts and images that are placed in the mind. If reinformed through physical (effort and action) and spiritual (confidence that the universe can and will provide) energies, without fail, you will produce desired outcomes because you have met the frequency of the desires you wish to see in your life.

Since energy is an electrical vibration it cannot be fooled. Any misalignment of energy in one field affects the personal overall vibratory

8

frequency of the individual. Thus, your entire molecular structure is affected when one or more consciousness fields is not operating within its proper vibrational frequency. Misalignment in the consciousness fields delays manifestation of desires into physical realities until such a time that they do align. The Law of Attraction and Vibration will ensure that this is so. This is not a personal decision. This is impersonal science that works strictly within universal laws.

Although the collective vibrational frequencies offer premium results small gains can be made in each of the vibrational fields individually. Raising personal vibrations in one of the **mental, emotional, physical/sensory** and **spiritual** consciousness frequencies **increases** the frequency and power in that domain. If the person moves up in frequency it means that he or she is vibrating at higher speeds within that domain. This means that if you have raised your mental frequency you will have an expanded mental consciousness domain as a result, and may increase your problem-solving abilities (think things through and come up with a better solution), but you still may not be able to process the information emotionally on a rational level, which will hinder the manifestation process.

Anytime there is a decrease in any one field, there is a lowering of frequency in that domain. For example, through depression, anger, resentment, guilt, regret, hopelessness, lack of faith and so on it means the speed of the vibration of person has slowed and he or she is falling into denser, lower energies. The person's life experience will reflect the lowered energy which usually results in heavier outcomes in that domain and vast decreases of power to manifest collectively. In the low vibratory frequencies, people will find much less control over life, and what appears in their physical reality because the lowered domain will reflect lowered energy and trigger lowered frequencies in the other domains.

It is vitally important to be cognizant of your thoughts, the images in your mind and feelings because every moment you are alive, they determine your lived experience. Increasing personal vibrational frequencies will improve peoples' lives, grant them control of their life, eliminate fear, bring joy, and offer the confidence and the power to create the future they want to face. But many people still question this wisdom, and some still refuse to believe that creating the life they wish to live cannot be possible for them. That creating as the Source Consciousness is outside of their capability or they are unworthy of such power.

Dr. David Hawkins renowned author, lecturer and expert on mental processes indicated that there are generally two types of people in the world; the believers and non-believers. To the believers, everything stems from good faith, and is probably true until proven false, and to the non-believers nothing is true unless proven so (Hawkins, 2002). Hawkins (2002) further contended that, "the optimistic manner stems from self-confidence, while the pessimistic approach stems from fear." This has much to do with the persons' overall vibration. If he or she is vibrating in low dense energies of lack and survival, usually frustration, anger, sadness and fear reign in that domain. Life experiences are usually filled with lower, less desirable outcomes because that is what they expect and the energy delivers. People in low vibrations are stuck in pessimistic outlooks believing there is no way out and continuously cycle in lack and survival energies until they realize that they have the power to completely change their life.

Believing one does not have control of their life is flawed thinking. Not only is there a way out of any lower vibration, but it can be achieved with relative ease. Higher frequencies breed self – confidence, and the unshaken belief that when applying the principles of energy correctly, there are no limits to creating the life you wish to live. White (1965, p. 9) contended that "fully half the things we do daily as a matter of course today, would even as recently as two centuries ago, have been considered magic without explanation, except as the product of occult forces … The continuity of history is unbroken in that respect … The superstition of the past is the science of the present, the prover of the future … as knowledge overtook these things and found them to be natural law … as humanity absorbed them and they became commonplace of existence" (White, 1965, p. 9). Thus, as history illustrates, often people must learn to believe and try things they don't quite understand.

NEVER FEAR. Illumination, knowledge and power will come with effort but a belief system that you can create anything you desire is also necessary. Belief turns into faith; faith turns into knowing. Knowing means that there is nothing unnatural about using energy to create, that you are already doing this every day, but now you will do it with a specific purpose. You understand that you can mastery energy and achieve unification with the highest powers of the Source Consciousness/God, the power that is now at your full disposal. Again, it is the same power that the Source uses to create, and this power is available to all that understand and work with energy.

The direct benefits of health, well-being, abundance, love and prosperity to people living in higher vibrational frequencies were confirmed by many other scholars, scientists and experts in the field. Edgar Cayce noted that "life in its manifestation is vibration." For many decades, Edgar Cayce, known as the "father of holistic medicine," and a well-documented psychic, referenced vibration as a powerful tool for healing, general health, and the treatment of illnesses and diseases. Cayce particularly emphasized the importance of thought in keeping healthy and vibrating in high frequencies (Cayce & Cayce, 2004). He was convinced that every human thought had the capacity to create either miracles, or crimes because of the impact of their vibration, and contended that if a person opens themselves in an intentional way to increase their vibrations, wonderful things can be created. He often admonished, "know that thoughts are things, and as their currents run ..." (Cayce, 2010) so are their matching outcomes. Thus, **people should** always **monitor** and **govern** their **thoughts** and ensure that they are of the highest order, meaning the highest vibration.

Higher thoughts, activate higher emotions, bring awareness and sharpen senses. The higher you shift in your energies, the quicker the upsurge to a higher frequency and access to the power of rapid manifestations. Dr. Wayne Dyer, an influential teacher, and the 'father of motivation' shared in his lectures that if you want something, since everything comes in response to vibration, shift out of lower vibrations into the higher frequencies and live and make decisions from those mental and emotional planes.

If you do, your life will immediately improve in every way because you will attract what you want by aligning yourself with the same frequency of your desire. Hawkins (2002) in his book, *Power vs Force,* contended that your vibration or level of consciousness is more important than you realize because you can only create from the frequency that you exist. Hawkins (2002, p. 37) further asserted that, 'man is immobilized in his present condition by his alignment with enormously powerful attractor energy patterns, which he himself **unconsciously** sets in motion. Being in a bad mood, or feeling unworthy sends energy signals unconsciously to the universe and they are registered as low vibrations. Through the power of the Law of Attraction and Vibration, these low energies will be returned to you, in one swift boomerang reaction and you will continue to be in a bad mood, until you raise your vibrational frequency. In order to **increase** your **power,** you must raise your vibrational frequency, **consciously** through your mental, emotional, physical and spiritual consciousness fields and the LEP Frequency Tool will guide every reader to do just that.

Your vibrational frequency determines your collective consciousness expansion and thus the power you can access to create, and the speed in which your desire manifests. Similar to the string theory which theorizes that the primary forces of nature are just different creations of the same vibrations within one Source Consciousness, the law of nature confirms that everything has a vibration and that all vibrations come from one central vibration manifesting in various forms. Every person lives and vibrates at their own rate, but we are of 'one' consciousness, of the same Source just on different vibrations so we, and everyone around us, appears in various energy forms as we move about our business on the planet either creating our own lack and survival or abundance, peace and joy.

The existence of Source Consciousness, God, Allah, Universal energy, regardless of the name or label assigned to this powerful force of ALL THAT IS is often a contentious subject of debate. However, even science confirmed the existence of a Universal Source of power, a divine

Consciousness that controls all life. The scientific evidence that God, or the Source exists was presented by Dr. Max Planck (1959) in his remarks when explaining the existence of Spirit. Dr. Planck was adamant that an omnipotence Consciousness controlled human kind, the universe and eternity, and that "we must assume behind this force (energy) the existence of a conscious and intelligent spirit. This spirit is the matrix of all matter" (Planck, 1959). This spirit is the Source Consciousness, the pure energy of ALL that is. Thus, since every human being comes from that Source Consciousness, every human being is 100% energy and of the same energy as the Source Consciousness and has access to the use of Its power according to his or her vibrational frequency. There is no favoritism involved. There is no bribery or like or dislike. No one is loved more or less. It is science. It is all the energy of vibration.

You reap what you sow. The faster the vibration, the higher the consciousness and the speed in which you can produce your wishes through an alignment of the **mental, emotional, physical/sensory, and spiritual energy** fields. Rising into higher frequencies assures a higher consciousness which offers answers and solutions beyond your current understanding to any of your problems. No need to turn to psychics, astrologers, tarot or fortune tellers and the like for tales of direction to your life, or outcomes of your potential future which will only confuse you or cause you to make wrong decisions based on the wrong information you received from people who have no idea what your future holds, what you really want, or what is best for you.

You hold your own future by working with energy. Your lived experiences are determined by how you use that energy. It is a conscious process. When you use the **LEP Frequency Tool** as instructed you will live from your highest consciousness in a world where you can get all the answers you seek. You will create and recreate your life the way you wish to live it, without limitations, or restrictions. You will hold the ability to reinvent your reality, eliminate that what you don't want, and manifest what you do to your specifications. You will create the future you want to face! If you are still reading, this book is resonating with you, and is for you, whether you think so at the moment, or not.

13

People often move in a hypnotic state outwardly meeting their responsibilities, completing their to do lists and trying to do the best that they can. But inwardly they know they are in search of a better life experience. In one of his lectures, Dr. Wayne Dyer asked, "do you want to live 90 years? Or do you want to live 1 year, 90 times? Take a moment, and think about that. What is your answer? Is living one year 90 times really living and taking advantage of this beautiful experience called life? Or are you just existing? Or are you living a life of endurance? Is endurance joy? No. Endurance is different than living. Endurance is a lack of growth; it is a stale existence. **Think about it**. What is your life like? The **LEP Frequency Tool,** if used correctly, will provide you the opportunity to live your best life every year! Not to endure, but to live your life with passion and excitement and not in a hypnotic trance of moving about in life fulfilling never-ending responsibilities.

Referencing the material from '*The Life and Teaching of the Masters of the Far East,*' by Spalding (1964), Dr. Wayne Dyer warns humanity that we are indeed moving in hypnotic trances, "it seems that humanity is running on automatic pilot. The average individual is in a hypnotic state...that is the majority of men and women are not living life as it was intended at all, not one in a million feels the freedom to live how he inwardly feels he should live. He has come under the world's opinion of himself and this opinion is what he obeys, rather than the laws of his own being." Dyer, continued that, "in this respect and to this degree, he is living under a hypnotic spell. He lives under the delusion that he is a mere human being living in a merely material world and only hopes to escape it when he dies and goes to what he calls heaven. This is **not** the determination intended in the plan and purpose of life. Obedience to one's inner nature, the expression of life, as he instinctively feels it ought to be expressed is the very foundation of life" (Dyer's summarization from *The Life and Teaching of the Masters of the Far East*).

This book presents **readers** the opportunity to live the life they were meant to live, and the future they want to face! Within the pages of this book the readers will use the **LEP Frequency Tool to pinpoint** where they live whether in the **Lack and Survival, Dedication,**

Absorption or Connection Consciousness fields. **They will identify** and **assess** their **personal vibrations** in each area of the **mental, emotional, physical/sensory and spiritual consciousness**
frequencies so that they can use, manage, direct and focus energy
to increase their personal vibrational frequencies effectively; thereby
quickly increasing their power to create any constructive desire.
Moreover, they will master the use of the divine energies of the I AM
presence, and the Violet Flame properties which are so integral to the
creation, manifesting and healing process.

It is important to understand the process of ascending into higher
frequencies, regardless of where you find yourself (Lack and Survival,
Dedication, Absorption, and Connection Consciousness). All levels of
consciousness express themselves in form. Each one is a stepping
stone. When you shift out of one frequency and align with a higher
frequency, you have transformed into a higher vibration of expanded
consciousness, thus more power is available to you. Shifting means
transforming. Alignment means you are in harmony. When you are
transforming and aligning, you are moving through the energy fields
of Ascension. The fields of ascension hold fractures of energy that
must vibrate at the same frequency for progress to be made. The
fractures that are needed to be in harmony so that you can raise your
vibrational frequency and ascend are the mental, emotional, sensory/
physical, and spiritual energies. The combination of these energy
fields is the requirement for a collective (quickening) rising of overall
frequencies that will propel you to highest energies. Thus, it is the
alignment (harmony) of the fractures that will move you through each
consciousness field until you reach the Connection Consciousness
and are ready to live in the ascended reality where life is bliss, "all" is
possible, and the power of the Source Consciousness is fully available for your use for any constructive desire.

When readers are diligently working with the parameters of
energy there are no bounds to what can be achieved. There are no
limits to heights that can be reached or the power of creation that
can be attained with the proper understanding of how to use the **LEP**

Frequency Tool of consciousness to increase personal vibrational frequencies and create any constructive desire. This book provides clear directions and guidelines, and offers visual flow charts which includes information that can be easily followed on how to raise, and maintain high vibrational frequencies, permanently. Not only in this lifetime, but the progression in frequency attained in this embodiment will carry over to the spiritual realms, thus assuring a higher place-ment of your soul-self in the divine realms.

Again, it is worth noting that if followed correctly, The **LEP Vibrational Frequency Tool** will assist readers how to swiftly **raise** their **personal vibrational frequency**. Live and make decisions from that higher plane and effortlessly direct energy from their conscious-ness to manifest desired realities and live the life they wish to live and the future they want to face every minute that they are alive. Moreover, the various and user friendly **LEP Vibrational Frequency Assessments** and **Supplements** included in this book make it easy to always identify **current** and **overall** personal frequency. The read-ers can select and assess a particular vibrational frequency in each of the **mental, emotional, physical/sensory** and **spiritual** conscious-ness, individually, and identify the frequency of their vibration in that field, or at any giving moment determine their overall personal vibra-tional frequency.

The information within these pages is scientifically derived, and objectively organized, but it was also personally experienced. Additionally, because LEP books are meant to teach, educate, and use as guidance materials, they are written in a rhetorical manner, with a deliberate attempt to reinforce information to memory. This tac-tic to readers may seem repetitive in nature, but the repetition is a lit-erary device that makes the concepts clearer and more memorable. Thus, this *Only Good Comes To Me* (#OGCTME) self-development book is written in a way that allows for understanding and quick imple-mentation of the **LEP Frequency Tool** to immediately change their lives through the readers' own consciousness.

If you are unhappy in any way in your life, this book is for you. You deserve your "happily ever after." So, don't spend every day reliving your past, or wonder how your life could be different. The **LEP Frequency Tool** is a powerful consciousness instrument that, if followed correctly, can produce tremendous results with great speed. But it does not work alone. It needs the readers to provide the effort, determination and the 'will' to create the life they wish to live and the future they want to face through activating higher vibrational frequencies, and making a commitment to working and living within the higher consciousness energy fields. The time is now! I applaud you for having the courage, confidence, strength and determination to make your "happily ever after" happen without further delay. #onlygoodcomestome

Introduction of the LEP Frequency Tool

The **LEP Frequency Tool** is a tool of consciousness. Within the human system there are various dimensions of vibrational frequency consciousness' that the **LEP Frequency Tool** can employ to access immense power that was and always will be available for each person's use. The consciousness levels include the mental, emotional, physical/sensory, and spiritual vibrational frequency domains. These energies control many points of consciousness throughout the person and can be tapped into to help bring desires from the consciousness into physical realities. The key to gaining power to use energy to create desires through these consciousness levels is the effectiveness of alignment of the energy systems in which they are utilized.

Consciousness, itself is invisible and has no form but it is extremely powerful once people understand how to raise its vibrational frequency to meet their needs. The problem is that humans are taught what to think instead of how to think (McNight, 2013). Knowing how to think, meaning raising your collective vibrations within the mental, emotional, physical and spiritual consciousness frequencies through the LEP Frequency Tool will open a world where miracles are every-day experiences.

There is no lack. Life was never meant to be an exercise in sur-vival. There is only the inability in the consciousness to perceive that the power is there for the taking but the energy system of all con-sciousness frequencies must be synchronized in the same frequency for the taking to occur. If for example, thoughts and emotions are out of alignment, they can block the frequency from forming an intent to be sent and desires have no chance of being manifested on the earth plane. Meaning if you think you can do something, but feel that you can't, your consciousness fields are out of alignment which can greatly delay or completely cancel out the manifestation process. If the systems are effectively aligned, they can function at top speed and bring desired manifestations from the consciousness into physi-cal realties very quickly.

There are no limitations in the physical universe. If the mind that has been trained what to think, or is taught belief systems with limitations, in that mind limitations are experienced (McNight, 2013). McNight (2013) contents that the power of the human mind becomes that which it thinks itself to be. Think high, think positive, think prosperity, think health, think life without limit. At the base of every human system lays the principle of universal knowledge that is available to all human beings because every cell in the body is a pattern of the whole, hence it has access to the whole (McNight, 2013), thus think BIG.

Each soul has its own vibratory soul print. Each person's vibra-tory rate is completely different from any other's just as all fingerprints are uniquely different (McNight, 2013), but each person uses the **LEP Frequency Tool** in the same way because the **LEP Frequency Tool** is a tool of consciousness. It uses and responds effectively to all vibratory consciousness frequencies. To access your personal power of creation and learn to align vibrational frequency between all domains of the mental, emotional, physical/sensory and spiritual frequencies for intended desires in the mind to be brought forth into physical realities, consciousness tools, such as the **LEP Frequency Tool,** must be used without delay.

Creation of your perfect reality and living a life *well lived* is your birthright. If used properly, the **LEP Frequency Tool** is a superlative consciousness instrument in changing peoples' lives with great speed, and in creating the future they wish to live. It is very easy to use, once a full understanding of how to work with energies to raise vibrations is attained. The LEP Frequency Tool offers you the opportunity to claim your birthright without fear and limitation, and create miracles in your own life because it teaches the readers the correct use and application of energy in the consciousness, to produce tangible results in physical realities. Miracles are manifestations of directed energy and can be easily created through the appropriate alignment of vibrations of thought, imagery in the mind and strong supportive feelings backed by effort through physical action and faith and confidence in spiritual universal laws.

The LEP Frequency Tool of consciousness offers readers the training and freedom to create their own wishes and lived experiences. It offers the exploration of limitless boundaries of higher frequencies which is the birthright of every human being. There really is no space or time when working with higher vibrations. Spatial concepts are only the illusion of earth life. In truth, a special flow of energy is released when you work on the assumptions that there are no limits (McNight, 2013) to what you want to appear in your experience. When you work with the LEP Frequency Tool do not worry about time because it is a tool of consciousness, just have faith that it is working on your behalf, and that your manifestations will appear in their perfect time.

The **LEP Frequency Tool** of consciousness includes three parts. The **Prep**, the **Means,** and the **Mechanisms**. All readers should begin with the **Prep** instructions included in this book. It is recommended that readers complete the Prep Assessment (A1) to gauge their Preparation of their current mental and inner alignment ***before*** working with higher energies. Through the practice of **Prep**, individuals learn how to raise their vibrations in various energy consciousness domains by understanding and adjusting thought patterns, emotions and signal transmissions so creation of desires is possible.

Thoughts and emotions are an internal structure. They can only be perceived through an internal process. For example, personal thoughts and emotions housed in the human body only exist for those who are experiencing them (McNight, 2013). They do not exist for those who do not experience their existence. Thus, they are only real and can used by the person who is thinking, feeling and acting upon them. Hence knowing how to align them internally vastly assists in the mental and inner preparation required to move the person into higher energies with greater speed. Meaning that outer manifestations are created by internal structures. Knowing how to prepare for higher energies places individuals in a much stronger position when the creation of manifestation process has begun. Do not skip the Prep! You must prepare for the journey ahead!

The **Means** offers the **how**. The **Means** includes the energies of **thoughts, images**, and **feelings** and identifies the person's current vibrational field of *Lack and Survival, Dedication, Absorption or Connection* consciousness. The vibrational fields within the **Means** energy activates the **mental, emotional, physical/sensory** and **spiritual frequencies** in every person, and uses them as **Mechanisms** to either live a life of lack and survival, or a life of well-being and abundance. Thus, the **Mechanisms** provides the **way** in which the **4 consciousness** frequencies of **mental, emotional, physical/sensory** and **spiritual** energies can be aligned to create desires in a conscious mind, and produce tangible results in a physical world.

Any rise in frequency, in any of the mechanism's **4 consciousness frequency** energies opens the door for profound changes within the persons' life within that energy field. However, in order to move to the next frequency and maintain its higher vibration, a collective alignment of all **4 mental, emotional, physical/sensory** and **spiritual** consciousness frequencies is necessary. Meaning that moving up in one energy field such as mental will bring some expansion of consciousness but it is not enough to elevate the person to a higher frequency that can tap into greater power, as this can only be done through a collective rise in all 4 consciousness frequencies. Thus, it is vitally important to continuously work with the energy and follow instructions in this book to raise all your frequencies in the, mental, emotional, physical/sensory and spiritual consciousness domains so that you may have access to greater power that is waiting for your use.

The **LEP Frequency Tool** is extremely beneficial to all readers who want to use the power of energy to change their life because it assists in creating energy patterns that are harmonious between themselves and *all* consciousness frequencies. This allows for unlimited potential and power to flow to you. As you live and move in higher energies, higher energies are attracted to you, which greatly improves your life and assists in your creation process. With continued application, great strides can be made. To stay on track each reader should periodically assess their vibrational frequency by completing the included **Assessments** and **Supplements**.

It is not difficult to identify personal vibrational frequencies. Anyone reading this book who takes the various **LEP Vibrational Frequency Assessments** and **Supplements** included in this book will reach their own conclusions, based on their own results. The included assessments are worthwhile, as they will illuminate the path ahead, and will always reveal your current personal vibrational frequency so that you can make the necessary improvements and course redirections. All the assessments are conducted in real-time and will include results only for the current measure. At each completion the assessments are the same, but your answers may not be depending on your mood, alignment of your various energy fields and so on. It is important to address any decrease in vibrational frequencies immediately. (It is recommended that readers assess themselves regularly by completing the assessments often, and use the supplemental information to add to, and enhance their life experience).

LEP FREQUENCY TOOL

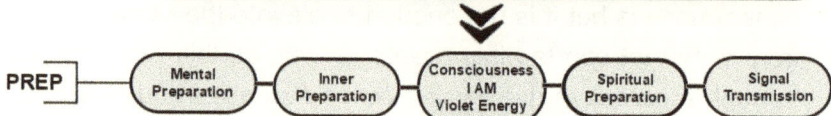

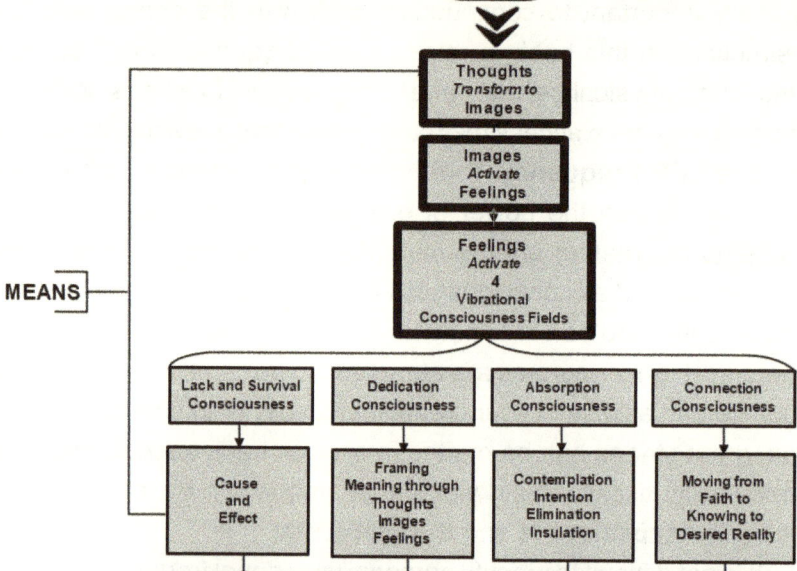

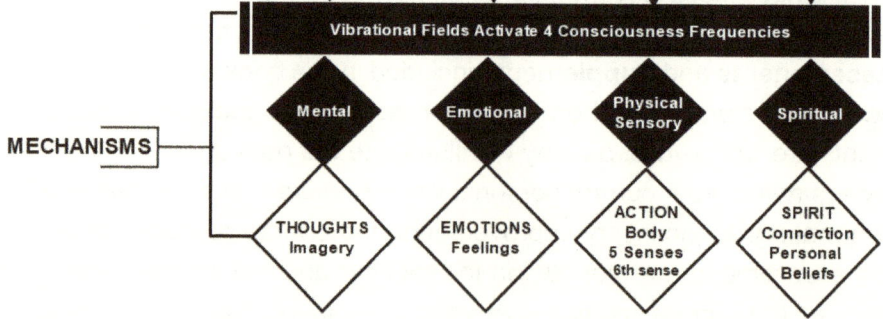

PREP

| Mental Preparation | Inner Preparation | Consciousness I AM Violet Energy | Spiritual Preparation | Signal Transmission |

MEANS

Thoughts *Transform to* Images

Images *Activate* Feelings

Feelings *Activate* 4 Vibrational Consciousness Fields

| Lack and Survival Consciousness | Dedication Consciousness | Absorption Consciousness | Connection Consciousness |

| Cause and Effect | Framing Meaning through Thoughts Images Feelings | Contemplation Intention Elimination Insulation | Moving from Faith to Knowing to Desired Reality |

MECHANISMS

Vibrational Fields Activate 4 Consciousness Frequencies

| Mental | Emotional | Physical Sensory | Spiritual |

| THOUGHTS Imagery | EMOTIONS Feelings | ACTION Body 5 Senses 6th sense | SPIRIT Connection Personal Beliefs |

2

The Tools

You are the determiner of your life. There is only one thing that can stop your progress and that is you not accepting that you are free of all limitations, and can expand your consciousness and energy frequency to improve or change your life at any time. All the resources you need, you currently possess. The **Tools** in the form of your **Consciousness,** which includes the '**I AM**' spiritual energies, and the healing properties of the violet energy, in particular the use of the **Violet Flame,** and **LEP Frequency Tool** will teach and guide you on how to increase your vibrational frequency and create the life you wish to live, and the future you want to face. The tools stand at the ready to assist and are available for use. But it is the readers' will and determination that will ultimately decide if he or she will pick up the tools, and use them as resources to create, or whether a life in lower energies of lack and survival is imminent.

Consciousness

Consciousness is the ultimate Source of all existence, and is a condition beyond time and space. The field of consciousness, itself, is infinitely powerful when it interacts with matter on this planet because out of consciousness arose awareness (Hawkins). Consciousness is realized in the prefrontal cortex because this is where humans process it. According to Dr. Hawkins, consciousness is responding to the stimulus of awareness. It is everything you see, hear, taste, smell, create and experience through your conscious awareness on this planet and beyond. It also includes the spiritual realms because consciousness is the infinite field that is the matrix of all our experiences that goes beyond death (Hawkins). Dr. Hawkins contended that it is the basis of subjectivity because through subjectivity, which is our vessel of perception, we are aware of our consciousness.

The higher the vibrational frequencies, the more expansive your consciousness becomes and the greater the power you possess because the measurement of consciousness determines your vibrational frequencies. Therefore, the higher the frequencies because your consciousness has expanded, the more positive your experiences and interactions with energies and the more power is available at your disposal. According to Dr. Hawkins everyone has a personalized section of consciousness which is you and is limited in that personalization until you move higher in vibrational frequencies and expand your consciousness where you will access more power.

Living in your highest vibration of consciousness in your current embodiment not only assures a joyous and prosperous life in this lifetime, but the frequency in which you live in your current embodiment reflects on the spiritual energy placement in the eternal realm (Newton, 2003), regardless of whether you believe in reincarnation, or not. Dr. Michael Newton, (2003) a renowned psychiatrist and author depicting life after death described vibrational frequency as the end all. He explained that energy is just the vibrational force that your spirit is evolving in at all times and that the higher the vibrational force, the higher the amount of energy one has because every soul has a specific energy field pattern which reflects an immortal blueprint of its character. His point was that we are born with a certain vibrational frequency and it is up to us to make progress on this earth and raise our vibrations so that, "when we die, our soul vibration will lift us to the spiritual plane that is most compatible to our vibration" (Newton, 2003). Thus, it makes sense to consciously put in the effort and raise your vibrational frequency, since it not only creates your desires in the current embodiment, and the life you wish to live, but the frequency is retained, when you die progressing you to higher vibratory states in the spirit world. Humanity is at a disadvantage because the human body was created to exist in a lower vibration, but frequencies can be increased by expanding one's consciousness through awareness and the **LEP Frequency Tool** to not only enjoy the current life to the fullest, but advance in the spiritual progress when the physical body dies.

In sum consciousness is always aligned with awareness. However not everyone defines consciousness in the same way. Scientists, scholars, and experts in the field often disagree on the definition of consciousness because as Schrodinger, who won the physics Nobel peace prize in 1933 contended, "consciousness cannot be accounted for in physical terms... nor can it be accounted for in terms of any-thing else." Consciousness is the vehicle through which tremendous energy of the Source Consciousness/God/Universal Energy, or what-ever name is chosen by the beholder, can be consciously directed through the awareness it has of it. Your lived experience on this planet is *consciousness* in action. Hawkins (2002, p. 94) indicated that "there is no localization of consciousness; awareness is equally present everywhere."

Disagreement on what consciousness is continues. But most sci-entists and scholars agree that consciousness is necessary to life. Max Planck, regarded matter, as derivative from consciousness and considered it fundamental to the existence of the universe (Planck, 1931). Planck (1959) argued, 'that we cannot get behind conscious-ness. Everything that we talk about, everything that we regard as exist-ing, postulates consciousness, and that consciousness is the Spirit of all matter' (Planck, 1959). Thus, Spirit is the Source Consciousness. It is God, the energy of All that is. It is the energy of intelligence and force behind the existence of *all* consciousness.

The **LEP Frequency Tool** is a tool of consciousness which is why it is so effective in the manifestation of desires process. You are connected to the Source Consciousness through your own con-sciousness, which is the spiritual energy of your 'I AM" active pres-ence within you. Your 'I AM' is your higher authentic-self, vibrating in spiritual energy. It is not who you are in this world by career, label, or status. Your spiritual consciousness is the true make up of your soul, who you really are and the type of person you can become and what you attract to yourself. If you do not like the current qualities of your-self, you can change who you are and what you want to accomplish by changing your consciousness through awareness of your strong connection to God, the Source Consciousness. If you want to connect to the Source and change who you are and what you are attracting to yourself swiftly, think kindness, compassion, forgiveness, love, and caring for yourself and others. Eliminate all anger, selfishness, greed, and influences from the ego.

To gain happiness, joy, prosperity, peace and greater power align yourself consciously with the Source Consciousness. You are forever linked to this Source, from whom everyone and everything originates, and since you are a part of the Source, you have all the powers of the Source and can create your life how you see fit in happiness, joy and peace. It is wise to remember that "conscious-ness automatically chooses what it deems best from moment to moment because ultimately that is the only function of which it is capable" (Hawkins, 2002, p. 29). Thus, if you do not control or direct your consciousness, it will direct itself from an auto pilot mode, or the ego and you will not like the results. Effort extended in any area brings results thus if you are focused on making money but are not aligned with the higher energies of the self, you will make money, but that money will not bring you happiness, joy or peace. It will bring you money and you will be left wondering why you are still unhappy and unfulfilled.

Decisions made from the ego, or fear and survival will not serve you. On the contrary decisions made from the ego will hold you cap-tive in the lower denser energies of Lack and Survival Consciousness until you change your consciousness through awareness that you must control the ego to have the power to be who you want to be and create what you desire. In order to move out of the lower consciousness energy where the ego resides it is imperative that the ego is addressed in your life. The ego can be the greatest stumbling block of human nature because it comes from the lower self (McNight, 2013). You must rise above it.

Presumptions in the mind are the result of the structure of the ego. Be aware of your ego and why it is surfacing. The ego is not hard to find. It reveals itself to you through inflated versions of yourself, judgments, or criticism of others etc. The ego is often an aspect of yourself that seem to glare out from another human being. So, each time you are critical or judgmental of another person ask yourself what it is in you that triggers this reaction, investigate and release these emotions. When you do you will also release these low energy emotions along with the power that the ego has over you and raise your consciousness. According to McNight, (2013), the ego is the self within you that sees only itself and believes that only what it is connected to is important, and anything that it isn't connected to it considers undesirable and as something that works in opposition to it. Anything outside of its own world is to be judged and condemned simply because it isn't a part of its lower ego consciousness (McNight, 2013). Choose kindness, unselfishness, forgiveness, love, and compassion for yourself and others and you will disarm the ego and be free from its clutch.

Much of humankind are stuck in lower vibrational consciousness levels because they are unaware that they have the power to easily change their lives by increasing their frequencies. They are unaware that they are controlled to a great extent by the ego, which is always associated with the lower energies. Thus, they are operating at very low consciousness levels of individual realized vibrations. For most people this is just habit. Some are stuck in lack of motivation or desire, or are simply worn down through prior experiences of life to a point where they become complicit, or they no longer care. This creates and environment of endurance but not living. Some people in lower levels of consciousness move through life, functioning, and existing, but not living and experiencing the best that life has to offer. Regardless of why people are stuck in lower consciousness is not nearly as important as the knowledge and awareness that anyone can raise their vibrational frequency at any time and experience the life, they desire simply by being conscious that they have this option.

Humankind has immeasurable resources that flow from the Source Consciousness to their own conscious mind at their disposal, they are just not aware of this fact. In order to partake of these resources, people must be aware of how to connect to and keep the link between their own consciousness and the Source Consciousness clean. To keep the link clean, establish and maintain a regular spiritual connection with the Source Consciousness. Dyer (2013) asserted that keeping the link clean between your consciousnesseses and the Source Consciousness is of utmost importance. He contended that, within your consciousness there are things that are not known but within the Source consciousness 'all is known' and available to you (Dyer, 2015).

Hawkins (2002, p. 34) was so concerned that this essential message was received by the readers that he emphasized that, "the individual human mind is like a computer terminal connected to a giant database. The database is human consciousness itself, of which our own cognizance is merely an individual expression, but with its roots in the common consciousness of all mankind." When referring to the Source Consciousness, Hawkins (2002 p. 34-35) further contended that, "the unlimited information contained in the database has now been shown to be readily available to anyone in a few seconds, at any time, and in any place. This is indeed an astonishing discovery, bearing the power to change lives, both individually and collectively, to a degree never yet anticipated." But one must be aware that they have the ability to access this database through their own consciousness. When you are aware that your conscious mind has this power you raise your vibrations, you expand your consciousness and can attract what you want to you because your consciousness can change your reality (Carroll,

1997). The choice is yours. You are an electrical being and if you "want to push upon the quantum parts of yourself…then change will take place…your reality on this planet is driven by human consciousness of choice" (Carroll, 2011 p. 244).

Effort is always measured by result. To use the consciousness as an apparatus in the **LEP Frequency Tool** you must be aware and have faith that you have this power. Do not let any outer discordant factors and appearances influence you in any way that you do not. Remain positive at all times, and know you are connected to the Source Consciousness and all the power of the Source can flow to you through your consciousness when you raise your vibrations but it is important to emphasize that 'efforts' must be extended. The readers must always remember that they are the governors of their life and must choose how they wish to live by directing their consciousness. Wherever your thoughts, images and feelings reside, there you are, so be conscious of any negative thought patterns or feelings. Should they surface, replace them *consciously* with higher, positive energies always being aware that the choice of who you are and how you live is yours.

Energy, Vibrations and Frequency

Energy is usually explained through physics in mathematical terms. It is usually understood as a 'the capacity to do work' paradigm where work serves as the creation of force and the distance moved by that force (Hawkins, 2002). According to Newton (2003), to fully understand energy scientists would have to figure out the all the elements of its creation and the consciousness of its source which to date is not possible. However, there is agreement among professionals from various vocations, scientists, educators, scholars, philosophers and the like, that everything and everyone is energy and vibrates at different frequencies. The frequencies determine not only how you look like but all of life experience. Edgar Casey contended that vibration is that same energy, same power, you call God. Brilliant scientists such as Albert Einstein, Max Planck, and Nikola Tesla believed in an energetic universe, and maintained that the secret of creation lies in the (electronic) wave, and if anyone wanted to discover how the universe operates one must think in terms of energy, frequency and vibration.

A basic understanding of how energy works is necessary for best results. Having at least basic knowledge on the role of molecular vibrations, in the manifestation of your desires or elimination of discord in your life, is an undertaking that every person in this embodiment must take if they are serious about creating and manifesting their dreams into existence. Dr. Wayne Dyer asserted in his lectures, 'it isn't what you don't know ... it is what you know for sure – that just ain't so ...'. This is an important concept because it means that everything you think is real is based on perceptions which are fluid. Your current reality is only 'current' for the moment because reality shifts and is always subjective and can be changed any time. And since perception is unique to each individual, vibrations determine people's perception which is formed through thoughts and feelings. A simple change of mind can increase or decrease vibrational frequencies and can subjectively create a new reality. Thus, if nothing is "real" this must mean that everything can be changed by aligning your vibration with the new frequency. How incredibly freeing is this concept which opens the door to unlimited potentials and possibilities? If you think your life is wrong or lacking, change it by changing your frequency.

Vibration is the way of creation. This is because people and everything in the physical and spiritual world is energy. In short, without overwhelming the readers, vibrations can be understood to be the speed in which electrons revolve around the nucleus of the atom. A molecule is made up of atoms which is matter, bonded together. In simplistic terms the atom is its own entity and when atoms bond together they are called molecules. When vibrations appear in a repetitive pattern, that pattern is called a frequency and determines (form) who you are, what you can do, how you see world, and what will manifest in your life

All energy is in motion. This means that molecules vibrate at different speeds. According to Bob Proctor the *Law of Vibration*, decrees that "everything moves, nothing rests, we literally live in an ocean of motion." When molecules vibrate at very slow speed you see it as your material (physical) world. When the molecules vibrate at much higher speed, they are invisible, such as your thoughts. Thus, everything you see and don't see is just a configuration and speed of the molecules. You bring desires from your consciousness into the physical world by changing the speed of its vibration, through thoughts, images in the mind, and feelings (trust and faith) supporting the belief that it will manifest. This is how you begin to connect to what is in your conscious mind so that you may bring it into your physical reality. Thus, essentially human beings, and everything on this earth, including the earth are just a bunch of molecules (matter) vibrating and attracting energies at whatever frequency was send because molecules are the makeup of energy.

Without vibrations nothing would exist. Thus, working with energies to increase vibrations to connect to the highest frequency possible, and think from that highest point of consciousness must be a priority in everyone's life. By changing the vibrational speed, you change the frequency and the world around you. This includes your potential to create manifestations in your life because energy reads vibrations and generates that frequency into your physical reality.

Connect to the frequency (vibrational speed) of your desire and because of the Law of Vibration and its secondary law, the Law of Attraction, it must come! Thus, in order to use the energy to create in the consciousness and manifest in your physical reality, at least a basic understanding of how energy works is imperative. In order to begin working actively with energy, as Rupert Sheldrake suggested, "first cultivating an intention to educate yourself on the universal laws governing the planet and how they function and how you may consciously apply them to the various aspects of our life" is needed. This means that the readers must be receptive in receiving the information relative to the energy and how it operates with various universal laws, such as the *Law of Forgiveness, the Law of Vibration,* and the *Law of Attraction*.

Human beings are just globs of vibrations in physical forms that have the power to increase or decrease their vibrational frequencies any time, and experience whatever they wish. The *Law of Attraction*, is the secondary universal law, and is also always in motion because you are continuously creating, whether you know it or not. You are creating your physical reality in every moment that you live with every thought that you have. The vibrations you send to the universe will be returned to you because of the *Law of Attraction* at the same frequency they were sent. These outcomes create your physical reality. For example, if you decided to pick a fight or hurt someone intentionally, be prepared for that energy to be returned to you in some form at the same frequency it was sent. In may not necessarily be from that person or that same situation, but that same frequency will reappear in your life as a discordant vibration and it will touch you in the same manner you have touched the other person.

The *Law of Attraction* always returns the energy in the way that it was received. If you want better results, use the energy of the *Law of Attraction*, and think, imagine and feel only positive, inspiring thoughts based in faith, forgiveness, kindness and love. In this way the things that you desire have the ideal conditions in which to appear in your physical world, and implementing the **LEP Frequency Tool** to create your new life full of happiness, well-being, joy and prosperity will be much easier.

Renowned clairvoyant, Edgar Casey taught that vibration is *One Spirit* in motion. It is one Consciousness of the Source vibrating and attracting like energies which determine all human lived experiences. Things and people seem separate from each other because they all vibrate at different frequencies. This is one of the reasons that perception is subjective, as people see themselves as separate from each other and everything else because of each individual's unique vibrational frequency, which alters perception and subjectivity. Thus, two people can look at the same thing and draw different conclusions because they are looking at it from different vibrational frequency points. Nikola Tesla often argued that everything in the universe is linked by a single pervasive organism, a consciousness of *All,* from which we are not separated, but are always connected to and with. Tesla, surmised that it must be so, for matter and consciousness are inseparable because they are united by participation (in Olsen, 2018). According to Tesla, (in Olsen, 2018) frequency and vibrations are the keys to understanding the universe. Tesla (in Olsen, 2018) described the universe as a kinetic system of energy in which human beings, because they are also 100% energy, can tune into from any location. Human beings can create anything that they wish. They are just not aware that they can do it, or understand how to use energy to do it.

Edgar Cayce, and psychologist, Michael Newton, among many other best-selling authors and motivational speakers, such as Wayne Dyer, Shakti Gawain, Louise Hay, David Hawkins, among many others experts in the field, all emphasized the power of attraction that energy holds. All people can and must use energy (vibrational frequencies) to manifest anything and everything they wish in their lives. The power lies in the vibration, and tuning into the correct frequency of that which you desire.

Consciously, tune into the correct frequency and it will materialize in your physical world. It may seem like a miracle, but "the miracle is really only a shift of frequency into a higher vibration that has snapped into view because you are now vibrating at a new level" Carroll, (1997). Dyer (2013) also stressed that abundance is not something we acquire; it is something we energetically tune into. Thus, since everything comes in response to vibration of energy, if you want something, you must shift into the vibration of your desire, through the alignment of **thoughts, images** and **feelings**, so that you can send clear **intent** to attract and align with the frequency of your desire and bring it from your consciousness into your physical reality because that is how energy works.

The 'I AM' Spiritual Energy Within

Consciousness and understanding of the energy processes are very important devices in the creation process, and in the use of the LEP

Frequency Tool. However, there is nothing more important than a true awareness of the **'I AM'** presence within each person that is the driver of monumental potentials in energy work. The **'I AM'** is God's presence and activity within you. It is your soul. The spark of spiritual energy that lives in the human body, but is always connected to the Source Consciousness/God. The words **'I AM'** are charged with intense spiritual energy. It is your spiritual link to God, the Source of All that is, was and ever will be. The expression, **'I AM'** as taught to Moses, (Exodus 3:14) whether through thought, feeling or spoken word releases the power of creation instantly (King, 1993). It is not through your physical body, which is just a shell, a vehicle to allows you to move about and permit your physical experiences in this embodiment, but it is through this link, that connects your **'I AM'** presence within you to the Source Consciousness, from which your life and all your power flows. "When you consciously connect to the 'I AM' presence within you…you are actually accepting the electronic structure which is then present in all manifestation" (King, 1993, p.93) because God, "is the Central Point of Life or energy within every atom, composing the substance from which comes all physical manifestations" (King, 1993, p. 92).

You are an electrical multidimensional spiritual being living in a physical world. You are having a physical experience through electronic activity which is the force qualified by consciousness, and activated on earth by your **'I AM'** spiritual presence. The electronic structure is beyond the physical domain (matter) (King, 2011). It is energy that includes both the wave functions of the electrons and the energies that are linked with them (King, 2011). But since individuals are both a transmitter and receiver of energy, through their consciousness and working with energy they can change their experience through increasing their vibrational frequencies by working through both their outer (physical) and inner (spiritual) activity, since they are both of the same energy. Max Planck vigorously maintained that all the physical matter is composed of vibration. Thus, through a union between your consciousness 'self,' your understanding of the importance of energy in your life, and your connection to the 'I AM' presence you have the ability to connect to the Source Consciousness and tap into the well of unlimited power.

There must be a willingness and determination on the part of the person to be open to hear and act, according to that *inner* voice. The inner voice is the spiritual energy inside each individual, the **'I AM'** presence," which is always linked to the Source energy that gives "all" power and life. It is through this energetic connection with the Source Consciousness that you can create. Rumi, shared "there's a voice that doesn't use words, listen… The soul has been given its own ears to hear things that the mind does not understand." The inner voice inside you is the energy of your **'I AM'** presence forever con-nected to the Source Consciousness. There is no separation between you, for you are of the Source. The **'I AM'** is the voice and energy of authenticity, and your link to use that power to eliminate discords or create anything you wish in your life. Always ensure a strong, perma-nent conscious contact with that inner presence, your **'I AM'** in every human condition that appears in your physical life, for you are God in action.

The **'I AM'** is the only energy that can be used to **invoke** all other energies of the Source Consciousness and make them available for your use. Raising your vibrations to match higher consciousness fre-quencies through the use of your **'I AM'** presence will allow you to invoke the **violet energy,** particularly **the Violet Flame. The Violet Flame** will help you open the door to the realizations of your dreams, and eliminate all discords in your life, and offer healing thereby giving you a true opportunity to live the life you wish to live and the future you want to face. It will also eliminate discordant karma leaving you free of discordant energy so that you may have your new beginning without discordant attachments.

The Properties of the Violet Energies

The violet energy, in particular the use of the **Violet Flame** is extremely powerful, and is another very important and effective element of the LEP Frequency Tool of consciousness. That is because the Source Consciousness consists of *one* energy that appears in myriads of colors depending on their energetic properties which determines the area of their strength and power. In the physical world, the violet light has the shortest wave length of light, and therefore has the highest frequency in the corporeal spectrum. This means that because the violet energy has the shortest wave length of light, it has the highest frequency in the physical continuum (Prophet, 1999). Thus, it has the ability to change matter at the atomic level by human beings which is why it is an integral part of the LEP Frequency Tool. Prophet (1999) maintained that since frequency is directly proportional to energy, the violet light also has the most energy, thus it has the greatest ability to create, heal or eliminate karma.

For those readers who take working with the *violet energy* seriously, you will find a powerful force entering your life. *Violet energy*, in particular the **Violet Flame**, helps in spiritual evolution in this embodiment and in the after-life by developing your mind, body and soul, through providing a supporting and sustaining platform to all life streams on the planet so that they may vibrate to their highest potential. It is a powerful spiritual energy that appears as a violet tint and can be directed to **manifest** personal **desires.** It also has the capacity to **eliminate** all **discords** from anyone's life, and adjust the energy harmoniously, outside of karmic cycles. The **Violet Flame** received Its name partly because of the tint of Its color, and because upon invocation through the person's '**I AM**' presence, "It descends as a beam of spiritual energy" from the Source Consciousness and "bursts into a spiritual violet flame in your heart" (Prophet, 1997) healing all discords and transmuting all negative energies into harmonious vibrations.

Since energy cannot be destroyed, it must be transmuted. The quickest way to transmute any discord, heal or eliminate karma is to invoke the **Violet** Flame because it has the powerful ability to correct past mistakes and balance all karma harmoniously. It transmutes the once discordant energy into higher vibrations, outside of karmic debt, where only good comes from the once discordant energy, whether the energy that was originally sent was intentional or unintentional. The **Violet Flame** is powerful spiritual energy, but does not work alone. The **Violet Flame** will work for us, but we have to work with it (Prophet, 1999).

Violet Flame Heavenly Alchemy

The **Violet Flame** is spiritual alchemy. It is heavenly alchemy because it has the capability to transmute energy (thoughtforms in consciousness) into matter (physical reality). It can also easily remove discordant vibrations, automatically, freeing the person to vibrate in higher frequencies. But the **Violet Flame** "can only be focused, projected and brought into activity by the **'I AM'** presence within each person" (Voice of the I AM, May 1936, p. 22) because it is their **'I AM'** consciousness that is fully connected to the Source and must be the driving force to activate the violet energy. The power of the Violet Energy has been noted by many notable experts in working with Its powerful energies, such as Guy Ballard (Godfre Ray King) and his wife Edna who were instrumental in the early teachings of the **'I AM'** activity. Elizabeth Prophet, an American inspirational leader, perfected the use of the **Violet Flame** for her readers, and Edgar Casey noted the power of the violet light in over 900 of his readings. However, the original archetype of the **Violet Flame** originated with St. Germain and was recorded by Guy Ballard, under the pen name of Godfre Ray King. Godfre Ray King's books were first published in the 1930's and continue to have a strong following because of their tremendous value in the applicability of the wealth of information they provide. According to King (2007) the **'I AM'** presence is the only force that can invoke and activate the **Violet Flame** energies. This is because the action that takes place in the use of the **Violet Flame** is an energetic activity that responds only to the high spiritual energies of the **'I AM'** command, and since you are of the Source, it is a call from God, the Source Consciousness to action, and the energies must respond.

Your desires and past deeds are nothing more than 'matter,' made of up whirling energies of the Source Consciousness, that, if discordant, the **Violet Flame** can transmute into positive energy. The **Violet Flame** is spiritual energy that can be directed and focused to achieve wanted outcomes and corresponds to the violet energy (light) of liberation and transmutation. It offers freedom from all chains, limitations, discords and karmic debts.

The **Violet Flame** is an incredible power at your disposal that, if used regularly, will grace your life with tremendous blessings as it helps you create the life you wish. It will also restore balance and harmony in your world by eliminating discords. When invoking the **Violet Flame**, through your **'I AM'** presence, marvels and miracles will take place in your life in a very short time. Limitations, restrictions, fears, anxieties and the like, will disappear and you will be able to create your desires with joy, without restrain, your ego dictating to you, or outer influences getting in the way of the best results that can be attained. King (2013) contended that when you invoke the **Violet Flame** through your **'I AM'** presence to eliminate something in your life, this calls upon the Law of Forgiveness and throws it back to the Cosmic Law for adjustment, wherein it is adjusted outside of the individual karmic activity (King, 2013). This lifts your burden because it eliminates lower vibrations from your energy fields, leaving you inspired and invigorated to create a better reality. King (2012) asserted that the use of the **Violet Flame** is the greatest blessing to mankind on this earth because it dissolves and transmutes all discordant creations, past and present and only leaves harmony in its wake. Thus, the person is clear, and free from any lingering lower vibrations that might have attached themselves, such as guilt, or regret, past transgressions and the like leaving him or her to create their wishes from much higher frequencies, free of the heavy energy of past baggage (which greatly affect the speed of their manifestations in the physical expression).

All discord, whether intentional, or unintentional, is caused by humanity. The concept of discord does not exist in the high consciousness fields. Humanity has created forms made of substance, energized by feeling and projected into the atmosphere about them (Voice of the I AM, May 1936, p. 17) which materialize as discord.

Without exception, every human being has made mistakes at one time or another in their journey through life. "All have felt discord and sent it forth in thought, feelings and spoken word" (Voice of the I AM, May 1936, p. 17). Yet, people are mostly unaware of how what they say and feel, and the inability to forgive themselves and others, selfishness and greed, or thoughts of guilt or regret really affects their existence today, tomorrow and in eternity. "Individuals have not the slightest concept of what they have created through their thought, feeling and spoken words, even in their present lives, let alone all the hundreds and possibly thousands of embodiments they have lived through previously" (Voice of I AM, 1936 May, p. 16). Sometimes the discord felt is so intense it affects every aspect of the individuals' health, physical and mental well-being for their entire lifetime and beyond. Other times the mistakes are on a smaller scale, but even small mistakes such as selfishness, greed, regrets, or guilt can trap you in lower energies and will forever hold you captive, unless you eliminate them from your energy fields through the use of the Law of Forgiveness, 'I AM' presence and the Violet Flame energy.

Long term discord suffocates soul growth and the ability to function in the physical world. All discord, especially if prolonged can cause continuous existence in low vibratory frequencies, severe psychological damage, self-esteem problems, lack of confidence, depression, extreme anxiety and eventually may end in the person unable or unwilling to function in life. Thus, it is extremely important to start freeing yourself from these attached low vibrations, and leave the past firmly in the past. If you are stuck in these low dense energies how can you possibly create the life that you want to live? Start using the LEP Frequency Tool of consciousness as soon as possible, so that you may be free of all discords and raise your vibrational frequency to attract what you truly desire. If not transmuted, these lower forms of energies will continue to manifest in emotional ways such as extreme feelings of depression, and mental ways such as a bleak perception of life and hopelessness. Moreover, it can also set you back in spiritual ways resulting in deficient beliefs in the Spirit or lack of trust and faith in the Source/God. Often times these low vibrations can manifest in physical ways such as illness and dis-ease affecting your physical well-being.

Use the LEP Frequency Tool to invoke the violet energy. The **Violet Flame** when called upon through your **I AM** presence will first shatter, dissipate and consume all wrong creations in your life. All discord will be dissolved and transmuted for good so that you may begin with a clean slate and begin controlling what shows up in your lived experiences, so that you are fulfilled and happy. As Dr. Wayne Dyer admonished, don't get to the end of your life and say "what if my whole life had been wrong?" there is no greater tragedy.

Use the LEP Frequency Tool of consciousness and ensure that your life is what you want it to be starting now, today, this minute. The **Violet Flame** will help you manifest your desires and eliminate discordant energy from your energy fields because it transmutes discordant energy into higher vibrations outside of karmic debt leaving you free to start your life anew. The **Violet Flame dissolves,** as it **shatters**, **eliminates,** as it **dissipates**, and **transmutes** into **higher energies** as it **consumes** wrong creations. Use it often, so that you can be free from all low energies, baggage or debris that may still be attached to you through thoughts and feelings, and thus, lowering your overall vibration and affecting your ability to create the new life you desire.

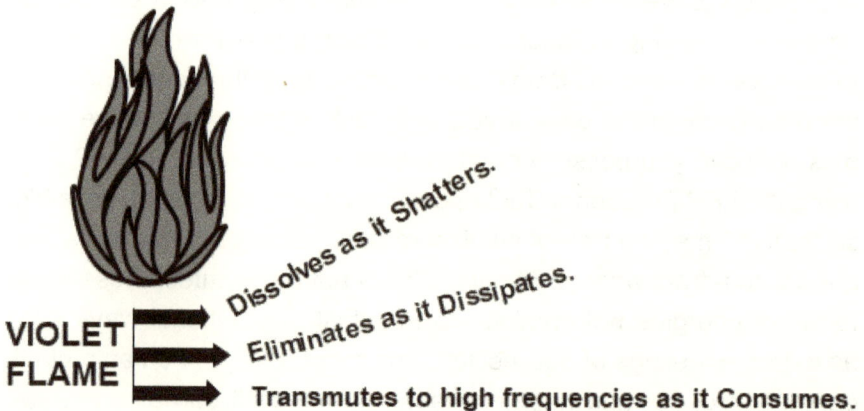

VIOLET FLAME

Dissolves as it Shatters.

Eliminates as it Dissipates.

Transmutes to high frequencies as it Consumes.

Since discordant energy cannot be destroyed, to transmute its properties, it is easier to shatter, dissipate and consume it through invoking the **Violet Flame.** When shattering the focus of the discord; the consuming is then easier (King, 2012). When something "shatters," it breaks apart to tiny energy particles. To "dissipate" means to eliminate it from your life, and to "consume" it means to transmute it to higher frequencies, since energy cannot be destroyed. If you use the **Violet Flame** with steady determination to shatter, dissipate and consume uncomfortable, specific or all wrong creations in your life, you will be relieved from all distress and discords in a very short time.

The **Violet Flame** is also often used for creation of desires, as the *violet energy* can be explicitly directed and focused toward a specific thoughtform. The thoughtform, backed by a firm image in the mind, and supportive feeling, becomes an alchemy instrument for manifestation of any desire, once activated by the **'I AM'** presence of the person. The desire, when held steady, and unwavering, becomes the conscious thought directing, for you cannot manifest a desire without conscious thought of the desire (King, 1993, p.92). Your feelings support the thoughtform, and manifestations formed in the consciousness motivate physical action. If supported by spiritual knowing that you are connected to the Source you open the door to unlimited power, as thoughtforms in the consciousness manifest in physical realities. When you have learned to comfortably work with the **Violet Flame**, you can bring forth from the consciousness anything you desire into your physical reality but it must be constructive. Be prepared to receive the answers to your call while remaining grateful, confident and trust that it will come in its perfect time.

People, situations, and often your entire life, will change quickly as higher agreeable energies enter your life. Problems that seemed insurmountable, whether financial, with relationships, children, health, life satisfaction or a particular issue will turn around seemingly out of nowhere and things will harmoniously begin to fall into place. But you will know that this is no accident that it is you who is now creating the future you want to live and face.

Use the guidelines and prescribed decrees included in the later chapters of this book, or create your own to direct and focus the violet *energies* to your needs, and extraordinary results will follow. The **Violet Flame** is so completely infused with the vibration of love and harmony that it will answer every constructive call. When you work with the **Violet Flame** you take command and full authority of your inner and outer self because you are working directly with your **'I AM'** presence, which through the **Violet Flame** produces results within your physical reality.

The LEP Frequency Tool in Detail

The **LEP Frequency Tool** is a consciousness instrument. It instructs readers on how to raise their personal vibrations by raising their **mental, emotional, physical/sensory**, and **spiritual** frequencies in order to manifest desires in their physical experience and/or eliminate discords in their life. The **LEP Frequency Tool** received its name because without the **Lived Experience Phenomenon (LEP),** vibrational consciousness on this planet, as we know it, would not exist. Each reader moves at a different vibrational speed in their life, thinks, feels and acts from that point of consciousness.

The vibrational frequencies are measured by the expansion of their consciousness. Different vibrational frequencies identify expansions of consciousness which determines their awareness levels and offer various points of power and the speed in which the desired results are attained. The higher the frequency, the more expansive the consciousness and awareness, thus the closer to the Source Consciousness, and the greater the powers that are available for the person's use. Using the **LEP Frequency Tool** lifts people to a higher consciousness because it increases frequencies in the Mechanisms' four consciousness frequencies (1) **mental;** (2) **emotional;** (3) **physical/sensory** and; (4) **spiritual,** which collectively raises the persons overall vibration so that desires in the conscious mind can be manifested in physical reality.

The **LEP Frequency Tool** is simple to use. It consists of three primary components: (1) **Preparation (Prep);** (2) **Means** and; (3) **Mechanisms.** The **Prep** prepares the readers for the shift to the incoming higher energies. The **Means** identifies the person's vibrational frequencies which reflects their current life (consciousness), **Lack and Survival, Dedication, Absorption** or **Connection Consciousness,** as experienced through the **4 Mechanisms** of **mental, emotional, physical/sensory** and **spiritual** consciousness frequencies. Each of the **4 Mechanisms** carries its own vibrational frequency. The combined total is the persons overall vibration and determines in which consciousness field they will reside, **Lack and Survival, Dedication, Absorption** or **Connection Consciousness** and how much power is available for their use.

Anyone can quickly move up the levels of consciousness by increasing their vibrational frequency. Results are strictly attributed to the effort put in and the disciplined manner in which the instructions are implemented. It is important that each reader understands that no matter where you currently are on the vibrational frequency rating, you are in a position to quickly climb higher. The **LEP Frequency Tool** of consciousness, if used as instructed, will change your life faster than you ever imagined or thought possible. Below you will find a brief introduction to each of the components, the **Prep, Means** and **Mechanisms**. Later chapters will provide complete information and instructions on how to utilize the **LEP Frequency Tool** in each of the **mental, emotional, physical/sensory** and **spiritual** consciousness frequencies to raise the readers' vibrations to their highest potential.

The **Prep** component is vital to the outcomes of your efforts because it prepares the mind to work with new higher forms of energy and must never be skipped, or omitted. The **Prep** component contains **mental, inner and spiritual preparation** and **signal transmission**. Everyone who ventures to increase their vibration must prepare their thoughts, and emotions, insert strong faith and trust into their life, and change or modify the signals they are sending to match the higher vibrations they seek. By preparing their mental, emotional and spiritual fields, all readers will begin to think, feel and trust from a higher consciousness, thereby aligning with, and attracting higher energies to them with greater ease.

In preparing your thoughts and emotions you are simply clearing the mind in preparation to receive information from a higher consciousness. It is important to note, and for the readers to remember, that in this first step of **Prep** when working with the **LEP Frequency Tool** you are *not* changing your thoughts but *preparing* your thoughts. This means it does not require heavy mental and emotional shifts.

The **Means** component identifies the current vibrational consciousness fields through the *How Do You Live?* assessments and provides instructions to the readers on **how** to control and direct the energies of **thoughts, images** and **feelings** to only attract the highest vibrations into their lives. **Thoughts** *transform* **to images. Images** *activate* **feelings. Feelings** *activate* **4** specific **consciousness vibrations** that are general to every person alive on the planet: (1) **Lack and Survival;** (2) **Dedication;** (3) **Absorption** and; (4) **Connection**. Identifying *how you live* within these consciousness fields, through the **Mechanisms** of **your mental, emotional, physical/sensory, and spiritual** consciousness frequencies is crucial to ensuring that adjustments are made to elevate you to higher energy fields where the manifestations of your desires can be achieved.

The **lowest** and densest consciousness level on the earth plane is the **Lack and Survival Consciousness,** which includes the *cause-and-effect* paradigm. It is the lowest energy field where most of humanity move. If any reader is vibrating in the **Lack and Survival Consciousness,** (see Assessment A2) a rise in frequency within the mental and emotional consciousness fields to increase personal vibrations must occur before you can go much further. It is the only way to sharpen the direction of energy to where you wish it to go, and insulate yourself against discordant energies, now and in the future before you can move on to the **Dedication Consciousness** where manifestation has the potential to occur.

The **Dedication Consciousness** vibrates at **moderate** energy fields. The **Dedication Consciousness** operates within the mental and emotional fields and focuses on control of **thoughts, images**, and **feelings** from the highest consciousness perspective, allowing for greater mental and emotional maturity and response, in every situation, which always yield better results. **Dedication Consciousness** must be mastered before any real power of manifestation can take place. The ability to control and manage **thoughts, images** and **feelings** in the **Dedication Consciousness** provides an indispensable foundation for all readers, but particularly those, who are moving into, or already are, in the higher energies of the **Absorption Consciousness.**

The **Absorption Consciousness** field includes the powerful spiritual energies of *contemplation, intention, elimination and insulation.* Being proficient with the energies of **thought, images,** and **feelings** and mastering the **Dedication Consciousness** fields greatly increases the speed in which manifestations occur because the high spiritual energies of *contemplation* and *intention* can align much quicker to the higher frequency of the desires, and thus attract them to physical realities at faster speeds. **Elimination** and **insulation** assure a peaceful life without the disturbance of discordant energies.

In the **Connection Consciousness** your cellular structure changes and is now vibrating permanently in much higher consciousness fields. The **Connection Consciousness (peak** energy) provides the opportunity to live permanently in an expanded consciousness of the Source where you are creating and making decisions from your highest energy potential without falling and causing the waste of your accumulated power and decreasing your vibrational frequency, hence decrease your power. In the **Connection Consciousness** you are fully **connected** to the **Source Consciousness,** and have shifted your vibration from **faith** to **knowing. Knowing** has turned into living your **reality** as you envision it per your specifications. Erasing all doubt, and **knowing** that all your constructive desires will come to you, the **Connection Consciousness** provides you the opportunity to continually maintain and live in the highest of vibration available to you in this embodiment. This is the state of bliss.

The **Mechanisms** component supplies the **through** or the way. Once the readers have a firm idea of their vibrational frequency through taking the *LEP How Do You Live?* assessments, and know what consciousness, field of **Lack and Survival, Dedication, Absorption** or **Connection** they currently reside in, they are ready to *activate* the **Mechanism** of *mental, emotional, physical/sensory* and *spiritual* energies through which they can quickly and permanently raise their vibrational frequencies. With each rise in frequency, the readers will be able to control the flow of energy and manifest any constructive desire.

Each consciousness frequency carries with it its own properties that will be greatly enhanced in higher energies. For example, the **mental** consciousness frequency includes all cognitive processes, thoughts, visualizations, images and so on. The **emotional** consciousness frequency includes emotions and feelings. The **physical/sensory** consciousness holds the frequency of action and motivation, and all physical and bodily functions. It also includes the 5 senses, sight, taste, smell, hearing, and touch, along with the sixth psychic sense. Lastly, the **spiritual** consciousness frequency involves the spiritual energy of the Source Consciousness that you are always connected to through your 'I AM' presence within, your belief systems and a clean link to spirit. A collective vibrational increase of the **mental, emotional, physical/sensory** and **spiritual** frequencies will raise the individuals' vibrational frequencies and include expansion of power and consciousness.

Vibrating high within all energies of the **mental, emotional, physical/sensory** and **spiritual** consciousness energies is easily attained through the use of the **LEP Frequency Tool** of consciousness. In these three components, **Prep, Means,** and **Mechanisms,** you have all that is necessary to raise your vibrational frequency, without delay, and can begin creating what you desire, or eliminate energies that cause you discords or pain. **The LEP Frequency Tool** moves the reader from being a passive observer in his or her life, or one who continuously operates in the world of lower energy fields, to an individual who is mastering the lower vibrations and shifting into higher and higher frequencies of joy to create that which in the past was thought impossible.

The serious readers who begin working with energy will quickly realize that using the **LEP Frequency Tool** to raise their vibrational frequency to manifest their new reality yields greater rewards and power with each new shift. The speed will depend on efforts extended. But with a steadfast effort to work with energy wonderful results are eminent. Dr. Dyer was so certain of the power of vibrations that he declared 'that nothing can stop my creative ideas from materializing... I've banished all doubt. I'll soon be seeing evidence of my manifestations everywhere...' In many of his lectures, Dr. Wayne Dyer, insisted that it could not be any other way, as everything is energy and it's all vibration. Dyer (2013) further contended that if, you shift your energy frequency to a higher vibration, live and make decisions from that mental plane, your life will immediately improve in every way.

Your brand-new life awaits. Get started without delay. By working with the **LEP Frequency Tool** of consciousness as outlined in this book to raise their vibrational frequencies and live in higher planes of consciousness the readers can achieve the joys and successes in the current embodiment while also assuring a higher spiritual growth and elevation in consciousness in the eternal/spiritual levels when the physical body dies. This occurs because the higher the frequency in which you live in your current embodiment, the higher the spiritual energy placement (consciousness) in the afterlife (Newton, 2003), regardless of whether or not you believe in life after death.

Energy is impersonal. Personal beliefs are of no consequence to energy on whether you believe in reincarnation. If you choose not to believe in reincarnation, it matters not. Your placement in the afterlife will always be determined by your frequency, not your belief systems relative to reincarnation. Energy just is, was and ever will be. It is here for your use; it is up to you if you will use it to create the life in which you wish to live, or be stuck in the lower frequency unhappy and unfulfilled.

LEP (LIVED EXPERIENCE PHENOMENA) FREQUENCY TOOL

PREP

- MENTAL PREPARATION
- INNER PREPARATION
- CONSCIOUSNESS
- I AM
- VIOLET ENERGY
- SPIRITUAL PREPARATION
- SIGNAL TRANSMISSION

MEANS

- THOUGHTS TRANSFORM TO IMAGES
- IMAGES ACTIVATE FEELINGS
- FEELINGS ACTIVATE THE 4 VIBRATIONAL FREQUENCIES
  - o LACK AND SURVIVAL CONSCIOUSNESS
  - o DEDICATION CONSCIOUSNESS
  - o ABSORPTION CONSCIOUSNESS
  - o CONNECTION CONSCIOUSNESS

MECHANISMS

4 VIBRATIONAL FREQUENCIES *ACTIVE* 4 CONSCIOUSNESS
FREQUENCIES

MENTAL	EMOTIONAL	PHYSICAL/SENSORY	SPIRITUAL
Thoughs	Emotions	Action	Spiritual Connection
Imagery	Feelings	Body Senses	Personal Beliefs

3

The Prep

LEP PREP SNAPSHOT

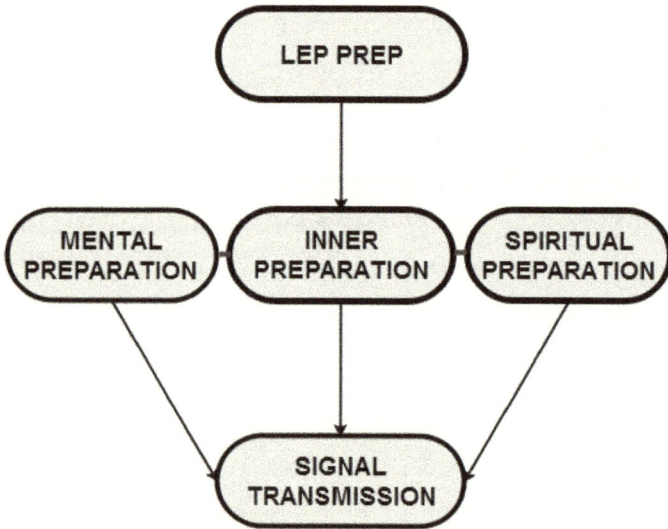

```
                    ┌──────────────┐
                    │   LEP PREP   │
                    └──────┬───────┘
                           │
                           ▼
   ┌────────────┐   ┌────────────┐   ┌────────────┐
   │   MENTAL   │   │   INNER    │   │ SPIRITUAL  │
   │ PREPARATION│   │ PREPARATION│   │ PREPARATION│
   └──────┬─────┘   └──────┬─────┘   └─────┬──────┘
          │                │               │
          │                ▼               │
          │         ┌────────────┐         │
          └────────▶│   SIGNAL   │◀────────┘
                    │TRANSMISSION│
                    └────────────┘
```

The Prep

Prepare. When embarking on increasing your vibrational frequencies, **mental, inner and spiritual preparation** is not an option but a mandatory requirement. The spiritual energy must flow freely from the Source Consciousness through your mental, inner and spiritual consciousness fields so that you can prepare the mind and emotions enough to work with, and attract higher spiritual energies. For this to occur, a check-in on thoughts, feelings, verbal expressions and the way vibrational signals are sent, must be exercised. During **Prep**, you must be disciplined and compel all thoughts, emotions and outer expressions, whether verbal or through body language, to only engage in high frequencies, and not focus on any negatively discordant energies. Additionally, ensure that all your **signal transmissions**, (the way you send energy consciously or unconsciously) is being sent from your highest frequency, meaning that your thoughts, and feelings must be of harmonious nature.

The **Prep** is an essential first step in raising vibrational frequencies and begins any energy work. Preparation rids itself of low, denser energies and replaces them with high vibrational frequencies of expectancy that will deliver the possibility of alignment with what you seek to manifest. The **Prep** with its **check-in** functions should be utilized before jumping into full energy work, whether you wish to eliminate discord in your life or begin creating new desires. In this clearing process you will be able to achieve your highest frequency possible so that you may begin creating from your maximum potential in the current moment.

Monitor yourself and practice! The **Prep** phase includes mental, emotional and spiritual preparation as you move in your physical body so that you can prepare to receive higher energies. In the Prep phase you will quickly realize that the correct attitude to be maintained is one of always being clear of discord in thought and feeling and in keeping the link to Spirit alive for that link is crucial and can be used as your support system.

You are not alone! Spirit wants you to excel for It is living through YOU, the soul. It is how the Source Consciousness/God experiences life on earth – through you, and helps guide you so that you may return to It in your purest energy form. The Source energy wants to do all It can to support you in all your constructive endeavors. Hence, there is a God-force in the universe, the Source Consciousness in peak frequency that is constantly working to guide you back to your true nature and rejoin It in the spiritual realm.

Preparation to receive higher energies includes, the mental, inner and spiritual prep and the understanding of signal transmissions. The **mental** preparation includes questioning, challenging and governing your thoughts to ensure that you are mentally at your highest vibratory frequency before you begin creating your desires. The **inner** preparation includes an emotional check-in with your feelings. The **spiritual** preparation includes a check-in on your belief system, and a specialized LEP meditation to assist you in the creation and manifestation process to clear all discords that may have attached themselves to you. It is recommended that all readers use the LEP meditations to clear all discords and/or to place them in optimum energy fields for creating desires. Meditation is crucial when manifesting desires because through the act of meditation human beings' expand their consciousness.

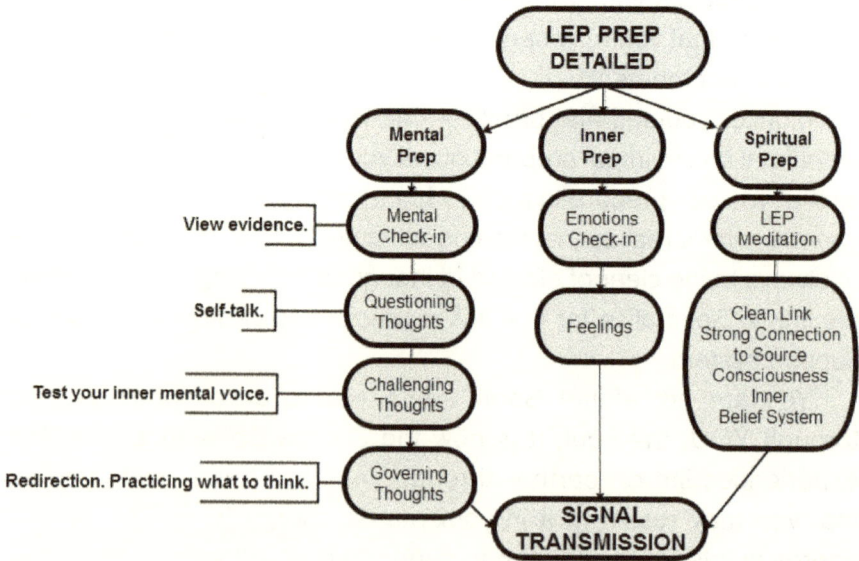

LEP PREP DETAILED

- Mental Prep
  - Mental Check-in — View evidence.
  - Questioning Thoughts — Self-talk.
  - Challenging Thoughts — Test your inner mental voice.
  - Governing Thoughts — Redirection. Practicing what to think.
- Inner Prep
  - Emotions Check-in
  - Feelings
- Spiritual Prep
  - LEP Meditation
  - Clean Link Strong Connection to Source Consciousness Inner Belief System

SIGNAL TRANSMISSION

Mental Preparation

Mental preparation includes **thought preparation. Thought preparation** is extremely important because thought is the molder of form, and the cause of all outer activity in the physical world. **Thought preparation** consists *of mental check-ins, questioning your thoughts, challenging your thoughts,* and *governing your thoughts. Mental check-ins view evidence* for and against the way you think. **Questioning your thoughts** focuses on *self-talk.* **Challenging your thoughts** *tests your inner mental voice* to make a determination if your thoughts are skewed and need modifications or realignment, and **governing your thoughts** focuses on complete redirection and *practicing what to think.*

In preparation, your mind is your equipment. To prepare the mind to create is equivalent to ensuring your equipment is in perfect working order prior to your start. This is why preparation should never be skipped! Your mind must include a mental preparation of harmonious thoughts of higher vibrations, and mental confidence that what you *intend* will come to fruition. The desire can only manifest in your physical world, if you have prepared, and became the designer and creator of it in your consciousness and letting go of all doubt. Dr. Hawkins in *Power vs. Force* (2002) offered a perfect example that illustrates that anything large or small can be manifested in the physical world out of consciousness, if one prepares the mind, and does not let outside influences, or doubt interfere with one's vision.

In one of his lectures, Dr. Hawkins recounted the creation of the Empire State building, "what happened on Fifth Ave in New York City in 1931 is there for all to see, and what happened in the consciousness of its creators also stands recorded in the database for all to see. To this day both exist complete, but in different sensory domains. By transferring 'concept' into concrete and steel, the architects simply enabled the rest of us to experience their vision." The Empire State building, as is everything else, was built in the consciousness and deemed an impossible project but yet it was brought forth into physical reality. For this monumental manifestation built in the consciousness to appear in the physical world, tremendous mental preparation by the architects was extended. Such is the power of mental preparation and fortitude of knowing that you can succeed and letting go of all doubt.

There must be awareness but no doubt. The first activity of **Prep** is to become conscious that you have the ability to raise your vibration to your highest potential while in this embodiment and create what you wish and/or eliminate any discords that causes you dis-ease. "Without having the consciousness of being consciously able to do it, there is no outlet for it to act ... to be conscious of a thing, gives it an outlet; and through this we can act" (King, 2012 p. 194). King (2012 p. 190) explained that, "your thoughts move through this consciousness outlet and mold your reality." If you are conscious of the idea that you can create or eliminate discords from your highest frequency, this lifts many roadblocks to manifestation and prepares the mind for the 'desired' expectations to appear in physical realities because of the Law of Attraction.

Thought Preparation Check-in

Check-ins are basic assessments that view evidence for and against the way you think. Essentially, check-ins are a quick temperature check of your harmonious vibrational thought patterns. Check-ins are not deep assessments, but rather a quick overview of the type of thoughts you are having. Periodic check-ins with your thoughts are mandatory, as they yield moments of clarity and an offer opportunity to redirect, if needed. Check-ins also ensure that your thoughts are of the highest frequency before you start working with the energy. Remember, your frequency determines the vibrations that will be returned to you in your physical reality. Thus, the goal is to vibrate as high as possible when working with energy, and keeping your thoughts free of discord. (It is recommended that readers complete the LEP Mental Check-in Assessment, A10) to identify your thought vibrational patterns.

Thoughts must be harmonious to vibrate in higher frequencies. Do your thoughts most often live in higher or lower vibrations? Checking-in with your thoughts reminds you to pay attention to what you are transmitting and receiving. Consciously checking in with your thoughts and monitoring their outputs allows you to catch, and eliminate, any harmful effects of discordant energy trying to invade your consciousness. If thoughtforms go unchecked, they have the opportunity to swirl, gather strength and return in their discordant forms and cause the unsuspecting individual undue stress, and disharmony due to their low vibrations. It will not be possible to lift you into higher mental vibrations and create desires when you are swirling in stress.

Just as discordant thoughts oppose the creation of your desires, harmonious thoughts manifest your desires. This is because as you think, your thoughts are connected to the pure mind of God, which is unlimited energy (McNight, 2005). In the creation of desires process "the mental energy bounces of the pure God energy and reproduces them in the form of script" (McNight, 2005). Thus, your thoughts (especially those that have strong emotional attachments attached to them) write your lived experiences and have the capability to manifest what you desire because they have the power to either increase of decrease your personal vibrational frequencies.

Check-in with your thoughts and do not allow them to languish in wrong or low energy conditions, for once they take root it is hard to uproot them. People often don't understand the disharmony that is taking place in their life. They think they are working hard, but don't understand why they are not happy, why things just don't work out, and question why they don't make more progress. It is because their thoughts run unchecked, controlling them and manifesting wrong creations in their life. Every person must control their thoughts to make any significant gains in producing the life that is desired.

You cannot create manifestations of higher energies while vibrating in low frequencies. If you wish to live in higher consciousness and create from that frequency, checking in with your thoughts regularly, and consciously eliminating, adjusting, and/or modifying lower thought forms, on the onset of their appearance is integral to your success and abilities to create your new reality. You are the creator of your thoughts; thus, you are the creator of your world. The type of thoughts you begin the day with will most often stay with you for the duration of your day. Think about this. The frequency in which you start the day will determine the pattern and energy flow for that day, unless you make conscious changes through thought. Starting in low energies will not only deter your progress in moving with quicker speed to the higher vibrations of manifestation, it will also affect your mental vibratory rate on a daily basis, and delay your progress into a higher vibration indefinitely.

Lastly, checking-in with your thoughts provides an opportunity to "clean house." It allows for taking a moment, to stop and examine the frustrations and irritations of life that fester in lower vibrational energy fields, sometimes unconsciously, or subconsciously, until you *consciously* bring them to light and resolve them. Sometimes the only way you will know where your thoughts fester is when you *consciously* check-in on them. If you don't like what you find, eliminate, or refuse them. As Louise Hay, (2012, video) affirms, "you can refuse to think certain thoughts," so refuse discordant thoughts, or thoughts that do not serve you, at their first appearance. Louise Hay contended in her many lectures that people have choices in what they think, "you are not a helpless victim of your own thoughts, but rather a master of your own mind. Whenever you think thoughts, they will align with the version of reality you created."

Check-ins are a very effective way to prepare the mind to create from higher energies. Because all inharmonious energies are eliminated upon examination. The readers mostly start with a clean slate and in a higher vibration. However, checking-in on your thoughts just to gauge their vibration is not enough, **questioning your thoughts**, **challenging your thoughts**, and **governing your thoughts** are also very important to ensure a higher overall mental vibrational consciousness. **Questioning your thoughts** allows for broader thinking and room for enlightenment. **Challenging your thoughts** helps with redirection, uncovers bias, and boosts creativity and growth. **Governing your thoughts** focuses on controlling, or exercising influence over all cognitive thinking processes, which if practiced diligently, *always* ensures a high vibrational frequency result.

Questioning Your Thoughts

Question your thoughts. Questioning is the art of learning through a broader spectrum, of getting answers for understanding through greater enlightenment. Questioning your thoughts is decoding information that only you possess. Decoding can be cognitively demanding and takes longer than check-in because you are not just identifying current vibrational energy. Questioning is a deeper activity; it queries whether the thoughts are serving you and the motivations behind them. Your thoughts should always be aligned with the version of you that you want, and your true intentions, and not from other stimuli, such as outer influences or your ego.

One of the most effective ways to question your thoughts is to listen to your **self-talk.**

Self-talk can be very persuasive, even when categorically untrue. Be aware of your "self-talk." When your mind drifts into discord such as judgment or criticism of yourself and others, or comes from the influences of the ego reign it back immediately. Self-talk tends to be slated towards lower forms of vibrations, and thus negative in nature. Look for any thought patterns or barriers that are limiting or directing your life in a way that is counterproductive to what you wish.

Any thoughtform stemming from fear, anger, selfishness, greed, anxiety, guilt, regret or any type of disappointment or limitations must be eliminated on appearance. If negative/lower thought forms go unchecked, they will throttle your potential and value as a person and harm and paralyze your efforts in raising your vibrational frequencies, leaving you unable to rise and move into a higher consciousness. Your inability to create from a higher consciousness will stifle your creativity, and most likely keep you in low vibrational fields, until such time you are ready to make progress once again and revert back to harmonious thoughts.

You must always question your thoughts and check to see if they are vibrating in lower vibrations. They are spiraling downward in frequency whenever your thoughts turn to the negative. King (2011 p. 8) contended that "when the mind accepts and agrees with a thing or condition, the individual decrees it to the world. Whatever you let the attention rest upon, you are agreeing with and accepting, because through the attention you have let the mind become one with it." There is great danger in this, as the more you think the same thoughts and they are of discordant nature, and you don't question them, the more you may become conditioned and draw to you, that, which you do not want.

Preparing thoughts is mental work that precedes all other manifestation processes because it allows you to question your thoughts which also shines a light on the incentive behind the thoughts. Your thoughts must be of harmonious nature if you are to make great progress in raising your vibrational frequency to produce positive results in a tangible world. Questioning your thoughts will not only assist you in broader thinking and offer new enlightenment through the answers, but it will also help you to understand yourself better and liberate your mind of energy that does not serve you. Thus, prepare you to receive higher vibrations.

Challenging Your Thoughts

Challenging your thoughts might be necessary. **Questioning your thoughts** uncovers discord, but many times through life's conditioning, discordant thoughts that have been accepted by the individual for some time become a part of them, and often take a bit longer to uproot. **Challenging your thoughts** helps with redirection, uncovers bias, boosts creativity, development and growth. Discordant thoughts or thoughts not aligned with your highest good must be challenged. By **challenging your thoughts**, you **test the inner mental voice** and decide if your determinations are skewed.

Challenging your thoughts can correct information that **check-ins,** and **questioning your thoughts** missed. Challenging your thoughts can uncover wrong, long-established thinking patterns and/ or incorrect conclusions. When challenging inharmonious thoughts, always look at the evidence in several ways and from the highest perspective to get to the truth of the matter. Often in challenging thought-forms, one must rise above their comfort zone and take the high road instead of reacting from the ego or pride

Challenging your thoughts involves the real truth, and not just the truth as established by your "ego." Ego and pride are lower forms of vibrations and live-in denser energies, but are very influential and powerful in planting thoughtforms in the mental consciousness of human beings. The ego's power structure is part of the imbalance in the earth consciousness which manifests itself in you, if not checked. When a person is not aligned with the higher energies of the mental, emotional, physical/sensory or spiritual consciousness they project a strong ego. The ego does not recognize the oneness of its existence with all the other levels of consciousness nor does it show appreciation or recognition for other important energy levels including all other forms of life (McNight, 2013).

Look for any other mental imbalances that project low vibrations and cloud your thinking. Moreover, don't fall into the trap and align yourself with lower forms of energies that send mental messages that you are inferior to others, that you can't accomplish something, that other people are more worthy than you, you don't have the right skills, looks, charm, or and so on. Ignore and challenge all images placed in your mental mind that do not serve you or will cause to think from a lower vibration. Challenging your thoughts means that when these thoughts do occur you instantly and head-on, challenge them by replacing them with harmonious thoughts that unequivocally send the message that you are *all* you wish to be, and have the power to create *all* that you desire.

Remove deeply the embedded thinking patterns and challenge the ingrained notions that limit your potential. Louise Hay (1994)

offers a quick and easy way to challenge any thought that does not serve you. In an interview, Louise Hay shared that she banishes all discordant thoughts quickly and easily. **"I say "***Out!* to every negative thought that comes to my mind. No person, place, or thing has any power over me, for I am the only thinker in my mind. I create my own reality and everyone in it" (Louise Hay). Be vigilant, recognize and identify your own thinking patterns, self-criticism and challenge your thoughts whenever you feel your vibrations dropping or you have a change of mood. Rise to the occasion and create the world you want by challenging any self-defeating thoughts, or thoughts that are not in your best interest that would restrict you or your power to create.

Challenging lower thoughtforms and not allowing them to exist in your mind is an effective way to retain your high vibrations and attract exactly what you wish in your life. Challenging lower thoughtforms may seem difficult at first, but it quickly gets easier with practice, as with any new skill. Be vigilant and challenge all discordant thoughts that do not serve, uplift, inspire, support and raise you up.

Governing Your Thoughts

Govern your thoughts! You are the governor of your life. "The individual alone is the governor and controller of the mind and will choose that which he or she will entertain; and will be at all times and forever, 'master of this condition now' because this particular activity requires no specific state of growth, but can be done successfully by anyone who will sincerely try" (King, 2012 p. 166). Thus, there is no excuse not to **govern your thoughts** and ensure that they always stay in the highest vibrational frequency possible. Dr. Sheldrake, a Cambridge trained biochemist, asserted that 'a thought fixed in the mind manifests when conditions are right.' The conditions are 'right' when the frequencies are aligned. If thoughts are not governed, but allowed to run free, uncontrolled, the harmonious conditions needed in the consciousness to create a desired manifestation will not take root, thus the desire will not appear, or be greatly delayed, leaving the person wondering why his or her manifestations are not showing up.

Govern your thoughts! It is up to each individual to actively participate and govern his or her thoughts to consciously contribute to create the right conditions by keeping vibrational frequencies high and aligned with that inner desire to outwardly manifest it in physical reality. The Divine process within the Source Consciousness is always at the ready, but it waits until you raise your vibrations to that of your desire, so that it can materialize it for you. Harmonious thoughts produce desires. If you govern your thoughts with sincere effort you will have prepared yourself to bring in higher vibrations and be at the ready to create whenever you wish because you will be existing in high vibrational frequencies where such power is readily available.

Govern your thoughts at all times because their power to keep you stuck in the lower energies of lack and survival is enormous. Discordant thoughts tend to sneak up on people, and before they know it, they are overwhelmed with mental states of depression, stress and frustration. By **governing your thoughts**, you have the capacity to stop this process before it gathers strength and causes much discord and inharmony which can disrupt your life. One of the more effective ways to **govern your thoughts** is to **practice what to think**, and refuse to allow any limiting thoughts to enter your mind. Dr. Dyer (2013) recommends that readers practice aligning yourself with the Source energy, and notice all your thoughts, and address those habitually misaligned ones.

Thoughts that do not make you feel good about yourself are misaligned. They must be reversed by either completely shutting them out/off or implementing a different way of thinking to replace the old habitual pattern. Throughout his lifetime Dr. Dyer (2013) contended that he *practiced* what to think. Dyer (2013) practiced thinking small and accomplishing big things, thinking in harmony and nature rather than the ego. It is always wise to remember that thoughts that are in congruence with the Source Consciousness and your highest self will yield great results. You cannot create great things in low vibrational energy, or find true and everlasting joy, abundance and well-being.

Thoughts can be difficult to govern because of the lightning speed in which they manifest. Thought is a quick, light mobile form of higher energy. It manifests instantaneously, unlike the denser forms, such as matter (Gawain, 1978), which can be more easily controlled, yet, it is the one place that each person has total control over. The writer, Aldous Huxley agreed that there is only one place in the entire universe that a person has complete control over and that is their thoughts. Your thoughts can be swayed and manipulated by your environment or others around you, but only you have the power to govern them and choose what you want to happen.

Governing your thoughts is crucial to your preparation to receive higher energies and success of creating what you desire in life because thoughts govern your actions. Your actions in turn govern your reality. Louise Hay contended that "we have to retrain our thinking and speaking into positive patterns if we want to change our lives and manifest something different." By **governing your thoughts** and eliminating any lower thoughtforms, you attract only those things and people who are in alignment with your highest ideals of yourself and have prepped the mind for the incoming higher vibrations.

Governing your thoughts also includes being consistently on guard for old thought patterns that try to make a comeback appearance once eliminated. Do not revert back to memories of where things did not work out as you intended, or dwell in any past mistakes, transgressions, guilt or regret. Flood discordant memories with love and forgiving thoughts and release them. This will allow the needed clearing, and cleansing. According to Dr. Dyer (2013, p. 606), "staying vigilant and continuously monitoring all thoughts causes you to notice what frequency you are transmitting and receiving. When you perceive that a thought is out of alignment, you can correct it; by doing so, you activate the Divine guidance because you're now thinking at the same frequency as the Source frequency... your job is to align with this frequency while simultaneously disabling the old thought frequencies."

Thoughts are the molder of form because they create your physical reality and the way you react and perceive the world. Moreover, "thought is interior speech and can be made a dynamo by which you can charge the body, home condition, or activity according to the consciousness or understanding you have of its power" (King, 2012, p. 188). Your inner thoughts, contain your habits, opinions and perceptions. Any thought that dwells on an idea creates that idea because thoughts create outer activity, you must **govern your thoughts,** and when you do you have prepared yourself to receive higher energies and can begin the process of creation.

Inner Preparation

In Proverbs 23:7 (NKJV) it is written, that "for as he thinks in his heart, so is he." **Inner preparation** is most important when working with vibrational frequencies because without *feeling* backing every *intent,* your desires will never manifest, or at best, be delayed until there is a match in the frequency between you and your desire. **Inner preparation** allows for greater and quicker successes because it not only sets the stage for desires to manifest, but is the enforcer behind every sent *intent.*

Inner preparation includes **emotions** and **feelings. Inner preparation** is also the domain of desires, beliefs, the most personal feelings, moods, sentiments, values, morals, ethics, Spirit, and meditation. **Mental preparation** is the dominant force that the individual is focused on, simply because human beings spend the most time in their heads, strategizing, planning, and/or envisioning what they want, how to do it, what it will look like when it is done and so on. But the **inner preparation** is just as important because it holds all past, present and future lived emotional experiences and often comes with great baggage of feelings that have attached themselves to the person and must be removed before effective energy work can occur, and your new life can be created. Stored baggage can include fears, anxiety, anger, depression, regret, and/or guilt, ill will toward someone, and so on.

Since **inner preparation** involves the **balancing of all emotions**, this is your opportunity to check-in on your emotions, and assess the health of your emotional consciousness. When working with **inner preparation,** control of emotions is necessary. According to King, (2007 p. 25), "it is a blight upon the life of mankind that so little control of the emotions is taught to humanity from the cradle to the grave. It is easy to give way to discordant feelings ..." but this must be brought under control. "This discipline requires determined, continuous efforts, for the thoughts and feelings of ninety five percent of humanity run uncontrolled and free" (King, 2007 p. 25). But in order to progress you must gain **control of your emotions,** and direct them. Not have your emotions direct you.

Emotions/Feelings Preparation Check-in

Checking-in with how you are feeling, and whether those feelings serve you and your highest good is vital in making quick headway in the rise of vibrations. Quieting one's self and checking-in with one's emotional consciousness prepares the perfect platform to clear and eliminate any discordant feelings that do not serve you and prepare you to receive higher vibrations. Remember, even though mental aspects even such as intelligence is the channel that information is received, it is feeling that molds its interpretation. Thus, emotional maturity and expansion, and balance play a large role in not only achieving but maintaining higher vibrations, and in the manifestation process.

Expanded emotional consciousness assists people to attain stabilization between their mind and feelings. It also helps them to better respond to discordant **emotions,** and keep their frequencies vibrating high. It is necessary that your feelings serve you, thus you must **control** them at all times, so that you may keep your vibrations high and attract what you want and not what you don't want into your life. The power of feelings is very strong because *feeling*, in many cases, *is believing*, thus a great influencer in a person's life. *Emotions* govern inner activity and any constructive desire that an individual wants to see manifested in their life must be backed by a supportive feeling.

Emotional check-ins immediately identify areas of emotional blockage that need removing. Emotional check-ins also provide you a quick overall frequency level of your current emotional vibration so that you can make the necessary adjustments. **Emotional check-ins** happen in real – time, require a total assessment of how you are feeling, and a complete attunement of why you are feeling that way. To be prepared to work with higher energies emotions must be monitored, governed and controlled. For assessment of your emotional vibrational frequency, it is recommended that readers complete the Emotional Check-In Assessment (A11).

Spiritual Preparation

Spiritual energy can often be hard to define because to many people it seems so ambiguous. Many people tie spiritual energy to religious aspects. Some do not affiliate spirituality with organized religion, at all. For others still, spiritual energy relates to science, atoms or quantum energy. Spiritual energy, in the current sense and for the purposes of this book, is defined as pure energy of the Source Consciousness from which human beings originated and are forever connected. It is the 'universal life force' flowing from the Source Consciousness into everyone's 'I AM' presence, the activity of the Source within you.

Spiritual energy receives its name because it exists in all living matter, in everything that is alive including you and all of humanity. Keeping the link clean between yourself and the Source Consciousness elevates you into higher energy frequencies with immense powers at your disposal. If you want to create with greater speed than you ever thought possible, or free yourself from the burdens of the past, or eliminate any discordant energies in your life, keep the link between yourself and the Source Consciousness strong by being aware of Its presence and Its power within you at all times. Any awareness' of the Source Consciousness as the working power in your life allows you to maintain, live and create in higher frequencies.

Spiritual preparation includes vibrational alignment with the **Source Consciousness**, and **meditation.** This means a **clean**, strong **connection** to the **Source** must be maintained at all times to receive optimal benefits. Dr. Wayne Dyer, in many of his lectures, emphasized the importance of keeping the link to the Source Consciousness open, and clean, if you want to manifest your desires in your reality. Dyer, admonished that 'we have the potential to create absolutely everything and anything we want – when we clean the connecting link.'

If you spiritually prepare, vibrational alignments will place you in the position to create because you will be ready to receive higher spiritual energies. Through **meditation** you will be the recipient of a calmness of the mind, which will yield a stronger connection to higher energies, where you will be able to prepare yourself by working with energy, fine-tune your desires, assume command of higher energies, and direct them where you want them to go. To keep the link, clean the use of the *violet energies* is recommended. In particular, use the Violet Flame Cleansing (S2) to shatter, dissipate and consume all wrong creations and keep your energy clean and as high as possible in the *currency* of every moment.

Spiritual preparation also requires an understanding and acceptance of the **'I AM'** spiritual energy within you. It also requires an awareness of the healing and manifesting properties of the *violet energy,* in particular, how to use and direct the **Violet Flame.** Additionally, **meditation** is essential to results. Regular **LEP meditations** are mandatory because they will quickly raise your consciousness and place you in the best possible position to either eliminate discords or create your desires. There is no going around this, if you want quick, and tangible results meditation is necessary.

LEP Violet Flame Meditation

There are many types of meditations and they each have a purpose. But for the purposes of working with the violet energy, **meditation** with the **Violet Flame** is strongly recommended. Meditation is necessary because it allows the person to achieve a state of mind where contact with higher energies is possible because it rests the mind enough to contemplate what they need and also to receive messages from higher frequencies. Ellen (2005) indicated that as you meditate, you enter into a deep the state of consciousness 'which is receiving the vibrations of love, wisdom, and guidance from your own divine essence. Your brain receives the frequencies of this truth through your spirit. The brain then sends pulses of these vibrations to the body through the central nervous system' (Ellen, 2005), which helps to relax you and form the meditative state. This elevated state of mind allows for creating either desires or eliminating discords through the power of *contemplation* and *intent*.

Meditation with the **Violet Flame** is similar to regular meditation. However, although it is similar because it requires that you find a quiet place where you are not disturbed, and the same process of elevating your mind enough to where relaxation takes hold it is more active in nature. The **Violet Flame meditation** is **action oriented,** rather than the more passive meditation of waiting for messages to be transmitted to you. With the **Violet Flame meditation**, you are consciously contemplating, visualizing and directing energy through your intent, and activating energy fields within your consciousness in order to manifest them in your physical plane. **Meditation** with the **Violet Flame** also differentiates itself from other meditations because of its specific focus of directing the energy to consciously raise **mental, emotional, physical/sensory,** and **spiritual** energy fields actively using them in order to create any desire in the consciousness and generate it in the person's physical reality, eliminate discord or karma. Custom made **decrees** on whatever you wish to eliminate or whatever you wish to create must **accompany** the **meditation** (see various samples included in the book).

You may use your own method of established practice of meditation on the onset to raise yourself to an elevated relaxation level. But generally when you begin to meditate begin living in the stop frame of the moment. This means each thought that arises you surrender it to the universe/God, along with each feeling, and each sensation. If you continue this pattern within minutes the mind begins to surrender itself as each thought unfolds. If you are having trouble clearing your mind focus first on surrendering whole stories in your mind that usually stem from the ego until your mind is clear. Surrender paragraphs, then sentences, and any other streams of thoughts or emotions that come up.

In this stop moment you have no problems and there is nothing on your mind. The energy behind thought is itself formless and begins itself as a thought, at the point release of the energy of thought (Hawkins). When you clear your mind, you clear your thought energy. This is an important step because the mind tries to anticipate the next moment, 'because it thinks it has to in order to survive, thus you are not experiencing reality but the ego's interpretation of reality' (Hawkins) which interferes in the relaxation state that is needed for meditation.

Meditative music is recommended and there are many options to choose from. Select wisely. By selecting music that really speaks to your soul, your imagination and visualizations will be at your highest potential. Harmonious music is of higher energies and is a tremendous asset in meditation because it allows for emptying the mind and offers a single point of focus; rhythm. From a neurological standpoint, your brain is listening to music and focuses on that as a default, which allows you to exclude everything else, and still the mind.

A word on lighting. Although commonly a darkened area such as a dark room is the preferred space to meditate by most people who practice the traditional meditative techniques, working with the *violet energies* produces the best results in well-lit areas. The amount of lighting is not as significant, but it should not be a dark space. The reason for a lit room is simple, "that which is of the Light always works in the Light (King" (1993 p. 158). "Darkened rooms are not used as a setting in which to produce that which they create, direct from the Universal Substance" (King, (1993 p. 157), the Source Consciousness.

During meditation, the **Violet Flame** which is ready to receive your instruction, through your **'I AM'** presence, responds to every call. When you meditate, focus on receiving high frequencies from the Source Consciousness because this transmutes anything discordant stuck anywhere in your spiritual self. According to Prophet, (1997, p. 42) one of the reasons that using the **Violet Flame** increases your vibrations is because, "freed of debris, the electrons begin to move more freely, thus raising our vibration and propelling us into a more spiritual state of being" and into a more relaxed state of consciousness.

Higher vibrations in meditation produce results because of the Law of Attraction. The invocation of the *violet energy* and your *decree* (which is activated through your 'I AM' energy) creates an instant convergence between your desire in the physical world, which is matter, and the *violet energy*, which is electronic spiritual energy of consciousness. If you are both vibrating at the same frequency, the convergence pulls the electronic energy into physical form and into your reality. Thus, when you meditate through the use of the **Violet Energy,** the elimination of discord or a creation of desired manifestation often could be instantaneous. However, a time for results should never be demanded as all desires are manifested in the physical world at their own perfect time, and your perfect frequency to receive them.

A prayer of gratitude and a grateful attitude should be shown at the beginning and ending of each meditation. **Decrees** are important in meditation and must be used to be clear in your *intention*. For example, if during meditation with the **Violet Flame** you wish to create a specific desire, as you meditate, enter into the heart of your own **'I AM'** presence. Allow your mind, body and emotion to receive Its spiritual vibrations and feel the power of you as the creator, as you visualize the **Violet Flame** in a dazzling illumination of brilliantly twinkling violet lights contemplate, see your desire in the Violet energy and send out your intention to the universe from that space. For example, if you wish to be free of financial stress and debt, during meditation, invoke the **Violet Flame** and take a lengthy amount of your time to visualize every bill and every financial obligation dissolving in the Violet Flames, or see prosperity or money flow to you everyday and in every way. See your bank accounts with healthy sums, money in your wallet etc.

In healing, surround yourself with the flame or even enter into it. Allow the violet light to lovingly wash over you, moving through you like a shower of beautiful violet healing light to rejuvenate, and invigorate every cell in your body, (or a specific ailment, or discord) that you want eliminated, so that you can be free and released of it or of all low and discordant energies. Prophet (1997, p. 2) contended that "the violet energy is an invisible spiritual energy that revitalizes and invigorates us. It can heal emotional and even physical problems, improve relationships and make life easier. Because the violet flame changes negative energy into positive, it is an effective healing tool…"

If time is of the essence, you can apply a quicker meditation with short direct decrees, which can also be very effective. For example, *Through my 'I AM' presence I invoke the Violet Flame to see to it that 'I AM' free of this financial stress and debt. See to it that it never enters my world again for the highest good of myself and all concerned. And so, it is decreed. See the debt dissolved in the Violet Flame, and that only good came of it. Thank it for the lessons it has taught you and release it. Feel the stress leave your body.* Decrees are rhythmic orders that call forth spiritual energies which are used with the **Violet Flame** to better direct energies. For examples of various decrees that can be used with meditation, see Supplements (S12, S13).

In your meditations with the **Violet Flame,** ALWAYS use visualizations. See them within the brilliantly flickering violet flames and imagine, visualize, and picture whatever you want created or eliminated whether it is money, opportunities, love, great health, abundance, perfect relationships or discords of any type. See it, feel it, and believe it. You do not need to worry how or when what you want will appear or when the discord will be alleviated for your desire will become your reality at the perfect time, place and space.

Signal Transmission

Signals are unseen messages in the form of vibrations that broadcasts your frequency of the *current* moment. The understanding that consciousness can create anything you desire must include the understanding that the signals sent through your vibrations are very real, and manifest very real experiences in your life. Be consciously aware of the signals you are sending whether through your thoughts, beliefs, actions, emotions, and so on, and make corrections whenever necessary. Dr. Dyer (2013) and Louise Hay (1995) contended that the 'power of your mind creates your world.' Keep your thoughts and emotions high by being optimistic and positive regardless of outer appearance. If you do, you will send signals of the highest frequency and be the recipient of amazing expressions in your life.

Signal transmission at all stages of life is vital to the success of all end results because of the Laws of Vibrations and Attraction. The signals transmitted by all living and non-living things can be seen as vibrational signatures which attract *like* energy to itself. Source Consciousness reads all mental, and inner vibrations and boomerangs "like" energies back to the individual at the same frequencies because the Source Consciousness is orderly and transmits within the frequencies it receives. Emotionalized thoughts are especially powerful signals because they carry potency which can manifest in intense negative or positive manifestations.

Since the individuals experience all energy in terms of 'high or low' in their expressions in life, it greatly affects them and everything surrounding them. How they think, act, believe, what they feel, how people treat them, how they treat people, the kinds of opportunities that presents themselves, how they get along, how they experience their day and virtually everything that shows up in their life will carry the same frequency. Thus, the signals sent through the combination of your mental and emotional vibrations are creating your reality, as a direct result of the Laws of vibration and Attraction.

Signal transmissions come in any form of mental, (through thoughts), emotional, (through feelings), physical/sensory, (through the way you use your senses or actions), and spiritual (inner belief systems) energy fields. The higher the transmissional frequency, the higher the vibration that will be returned to you. Remember, mental and emotional fields can control what comes to you if you allowed them to form and remain in lower vibrations without being checked. They only transmit to the universe what they are, not what you want them to be. So be very cognizant of your thoughts and feelings for they define the signals that are sent to the universe, and as a result shape your lived experiences.

Prepare yourself well, and be aware of the signals you are sending as they are a reflection of your current state of mind. If you are not attracting what you desire, start paying attention to the signals emanating from you. Congruence between your harmonious mental, emotional and spiritual fields is the only way you will send signals of the highest frequencies to the universe and be the benefactor of much higher vibrations entering your life.

PART 2
MEANS

4

The Means

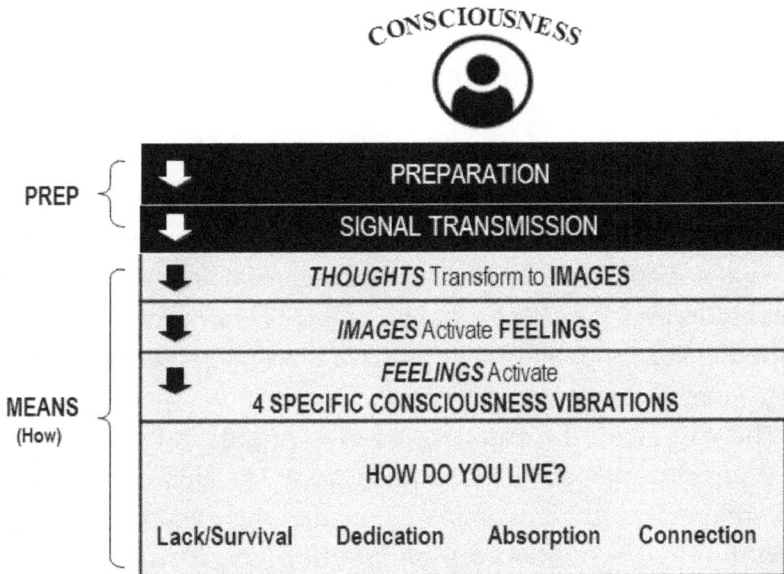

The Means

The **Means** offers the readers the "how." The Means includes the consciousness fields of **Lack and Survival, Dedication, Absorption and Connection Consciousness** and identifies current vibrational frequencies of the readers, and uses that information to activate the **Mechanisms** of their **mental, emotional, physical/sensory** and **spiritual** consciousness vibrations in order to help people raise their overall vibrational frequency. This vastly assists each person to expand their consciousness so that they may manifest constructive desires into their physical reality. The **Means** accomplishes this through control and direction of the energy of thoughts, images in the mind and **feelings**.

Thoughts transform to **images. Images** activate **feelings.** *Feelings* activate **4 specific vibrational fields** of L*ack* and *Survival, Dedication, Absorption* and *Connection Consciousness.* The **Lack and Survival** consciousness is the densest in the lived experience phenomenon and is where most humanity move. The **Lack and Survival** energies are of discordant nature because they are of the **lowest** earthly vibrations and move in the "**cause and effect'** paradigm.

The **Dedication Consciousness** which is the next level from **Lack and Survival** moves in **moderate** energies and includes the ability to silence the inner and outer mind that is usually out of control in the Lack and Survival Consciousness. In the **Dedication Consciousness** the person masters the ability to control **thoughts**, **images** in the mind, and **feelings**. This level offers the first opportunity to work with energies of creation.

The **Absorption Consciousness** is **higher** in frequency than the Dedication Consciousness because it contains greater power of creation. The Absorption level includes the expanded energies of *contemplation, intention, elimination* and *insulation.* Within the **Absorption Consciousness** the power to create desires, eliminate any discordant energy or balance karma outside of karmic cycles not only exists but is the operating apparatus that is used to fulfill any aspiration, wish or goal, providing it is of constructive nature.

The **Connection Consciousness** vibrates in **peak** frequency. The **Connection Consciousness** offers its occupants an existence of living with capabilities to have manifestations released from their consciousness into their realities, almost on demand. In this peak consciousness life is usually characterized by euphoria, an exhilarating way to live that elevates understanding, awareness, and vastly increases the power to create because the person has tapped into the Source Consciousness at their highest frequency. It is living in blissful energies of the person's full potential.

To begin using the **LEP Frequency Tool** of consciousness assessing your current vibrational frequency is necessary. The included, *How Do You Live?* assessments will identify the readers' personal vibrational frequency fields and determine if they live in the *Lack and Survival, Dedication, Absorption*, or the *Connection* Consciousness. This knowledge is necessary so that they can begin to make changes and modification to increase their vibrations and experience a better life. Moreover, knowing where you vibrate in the current moment will assist you to make the necessary adjustments in your **mental, emotional, physical/sensory** and **spiritual** consciousness and help raise your overall frequency, so that you may see outcomes of your desires in your physical reality with greater speed, and create the future that you want to face.

Thoughts Transform to Images

Thoughts transform to images. As the atoms form the body or outer environments for, and of the individual, so do individuals' thoughtforms create the inner and outer reality of the person. In the book by Wattles (1910), "*The Science of Getting Rich*," the author contended that a man can form things in his thought, and, by impressing his thought upon formless substance, can cause the thing he thinks about to be created. It can be created and manifested because **thoughts** transform into **images,** and **images** activate **feelings, feelings** trigger the **mechanisms** of manifestation within the **mental, physical/sensory, emotional** or **spiritual** frequencies of consciousness. Harmonious **alignment** in **all 4** consciousness frequencies **raises vibrations** and unleashes manifestations from the conscious mind into physical realties.

Anything persistently held in your consciousness in thought and feeling will bring them into your use and world. It must because it responds to the Law of Vibration and Attraction. When you think or feel something you are vibrating at the same level as that something. Thus, whenever you allow your thoughts to dwell in the low vibrations, you are compelling them into your physical universe, and have opened yourself up to whatever energies were generated by that vibration. You are creating your desires as you are choosing your own thoughts, thus what is running in the programming of your mind eventually will manifest in your physical reality (McNight, 2005). McNight (2005) admonished that if you want to change your outer world you don't start with changing your external world but must first change your mental programming.

In addition to thoughts, images play a key role in the manifestation process. Impressing an image of low frequencies, such as unhappiness, anxiety, regret, guilt, sadness and the like upon your mental consciousness will attract these lower energies to you, almost instantaneously. The dense energies will appear in many forms such as a sudden change of mood, depression, bleak perception or outlook on life, lack of motivation, unexplained anger, even rage and so on. Paying attention to the "trends" of your thoughts and correcting all negative and discordant thoughts *before* they have a chance to make an imprint on your consciousness, will allow you to move much quicker into higher frequencies and begin the creating process.

Louise Hay, often referred to as the queen of New Age, an inspiring motivational author, speaker and teacher who educated millions of readers, since her 1984 bestselling book, and movie, of same name, "*You Can Heal Your Life*," emphasized the tremendous power of thoughts "accept the fact that every time you think a thought, and every time you speak a word, you are literally painting your future and creating your life…Train yourself to be aware of what you are thinking…our thoughts bring us back the experience…Even at the smallest level if we are aware of our thoughts, we can start to make changes." In the movie, an unhappy young woman finds a message card with the words, *I am willing to change*. From that moment, her life's transformation began as she became aware that if she wanted a different life, she 'had' to change, but more importantly, she was willing to change.

It is the same for all who are reading these words. Are you willing to change? Are you willing to do what some would call impossible? Yet, if you are resonating with this book you already know that it is possible. It all starts with your thoughts, and your willingness to change your life. In her many lectures, Louise Hay explained that, "most of us have learned to view our thoughts as the reflection of the outside world, a reflection of what is happening to us, but what if that is not how the universe works? What if with every thought you think, you are actually creating your present and your future? What if you are creating the story of your life with the very thought you are thinking now, then perhaps if we are willing to change the way we think, wonderous opportunities would reveal themselves to us and our lives would move in a whole new direction."

Every thought has a vibration. You must always be in control of your thoughts because your thoughts create images in your mind that are imprinted in your consciousness. These images are used as blueprints to manifest externally, what is created internally through thought. If the images are of lack and limitation, it will activate feelings of lack and limitation, which will attract those characteristics (low energies) into the persons' life, and their life will reflect, the Lack and Survival energies in which most of humanity moves. If the image is one of success, peace and happiness, the energy will bring more of the same.

The longer the images imprinted on the consciousness linger, the greater the chances of them taking root and the manifestation of those images coming to fruition. Some imprinted images may quickly out-picture, if the focus is changed. For example, if you think and have an image of yourself as a successful person but have a wishy-washy personality and are easily influenced by others no matter how strong the imprint in the mind that you are a success, it can be easily torn down by others and the image will quickly out-picture leaving you in the mental state that you are not a success but a failure. By the same token, if the energies are redirected elsewhere because the desire that was once held in the mind has now been replaced with new *intent*, (new desire) manifestations will take much longer to appear as the new intention now must gain traction.

In order to create a mental determination (an imprint in mind) must hold the desire steady until it manifests. It is always up to you. You are always the one that must make the effort to hold the imprints of your desires on your consciousness, which creates your reality. If you want your desire to come to you, be firm and do not be dissuaded by yourself or influenced by others. H old strong your conviction and never allow that image to be out-pictured by something else.

All human beings are the determiner of their lives and must always hold the image of success in their consciousness, whatever that means for, and to them. If the readers and LEP Frequency Tool practitioners hold the images, and with a determined stand, rise to meet the higher vibrations that are freely available to them, their life will be forever changed. "If you maintain this determination, you will find at some future time that the force set in motion never ceased for one moment to work to that end" (King, 2012).

If the image is held steady, everything you think about that is imprinted in your consciousness must manifest at some point in time because the energy never ceases to draw the "like" energy towards it. Therefore, if you wish your desires manifested, maintain your deter-mination. Hold your image steady, and do not allow doubt to enter your energy fields.

Images Activate Feelings

Energy cannot be fooled. Once thoughts and images in the con-sciousness are aligned with your feelings, they result in manifesta-tions in your physical reality whether you want them to or not. If your thoughts are of negative or discordant in nature, your lived experi-ences will be as well. You can only experience the energy you send.

Energy is not personal. Every outer experience is only a mirror of our inner thought patterns and images implanted in the consciousness and will be lived and relived at that same frequency. These images are very powerful because they provide the insights of how people really feel inside; the vibrations they live in, and signals they are sending.

Since energy reads your vibration, it can't ever be fooled. You can't tell the energy "I am only thinking positively and support those thoughts with positive images" because energy reads your vibration. It is not waiting for you to tell it what you really think or share with it the type of images you are planting in your mind because your thoughts and images activate your feelings automatically. Energy knows you better than you know yourself. It knows exactly what you are thinking, and seeing in your mind which activate your emotional consciousness.

Feelings are produced by emotions that were influenced by thoughts and images. Feelings are unguarded points of consciousness within a human being. Feelings are the activity of life and accumulative energy by which thoughts are propelled into the atomic substance, and thus do thoughts become things (King, 2007). Emotions create an internal reality which attracts the energy of your feelings in various aspects to you. Keeping only harmonious thoughts and images in the mind changes the point of attraction, and in turn, changes the feelings within the person because thoughts and images activate feelings. Thus, the universe does not respond to just your words, but your words are reflective of how you feel (Hay, 2007). How you feel is reflective of the vibration that you are emanating through your thoughts and the images planted in the mind.

The world is a magnetic mirror that attracts the same energy you sent in thought, images and your feelings. You may not be aware of it, but everything in the universe is reflecting back what you sent out. You are responsible for what shows up in your life because you are both the receiver and the transmitter of your energy and manifest according to your vibrational frequency in your physical life through **thoughts, images** and **feelings.** Louise Hay contended in her lectures, that "the truth as we now know is that your thoughts and beliefs, what you think and believe is what will come true for you … your thoughts create your life and when we get that, we can make enormous changes" (Hay, 2008). So, only include pictures and images of high vibrations in your mind because these images will activate your feelings, and draw those same vibrations to you. The images send out a resonance into the world of energy which assists in physical manifestations. If you vibrate at the frequency of your desire through your thoughts, images in the mind and feelings those desires, if they are constructive, will manifest. For higher frequencies can only manifest things of "higher frequencies." High frequencies cannot create against the grain, meaning desires of low frequencies. Thus, whatever you think and feel from higher frequency will come into form. Where your thoughts and images in your mind are, there you are, for "you are your consciousness, and whatever you focus upon you become" (King, 2007).

Feelings Activate the Four Consciousness Vibrations

Thoughts trigger images, images activate feelings of vibrations of **Lack and Survival, Dedication, Absorption and Connection Consciousness.** All human suffering, unhappiness and unfulfillment is a result of human constructs. If you change the constructs by using your thoughts, images and feelings, you increase your vibrations and automatically move into higher vibrational fields and experience a more fulfilling and happier life. There are **4** specific consciousness vibrations, **(1) Lack and Survival (2) Dedication (3) Absorption, and (4) Connection** that operate within any individuals' shift in energy that produces its own momentum, and attracts the energies of its kind.

The power of creation is very limited or almost unattainable for those living in the very dense energy of the **Lack and Survival Consciousness** (Assessment A2). The Lack and Survival consciousness field is the **lowest** energy field as it is particularly unstable with fluctuating moods, stress and energy that is not controlled as it operates within the *'cause* and *effect'* reactive sphere. Living in Lack and

Survival energy often brings the most discordant vibrations, particularly when individuals uncontrollably fluctuate between lower and higher forms of energy like joy and sadness, or peace and anxiety.

Dedication Consciousness (Assessment A3) is a **moderate** energy field. It holds the ability to silence the inner and outer mind, and control and manage *thoughts, images* and *feelings*; thereby retaining their higher vibration, attracting, and increasing the speed in which desires manifest. Dedication Consciousness is the foundation of all good things to come. It the start of the creation process and the commencement of available power to flow to you.

The **Absorption Consciousness** includes the energies of *contemplation, intention, elimination* and *insulation.* The **Absorption Consciousness** (Assessment A4) is a **high** energy that fully makes use of the skills learned to harness **thoughts, images** and **feelings** in the **Dedication Consciousness.** In the Absorption consciousness abundant power is bestowed upon the individual and they have the ability to manifest desires, eliminate discord or balance karma quickly and easily, and protect themselves against incoming discordant energy through the application of **contemplation, intention, elimination** and **insulation** energies. At this level constructive desires that were only possible for the individual in the past become assured.

The **Connection Consciousness** is **peak** energy and offers unlimited resources at your disposal. *Faith* is replaced with *knowing. Knowing* is replaced with the *reality you want to live.* You create from a sense of well-being. Nothing is restricted, limited or denied. All worthy desires are created in perfect order and harmony. People living in this **peak** vibration are much slower to anger. They understand that there is really no such thing as people, arguments, negative situations, or bad news. It is just energy that must be handled and controlled which they do with relative ease. Desires in the consciousness swiftly make their appearance in physical reality, and creating the future they want to face becomes effortless.

Each consciousness field, **Lack and Survival, Dedication, Absorption** and **Connection** is explained in detail in the next chapter. Your access to powers of elimination or creation of desires will always depend on where you live energetically. This cannot be faked; you cannot pretend to vibrate in higher consciousness and produce results. Energy only responds to like energy, and must be aligned, meaning that your **thoughts**, and **images** in your mind, and your **feelings** must be aligned, and through **contemplation, intention, elimination, and insulation** you WILL produce results!

Take the *How Do You Live? Vibrational Consciousness Identifiers* in Chapter 10 and find your current vibrational frequency. No matter where you are, you can increase your frequency at any moment and start creating the life you wish to live by following the simple instructions in this book. Assessments should be taken at continuous and regular intervals to ensure that progress is being made. Supplements will assist all readers in the progression of their journey into higher frequencies.

5

Means

HOW DO YOU LIVE?

Lack and Survival Consciousness

There is an endless supply of everything you can possibly need in the universe. There is no lack. There is only perceived lack. In the **Lack and Survival** Consciousness, which is the lowest vibration of basic existence, humanity moves in automatic rhythms of *cause and effect,* unobservant, unaware and often too preoccupied with life's challenges to care or even notice that they have the power to change their life.

The energies of **Lack** and **Survival** take many forms that manifest as negative lived experience and discord. As is the case with all energy, Lack and Survival Consciousness is impersonal. It does not discriminate against being single, in a relationship, finances, economic or social status, intellect, beauty, gender, culture, religion and so on. These low and dense energies effect all human beings who live in that consciousness field with the same low vibrations through the individual's **mental, emotional, physical**, or **spiritual** consciousness frequencies. The **low** energy of 'lack' shows up in various shapes and **causes** the **effect** of survival which may appear as discord in peoples' lived experiences.

To reaffirm, whether the readers are rich or poor, in a relationship or not, healthy or not and so on, is of inconsequence. 'ALL' who live in this energy will experience the low uncomfortable vibrations of this discordant energy in their vibrational fields through any or all of their consciousness frequencies. For example, just because you are rich does not mean that you are happy. Many financially secure people are miserable and feel lack. When vibrating at low frequencies no one is excluded from life's challenges because one has accumulated great wealth, is in a happy relationship, or loves their job. High energy vibrations must occur in all of 4 of the mental, emotional, physical and spiritual consciousness domains in order to bring joy, peace, well-being and abundance into your life. Consistent low vibrations will overwhelm the individual and squash the life force energy right out of them causing demotivation, stress, unhappiness, anxiety and a life filled with sadness, unfulfillment and struggle.

Many people in the **Lack and Survival** Consciousness live in the action mode of doing. Doing, doing, and doing but not getting anywhere professionally, financially, mentally, emotionally or in any other way. Or if they get ahead in one area, it doesn't bring them the happiness they thought it would, or another area of their life will begin suffer. It seems as if no matter how hard they try, the doors to professional opportunity, great relationships, wealth, health and well-being or just some sort of balance in their life, and happiness and peace are forever closed to them.

Some people are very driven, and make great strides and progress in areas they thought they wanted. They accumulate great wealth, or have acquired the person or the career they thought they wanted, or achieved some other goal that they long sought, but even when they got it, it did not bring them the joy they thought it would. Thus, they continue to live and cycle in "lack and survival" energies. They are now the people that seem to have it all, yet they remain unhappy, frustrated and unfulfilled.

The truth is that the "haves" are as often just as unhappy as the "have nots." Other people in the Lack and Survival consciousness field are just barely getting by as each day turns into the next and the endless array of tasks and responsibilities await them. Others, yet, have fallen on even harder times and just can't seem to financially dig out, or find the right person, or are experiencing illness or poor health. They are discouraged, exasperated and have all but given up. They are but a shell of a person living a discontented life with seemingly no way out of their own personal hell and feeling as if "all hope is lost."

People cycling in the Lack and Survival energies do not live fully, but exist to endure. Lack and survival are most obvious when one is laden with roles and responsibilities; for the most part created through external economic, or self-inflicted internal perspectives. Happiness at this stage is only a faraway glimmer of what life could be. In many cases, although the face may hold smiles and a light hearted attitude, and individuals may present themselves as fully functioning responsible adults to the external world, internally they are vibrating in very low energies, and are disappointed and disillusioned by life. These energies may manifest as mood swings, short temperament, impatience, frustration, deeply rooted unhappiness, tears, anxiety, depression, helplessness, lack of faith and hope, loss of esteem, stress, negative perspectives, illness and so on. These low energies are reflected in the persons' 4 **mental, emotional, physical, and spiritual** consciousness frequencies.

To a people living in **Lack and Survival** energies, life often feels heavy. These individuals cycle in these low effects **mentally, emotionally, physically** and/or **spiritually** at different intensity of frequencies but all feel their discordant forces. All successes to move out of **Lack and Survival** energy fields and into higher consciousness come through the determination and will to change the **causes** and **effects** of the energy in their life, which is the only force that will lift them into higher vibrations, and move them into a new and much more improved life.

Cause and Effect

If you understand that you **cause** the **effects** in your life, you can quickly modify the **causes** and get much better **effects**. The cause-and-effect principle is based on the theory that the outer manifestation is a representation of the inner energies. If your thoughts are negative, so is your lived experience on the physical earth. According to McNight (2013) once you can get your mental thoughts patterns in control in the physical realm, this will affect energies (your experiences) positively. Hawkins (2002, p. 27) further explained that the observable world is a world of "effects."

It is not the outer circumstances that determine your vibrational frequencies. It is the inner state (conscious and unconscious) that determines your outer circumstances because it can only attract similar frequencies. Ultimately, the only thing a person attracts is what he or she already is (Dyer, 2013) through the vibrational signals that they send from their mental or emotional consciousness fields. Troward (2007) in agreement with Dyer (2013) affirmed that what you attract into your world will always be consistent with your own state (Troward, 2007). Thus, your **cause** will match the **effect**. If you are vibrating at a lower frequency, the universe, which is impersonal, has no choice but to match that frequency and respond with the sum total of the energy (conscious and unconscious) that is aligned with your vibratory state. Thus, it will give you the **effect** that you **caused.**

There is no one to blame. Unequivocally, your vibratory state is the **"cause"** that determines the **"effect"** (what shows up in your life). You are the creator of all that enters your existence in some manner. King (2012, p. 10) contended that, you alone are the governor of your life and its activity and are commanded to choose what you desire to manifest." Life in the physical universe is all about growth and creating the world in which you wish to experience that world. But you experience that world through the results of your **cause**-and-**effect** actions. You can experience your life in the low vibrations of pain, suffering or sadness or you can experience it through vibrant energies of love, passion, prosperity and happiness. But you will always experience it through the **cause** and **effects** of the energies you yourself extend, and the signals you are sending.

When living in the Lack and Survival Consciousness field you are confined to low mental, emotional, physical/sensory and spiritual levels. To move out of this low energy it is necessary to release fears and negative concepts that live in those levels. Continual cleaning of the thoughts and emotions of fear, selfishness, greed, anger, hostility, regret, guilt or lack of kindness, compassion, forgiveness and love are essential. Discordant mental and emotional patterns must be broken and released to unblock the negative energy flow so that you can rise in vibrational frequencies and lift your consciousness to higher levels of energy where more power is available to you. If you work toward higher levels of light and love for yourself and others, forgive your transgressions towards others, and transgressions by others toward you, no matter how big, small or painful they may be, you will get the desired results. Begin to practice humility, compassion and kindness, and you will leave Lack and Survival energies and raise into the higher vibrations of love, and power with greater ease.

Each person has within them the highest capacity to love. Love is essential to gaining more power because the more you love the closer you are to the Source Consciousness from whom all powers flow. Love can pull you out of Lack and Survival energies because it promotes self-love, self-esteem, confidence, self-trust and a non-judgmental attitude towards acceptance of yourself and everyone around you. Additionally, it moves people beyond negative feelings (energy) and fear. Moreover, letting go of all fear and focusing on the love vibration assists in the removal of blockages and the raising of vibrational frequencies by expanding your consciousness levels, which must be done, if you are to move up in vibrational frequency and harness more power. Love energy can help bring you out of the dense Lack and Survival Consciousness because it brings more awareness and power to you because of its pure love energy vibration. Love vibration is the highest level of energy within every life form and has the capacity to lift vibrational frequencies with great speed.

Send love and blessing to yourself and the world! Be careful and mindful of the energy signals you are transmitting to the universe! Always be conscientious of what you are projecting to the universe because these are the signals you are sending. Watch your thoughts, images in your mind and emotions for whether these energy forms are sent subconsciously or consciously they will return to you the same energy. Coming from a place of love and being aware that only you can transform your life is a good start because these signals are hopeful and rooted in goodwill and faith. Change your mind-set of "things are happening to me," to "only great things are happening for me because I am the controller of my lived experiences, and only good comes to me" and believe it!

Living in low energies is never productive and will only bring you more of the same. It will never assist you to achieve your desires but will keep you trapped in a life of endurance enslaved in the Lack and Survival energies until you consciously increase your vibrations. All readers that find themselves in the Lack and Survival energy field must take responsibility and action to rise in vibrations because only through your own efforts you can produce your sought-after results. Take Assessment A2, and find out if are you living in the Lack and Survival Consciousness field.

Dedication Consciousness

All creation starts in the consciousness. The **Dedication Consciousness** vibrates in **moderate** energies, as it launches mastery over **thoughts, images,** and **feelings.** The **Dedication Consciousness** is the beginning phase of everyone serious about working with pure energy to produce tangible results in their physical world. To begin to lift out of Lack and Survival energy fields mastery over your consciousness must be achieved.

All desires commence with thoughts, appropriate images, and are backed by supportive feelings so that they may produce desired results. Likewise, people's transformation from lower to higher energies, where all things are within their grasp because they have opened the door to power that they can tap, also begin with framing thoughts, images and feelings, to produce their desired outcomes. Your thoughts, images in your mind, and feelings must be harmonious and fully aligned to acquire the higher energies you seek to manifest your desires and live in the world you wish to face. **Harmonious** responses in the **mental** and **emotional consciousness** fields will **raise** your vibrational **frequencies**, and vastly increase your power to create anything you desire, or eliminate any discord in your life, regardless of whether that discord causes discomfort in your finances, love, health, career, and so on.

LEP Framing for Manifestation

Framing for manifestation requires a harmonious energy alignment of **thoughts, images** and **feelings.** Alone, the logical mind, which is singular, can process understanding. But it cannot manifest desires without the other perceptual lenses of inner emotions that spark strong feelings. Every moment that people live, they frame their experiences through their **thoughts, images** in their mind, and their **feelings.** And thus, **manifest** exactly what shows up in their life because these **experiences** will match the frequency of the mental and emotional vibration of the individual. In framing for manifestation of desires, vibrations try to find patterns within the mental and emotional framework of existing blueprints of a human being, so that it can attract to them what they want. The higher and more harmonious the vibrational patterns of your **thoughts, images** and **feelings** towards a desire, the quicker it will be attracted into your physical reality. This is the only way energy can work because in the law of physics, "like" can only attract "like." Thus, you can't desire something in the mind, but inwardly feel that there is no way that you can get, as in this scenario the energy is not aligned. If the energy is not aligned it greatly delays progress and will eventually thwart efforts.

Framing Thoughts

Thought is an energy system with a point of attraction. Whatever you think about expands and draws the qualities of that energy to you because of the magnetic nature of thoughts. Framing your thoughts positively will activate optimistic feelings, which will activate alignment with a higher vibration and send the signals of expectancy. Alignment with a higher mental vibration generates power and significantly increases the ability to create desires. Always be positive so that your mental faculties are always working in harmonious energies. Any negative or discordant thoughts, and/or images in your mind must be either immediately eliminated or reframed. Be alert for thoughts that creep in by force of habit and reject any idea that does not serve you or limits you in any way. If low energy thoughts appear, reframe or eliminate them immediately!

Framing thoughts for manifestation is simply conditioning yourself to frame all information (energy) from your highest vibratory potential. It also entails being more patient and not making any judgments on how to react. Make it a habit to allow your mental mind to inform you on how to best reframe a thought or an image to be better aligned with who you are and what you need, not so much what you want. Listen to your mental guidance system to discern, interpret and respond appropriately to the mental information or energy you are receiving. Training yourself to be mentally aware of the caliber of your thoughts, and the images in your mind opens you up to higher vibrations and quicker manifestations of your needs.

Louise Hay (1994) in her book *101 Power Thoughts,* informs us "that the thoughts we think and the words we speak are constantly shaping our world and our experiences. Many of us are in an old habit of negative thinking and do not realize the damage we have inflicted upon ourselves." The most severe damage occurs from negative thinking patterns that keep people imprisoned in lower vibrations, such as the Lack and Survival Consciousness. However, as Hay indicates, "we are never stuck because we can always change our thinking." Reframing negative to positive thoughts significantly increases vibrations, and the overall mental frequency of the individual. Positive, uplifting thoughts calibrate much higher. The highest calibrated frequencies of thought, which are measured through simple kinesiology methods, reveal that faster vibrations are closer to the dimension of Source Consciousness. This places you in a higher frequency and position to create.

Any lower thoughtforms that linger lower the mental frequency of the individual. A low thoughtform is any energy that distorts meaning, and holds limiting beliefs, judgments, criticism, discords, or any deliberate negative perceptions of yourself, or others. Reframing these thoughts is essential, and must be done! If not, they will attract "like" energy, and the person will be swiftly pulled into the low energy fields of discord and lack. To achieve a high mental frequency, practice harmonious thinking, and you will maintain a high vibration. Anytime you feel your vibrations drop, immediately check-in on your thoughts and the images in your mind and reframe as necessary.

There is a rainbow in every discordant situation. Find it! Reframing thoughts to raise their frequencies entails viewing everything from a positive perspective. When a past experience comes up that is full of pain, understand that you learned from it and reject its continuous presence in your mind and heart! Forgive yourself or others and move past it. The past is in the past and must stay there. With the sudden appearance of new intense lower energies this can be difficult, thus simply redirect quickly by sending thoughts of love, and peace to the experience or even the world. This will immediately balance your mental consciousness and raise your vibrational frequency.

Being kinder and gentler in every thought you have about yourself and others is an enormous frequency booster. The more loving and kinder you and your thoughts are, the higher you will vibrate, and the quicker your frequency will rise. A book that is highly recommended for all those who need a more intense direction on how to reframe thoughts is Dyer's *Change your Thoughts – Change your Life.* Dyer (2007) offers excellent examples of how to reframe negative thought patterns. Dyer (2007) quotes La-Tzu with the words that are so suited for this time, "this is oh so easy, so simple to understand and practice, yet so few are willing or able to grasp the essence ..." (Verse 70 Lao-Tzu's – Tao).

Navigating the internal and external energies and life's challenges can be mentally difficult. But any discord framed with thoughts from a higher consciousness will always trigger

the correct response and course of action, which will allow the person to retain their high frequencies and/or even increase them. To illustrate how a change of a mental outlook in everyday life could help you keep your vibrations high even in discordant situations, read the following vignette. If you don't like your aunt Sue, but you will be in her company for the holidays, you don't have to mentally change your opinion about her, but you can reframe your thoughts to vibrate from a higher frequency which always comes from a place of love.

There is beauty in everything and everyone, and peace can always be found within. Reframing perceptions and focusing on positive qualities will actually raise your vibrational frequencies and expand your awareness of the situation. Hence, knowing you are going to see your aunt Sue; you also know it will be for a short time. The evening would be over soon enough, and the visit would provide you with an opportunity to increase your vibrations when you took the high road in every discordant situation that came up.

You will also grow from the experience. When you move into higher frequencies it doesn't mean you change people. It means you change yourself.

When you grow and change yourself you expand your consciousness. If you reacted with annoyance, frustration, anger, judgment, criticism and so on, your own overall vibrational frequencies would drop because **thoughts activate images, images activate feelings.** Thus, collectively by the time you leave your Aunt Sue your whole being would vibrate at a lower frequency which would change your lived experience. Reframing your thoughts will bring you peace over the situation and keep your vibration high because you will not be sucked into a lower frequency regardless of the situation that may occur. You will however, gain ground for the higher frequency brings with it more power and control and a much better lived experience.

Be cognizant of the thoughts and images in your mind, and be careful of hitchhiking thoughts that may lower your vibration. Hitchhiking thoughts are thoughts that lower frequency because they are filled with imaginary calamities that lower your frequencies and rob you of your power. Hitchhiking thoughts can appear as old hurts, disappointments, guilt, regret and the like, or various scenarios of reliving the mistakes you made in life, which only bring more 'like' qualities to you. These hitchhiking thoughts can hijack energy and cause much misery and high levels of sadness, depression, anxiety and illness, if they are not reframed and brought into higher thought patterns immediately. Do not allow them to dwell in your mind!

If you frame your thoughts in the way of "only good can come to me," then you will continuously live in a higher vibration. Take the stand that if discord appeared it must be good for you somehow, for **only good can come to you.** Hence, take the opportunity and use the appearing discord to increase your vibrational frequency by responding and **not reacting.** We must use every opportunity to frame incoming information appropriately, not as bad, but as energy that needs to be handled. If it showed up that means that there is something in there for you that you must handle from your highest potential, otherwise it would not show up. Creatively redirect and rethink, transcending what was once labeled as bad for good, and frame it as a gift, focusing on how it can "serve" you. If you do, you will remain in the higher vibratory mental frequencies and not lose any power, and very possibly solve the problem in the long run.

Framing Images

Framing images of **thoughtforms** in the mind will align them with higher vibrations and draw the frequency of that vibration to the person. Thus, framing a desire in the mind and supporting it with the image of it as if it already had manifested brings it from the conscious mind into physical realities. Thought supported by **images** of the desire that the person is trying to manifest should always be in the form of an unwavering picture of the desire and should **include sensory** information received from the senses of **smell, taste, touch, seeing** and **hearing** to fortify it further into existence. In this way the vibration of the desire perfectly matches the intention which attracts that frequency to the individual in whatever form the image imprinted in the mind holds. The image in the mind will trigger emotions and align the thoughts, images and feelings in a way that activate the Laws of Vibration and Attraction to ensure that the desire manifests from the consciousness into the individual's physical world.

The individuals, through control of their thoughts must make every effort to ensure that the pictures they are framing in their mind are only of the highest energies. Framing images in your mind through a higher vibration is vastly important to working with energy and creating the life the person desires and increasing and maintaining higher energies in your life because of the *Law of Vibration and Attraction.* What you think about and see in your mind, you create. **Images** can be **framed** to inspire and raise the mental vibration of any individual and increase their powers to **create**, or decrease frequencies leaving the individual with either great power to create or loss of power and the inability to create. High vibrational images attract like vibrations, just as low vibratory images attract the low vibrations, which often results in the creation of things you don't want in your life, rather than what you do.

In the **moderate** frequency of the **Dedication Consciousness,** it is important to be **aware** of **images** planted in the **mind.** Images are one of the most potent attractors and influencers of a persons' mental vibrational frequencies. Conscious control must be taken to ensure that the images in the mind are always aligned with the highest frequencies. At first, in the **Dedication Consciousness,** it takes a conscientious discipline to ensure that every image in your head is positive, meaning of the highest qualities, as mental pictures in human consciousness often run uncontrolled, but within a short time, the rewards will be worth the time expended.

Framing Feelings

Images can be **framed** to inspire and raise the vibration of any individual because they invoke feelings, which are crucial to manifestation. Low vibratory images activate the *Law of Vibration and Attraction* and as a result draw discordant energy to themselves, often without the person understanding what is happening and why they are feeling so poorly. **Feelings** are often the great **determiner** of a human being's vibrational frequencies, and vastly affect the ability to work with energy to create manifestations. That is because feelings that are derived from thoughtforms and images planted in the mind determine the **emotional life** of the person.

Human beings attach meaning in their life through their lived experiences via thoughts and images in their mind which trigger feelings. The feelings drive the implication of these energies, and very often can misread the situation based on faulty logic, which trigger faulty images in the mind that activate flawed feelings. When one allows the mind to dwell upon images of perceived discords and allows these feelings to generate with him or her, the person automatically drops in frequency and the energy forces them to lower vibrations where unwanted experiences will come into fruition, and the creation process is stifled. The better you can envision your desire using all your senses, and the longer you can hold the image of it steadfastly in your mind, and imprint it in your heart with positive feelings of expectancy the quicker the desire will be brought from your consciousness into your physical reality. This occurs because thoughtforms trigger images in the mind, and images active feelings and when all three are aligned they attract that energy to you in the form of your desire and bring in to your physical world.

Emotions originate in the brain, more specifically in the limbic system. This is why thoughts and images in the mind activate feelings which arise from people's lived experiences. Feelings are felt like a quick spark in the heart, and can occur even before one is even aware of what is happening. But whether the feeling was sparked through prolonged thought or a quick reaction it can initiate low vibrations. The more intense the feeling about something, and the longer it is held unwavering in the heart, whether it is positive or negative, the more quickly it will manifest, especially if backed with strong thoughts and images in support of it. King (2007 p. 23) contends that the "feeling activity of life is the most unguarded point of human consciousness." Framing feelings correctly and from the highest frequency is integral to responding and not reacting to situations or people. For responding is rooted in emotional maturity which is of a higher frequency, reactions are rooted in lower energies of spontaneity.

Human beings' emotional body and personal feelings must be controlled if the intent is to work with higher energies. Since emotions often ignite various feelings automatically, disciplined **control** of thoughts and images in the mind when **framing** emotional energies is integral and must be exercised at all times. Control of personal feelings in every situation raises the energy and the situation becomes clearer, and easier to control and manage. Again, controlled feelings are achieved through framing incoming information by responding and not reacting.

Reframe every negative feeling within you, and refuse to accept any discordant feelings from this point on. You can do this by governing your thoughts and controlling the images that you imprint in your mind. Respond rather than react to situations. This will result in much better life experiences, and an opportunity to vibrate high and feel good permanently as you create your new world. Use the new energies of positive **feelings** to support the creation of your desires. Because of the conscious application of **control** over the **emotions** in the **Dedication Consciousness,** the framing of desires from your highest vibration grants you the power to begin creating your life as you wish and to manifest the future you want to face.

Human beings are very emotional beings. Through lived experiences they are constantly creating new feelings that must be reframed if these feelings do not serve them or their highest good. It is up to all individuals to stay vigilant and guard their emotions because they are vital to maintaining and increasing their vibrational frequencies. "I tell you the need of guarding the feeling cannot be emphasized too strongly, for control of the emotions plays the most important part of anything in life" (King, p.22) because once feelings support the thoughts and images in your mind, your manifestations are sure to come.

Absorption Consciousness

In the **Absorption Consciousness** miracles can be every day experiences. Once individuals understand the importance of controlling and cultivating their mental and emotional consciousness, and can successfully manage their **thoughts, images,** and **feelings** they are ready to move into the **high Absorption Consciousness** fields. Moving into the Absorption Consciousness **activates** the spiritual vibrations of **contemplation, intention, elimination** and **insulation to** bring into physical reality, that which up until now has only resided in the consciousness.

Contemplation involves *introspection, self-evaluation, deep thoughts, and inquisitive inquiry.* In essence all energies which invoke *reflection* and *assessment.* The energy of **contemplation** jumpstarts the flow of power and begins the creation of your desires process because you have learned to **control** your **thoughts, images**, and **feelings** and keep them in the highest vibration which expands your consciousness and births new knowledge and wisdom. **Contemplation** is vastly important in the manifestation process because it clarifies, crystallizes and forms your **intent** *before* it is sent. This assures that you get what you really need, not what you think you want. Want is fickle, what you want today may not be what you want tomorrow. Or if you get what you want today you may not like it. But what you need you will always keep. Contemplation will illuminate your needs so that you can send out your intention to bring them into your physical reality.

Intention is the total sum of your **contemplation** and directs the energy of your desires. Dyer (2013 p. 217) felt so strongly about the power of **intention** relative to manifestation of all desires that he urged people, "to move into this awareness now and know in your heart, just as the farmer in *Fields of Dreams* knew, that if you build this inner dream, surely, it will come." The power of **intention** will lift you from living in the ordinary state of consciousness into a higher existence, but first you must **contemplate** your **intent** into existence. The power of **intent** is like a magnet, if used according to the **LEP Frequency Tool** of consciousness, and soon you will see evidence of your manifestations everywhere.

In addition to the spiritual energies of **contemplation** and **intention,** the high energy fields of the **Absorption Consciousness** also include the energies of **elimination** and **insulation. Elimination** will remove all discordant energy from your life and free you of life's baggage. This will allow you to vibrate at higher frequencies so that you may create what you need to appear in your life, without limit. The energy of **insulation** will protect you against any incoming discord that try to invade your energy fields and lower your vibrations.

Energy of Contemplation

Contemplation is the first energy field in the **Absorption Consciousness** and starts the flow that **creates intentions**. Contemplation is not just thinking, questioning, or pondering, but a real effort to visualize the right conditions which you wish to manifest. It is this **thought** backed with **images** and supported with feelings that creates your **intention.** Additionally, spending time in **contemplation through the process of meditation** on what you need before you can send out the **intention** to manifest it in your physical world is a necessary first step in the movement of energy from your consciousness towards the creation of your reality in the physical world.

Don't worry about anything. You are in the right place, moment or situation to improve your life through contemplation. Let go of all problems, past mistakes and transgressions, pain, unhappiness and the like. Release all thoughts that are not aligned with the vision that you are a good person, and have the power to change your world and your lived experiences and can create anything you wish.

Your willingness to **contemplate** and see yourself having what you need to manifest gives you the ability to put forth the pure **intent** to bring those energies to you. Huxley, an English writer and philosopher, explained that "contemplation is a condition of alert passivity, in which the soul lays itself open to the Divine." It is not rushing around in the outer world in a continuous state of activity 'doing,' which just leaves human beings exhausted at the end of the day. Noting the vast importance, the power of contemplation plays in the discernment of his life, Huxley, shared, "for until this morning I had known contemplation only in its humbler, its more ordinary forms – as discursive thinking; as systematic silence leading, sometimes, to hints of an 'obscure knowledge'. But now I knew contemplation at its height." **Contemplation** is where imagination can run wild, where you can test out any experience before bringing it into your physical reality. **Contemplation** has unlimited power in which anyone can create perfect desires, and have them materialized in the physical world through the direction of **intent**. Dr. Dyer (2013) affirmed, "it's as if by thinking about what you desire, you release a zillion little invisible, yet alert worker bees who guide you in the act of creation" of the very thing you desire.

Contemplation sets forth thoughts of *initiation*, *self-evaluation*, *reflection*, and *introspection* among others. It consciously weighs all *pros* and *cons* of any conscious inquiry, reflection or message. To contemplate is to rest suspension of all activity and allow the grace of the Source/God to empower you to visualize your perfect reality, supported by the corresponding feelings, and create the blueprint for your desires in perfect arrangement. According to Aristotle, "contemplation is the highest form of reality, and the ultimate value of life depends upon contemplation, rather than upon mere survival."

Thus, knowing the value of contemplation, at full effort, contemplate and imagine every detail of everything and anything you wish to appear in your life. Use affirming **thoughts,** positive **images,** and support it with the appropriate **feelings,** because strong emotions have a tendency to manifest desires faster, and sensory systems like color, texture, and so on to ensure a positive result. See it and feel it as it is already so. This will speed up the manifestation process from your consciousness into your physical reality. If you do not find time to contemplate and hold the picture of your desires steady, or cannot see yourself being surrounded by the exact scenario you wish to attract, the picture will quickly out-picture and be replaced with images of doubt, limitation, or lack and you will essentially close the door to your dreams and not be able to move into higher frequencies and create the world that you want.

Contemplation triggers your creations through your imagination. Unequivocally, it is the act of **contemplation** that activates **intention** and causes physical materialization. Dyer (2013) recommends that you "view your contemplative moments the same way you view your practice time for improving your skills at any endeavor." He further contends that "an hour a day throwing a bowling ball is action that leads to higher bowling average; a few moments several times a day musing about what you intend to manifest in some area of your life will have precisely the same effect on your manifesting average." Thus, spending time in **contemplation,** to clarify your **intent** is one of the most valuable tools for manifesting everything you ever desired in your tool box for life on earth, as it is the start of the creation process in the mind.

Contemplation opens the door for **intention** to gather strength and bring these energies to you in your physical existence. When you **contemplate,** scarcity and unfulfillment no longer exists. Only your vision of the reality you wish to create exists and takes center stage because it is supported by the powerful vibrations of **intent** and reinforced by your expectant **feelings.** You are well equipped with a mind that can contemplate any constructive thing based on your specifications and bring it into your physical reality.

Contemplation is often linked with meditation because of its holistic nature, and considerations, such as silence, and a setting appropriate to contemplate. Both of which are necessary for in depth and clear reflection so that an accurate intention may be formed. Contemplation offers many rewards as it assists to clarify and shape your desires because it is also clothed in enlightenment and awareness through evaluation of the 'self.' Personal assessments invoked by contemplation often shed light on situations, desires, personal preferences, and likes or dislikes. In many cases contemplation uncovers who you are as a person, and what your life's purpose should be. When you contemplate, you become quiet, still, get deep. Never rush within the silence. Relax, open your mind and heart and just allow yourself the time to discover what you really need in life to make you happy. Contemplate exactly how you want your life to look. See your desire, or your new life with vivid description, and feel as if it is already here.

Often time spent in **contemplation** and *re-evaluation* is the most rewarding and brings immense lucidity because it identifies what you really need to be happy, and what you want your life to look like. Take your time in contemplation, don't ever rush the process, but explore and experience all your desires completely and thoroughly before you create the intent. Is this really what you need? When you get it, how will it change your life? If you have trouble contemplating, or are feeling blocked, or just want better clarity on your true desires, journal your feelings and any limiting thoughts that appear.

Journaling often puts things in a better more enlightening perspective, as words on paper tend to be more focused. Be free as you contemplate, and know that all is probable, as "the mind cannot conceive anything that is not possible of accomplishment" (King, 2012, A p. 61). So, find a quiet place, close your eyes, and use creative visualization to let your imagination run free. Experience every scenario as if you are living it now. Experience your desires in their full glory with every scent, sound, and touch. See the colors and vibrancy of your intent, exactly as you wish it. Look at the pitfalls of achieving it, and ensure that it is what you really need, for if you **contemplate** it, send out the **intent** and hold that **vision** imprinted on your consciousness; it will surely come.

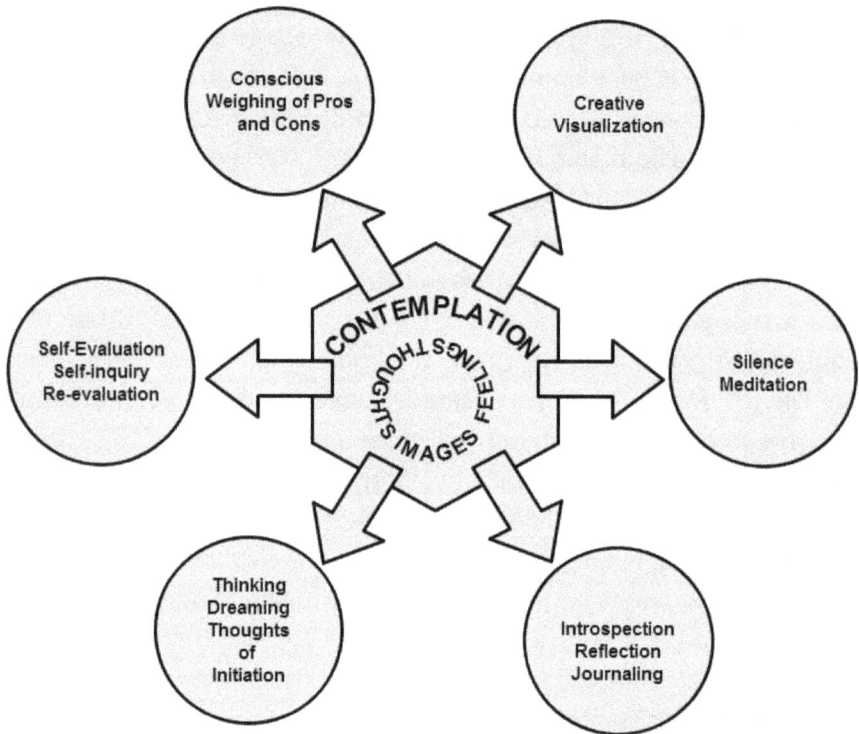

Energy of Intention

Intent is powerful. By changing your inner reference of what your true **intention** is you are allowing new results of a much higher vibrational frequency to enter your life. According to Dyer (2013) "the word **intention** has a connotation of nothing getting in the way. Regardless of what opposition there may be, the word 'intent' suggests and implies that something is going to happen" (Dyer, 2013). Thus, after **contemplation** and your desires are firmly identified, **"intention"** takes the lead and makes something happen.

In his book, *The Essential Wayne Dyer Collection,* Dyer (2013) details instructions on how to use the power of **intention** as a tool to assist people to co-create the life that they desire. He further explained, that through 'the power of intention, you'll see your dreams being fulfilled' (Dyer, 2013). But remember, in order to get what you want, you must be aligned with its frequency. For example, if you want more love, but you are not actively in a loving manner yourself, your power of intention is weakened. You attract into your life energies which are not the face of love. Consequently, more of what you don't love will appear in your life. If you return to contemplation and inquisitively reflect on what you need and why you need it, you can modify the intention at any time because you have shifted your attention to the new desire.

Deepak Chopra (1994) contended that attention energizes and intention transforms. Chopra (1994) further contended that whatever you put your attention on grows stronger in your life. Whatever you take your attention away from will wither, disintegrate, and disappear. This means that your **intention** cannot just be sent and forgotten about. The intent must remain in the **expectant** phase in your **thoughtforms,** mental **images** about it, and contain supportive **feelings** of it. Emotions, in particular are very powerful in the intention process. Dyer (2013) recommends using emotions as a barometer, a guidance system for your thought process and self-talk to catch discordant thought patterns because your emotions reflect your thoughts. To control your feelings so that you can work with **intent** you have to control your thoughts and the images you are planting in your mind.

Energy alignment is crucial to the manifestation process. If your alignment is off and you are not in line with your intent, change the pattern of your alignment by thinking higher thoughts of confidence that the expectations of your desires will manifest in their perfect time, and support them with higher images of yourself and feelings of confidence. Leave no doubt that it is so! This will increase vibrations and assist you to tap into the frequency that will match that of your intention.

If you are out of harmony with your intention you will not be able to vibrate at its frequency, and attract what you want. No amount of sadness, tears, anger, despair or even God will help the situation. In one of his lectures, Dr. Dyer contended that, "the field of intention doesn't know anything about non-well-being, it creates from a source of well-being. It doesn't know anything about fear, anxiety, or worry, it is only in a constant state of creation through the power of intention." It only brings you the energy that emanates from you, whatever that intention is on, at whatever frequency you release it. Thus, the lower frequencies will bring about lower experiences until the intent is changed, modified, or adjusted and matches the expectancy of your desire.

Ultimately, "you get what you intend to create by being in harmony with the power of intention, which is responsible for all of creation. If you think you can't manifest abundance into your life, you'll see intention agreeing with you, and assisting you in the fulfillment of meager expectations!" (Dyer, 2013). Thus, if you don't make adjustments to your intentions, and if you are unhappy with your lot in life, you will continuously exist in lower, denser vibrations and experience their discordant energies throughout your lived experience, until through contemplation, you change your intention. In the reality of the human consciousness everyone is already connected to everything they need or want in life; they just have to use the energy of intent consciously and connect to the vibratory field of their desire.

If your intention is to be happy, at peace, have love or want other people to be kind and patient with you, radiate those energies and these energies will return to you. One way to raise your vibrations so that you may send out your intent from your highest frequency to attract these energies to you is to respond with kindness, patience and love, regardless of outer appearances, to everything that comes your way, whether it is discordant or not. If you want your intention of a specific desire fulfilled, you have to be in higher frequencies. A quick way to bring higher energies to you and raise your vibrations so that you are at your peak frequency in order to create manifestation is to radiate love and peace to the world. See the image of yourself, and feel your whole body radiating good will. Your vibrations will increase and put you in the frequency you need to be in so that you may send out your intention from higher frequency and your manifestations can come to you.

Your intentions are your power to the life you wish to live and the future you want to face. Thus, remember, once identified through **contemplation,** to send your **intention, imagine your intent** using your **thoughts, images in the mind** and **feelings.** Consciously align with your intent, and use creative visualization and be as detailed as possible. Envision and hold the image steady by imprinting it on your consciousness so that it is continuously attracted to your energy fields. Take your time, and when ready mentally send out your intent to the universe. Reaffirm the intent through the use of decrees. Remember to hold the intent of the image steady in your consciousness, and do not allow doubt to enter!

Live as if your intention is already here! Dyer (2013) asserted that, doubt must be removed when working with intent. Shakespeare declared, "our doubts are traitors, and make us lose the good we oft might win ..." When working with the power of intent, all doubt must be replaced by faith and eventually by a knowing that, "all things whatsoever you ask for, believe that ye have received them, and ye shall receive them" [Mark 11:24].

When working with intent, it is not enough just to work with your mental and emotional energy fields through the power of contemplation and intention. You must also be razor focused and take any opportunity to advance your intention in the physical world. This means you must always be at the ready to do your part in and manifest your intention in the physical world by actively pursuing your intended desire in every way, shape and form through your physical action. For example, you can contemplate the perfect career, send out the intention, and the universe will oblige and you will come across that opportunity, but in order for you to receive it, you still have to physically apply for it. In another example, you can contemplate and send out the intention for the perfect person to appear in your world, but once the energy fulfills your intent and brings them in your world, you still have to ask them for a date, or accept a date in order to engage that person in your life.

Be patient with all manifestations, and never set a time for results. Allow the manifestations to come to you in the way the Universal energy wants to send it. This is where faith and trust come in. You have to have trust and faith that when your intention is sent from the conscious mind it will manifest in your physical reality in its own perfect time. The Universe has the complete picture, of when the perfect time for you will be, you do not. Trust and have faith in the Source Consciousness that all your constructive intentions will materialize. The Source Consciousness is ever present in you and your life and only wants the best for you. You must trust and have faith that it is so.

Thoughts, images, and feelings are crucial to form and send the intention to create in the consciousness what is desired in the physical world. But energy in the consciousness must work in unison with the actions taken in the physical world. Actively work to bring your desire to fruition through your behavior, intelligence, planning, networking, strategizing, and any other innate traits or talents you have to pursue your intention fully. Your behavior, motivations, determination and action to persist and take every opportunity to manifest what you intended in your consciousness to appear in your physical world are crucial to your ultimate success. Action and persistence intensify the energy and aligns it with your intention, which determines the speed of its appearance in the person's life. This means once they appear, the quicker you ask that person out, or accept a date, or apply for that job, the quicker you will succeed, and the thing that was once only in your consciousness has now manifested in your physical reality.

Be receptive to the energies, the power that you hold, and fully expect the desire to come to you. If you are vibrating at the frequency of your desire in your mental, and emotional fields and are taking appropriate steps and actions in your physical world to attain it, you will align with it and the desire will appear in your physical reality soon enough. Stay in harmony with the Source Consciousness by including your spiritual confidence in your expectancy that you have this power and it is working for you at all times, and your desire is sure to come.

Be mindful that nothing will stifle the energy of intention faster than a feeling that you do not deserve what you "intend," or having doubt that it will come. What you 'know' beyond doubt, will be realized in the future. This is the power of intention at work (Dyer, 2013). Dyer (2013) further contended, that by combining free will with intention, you harmonize with the universal mind. Being in harmony with your intent is important as it is the only way to meet its vibration and attract it to you. When life appears to be working against you, when your luck is down, when the supposedly wrong people show up, or when you slip up and return to old, self-defeating habits, recognize the signs that you're out of harmony with intention (Dyer, 2013). **Contemplation** must be resumed, and the **intention** reviewed and modified.

When intent is sent to the universe it is treated as a blueprint of desired energy. Reaching and maintaining higher frequencies and living out your dreams is assured because the power of your pure intent will lift you from living in an ordinary state of consciousness into a world where you decide what shows up in your life. Always, remember that 'intention is not something that we do, intention is something we connect to' (Carlos Castaneda). "If one advances confidently in the direction of his or her dreams, and endeavors to live the life that he or she has imagined, he or she will meet with a success unexpected in common hours" (Henry David Thoreau).

Advancing confidently in the direction of ones dreams often entails tremendous courage, determination, and an unwillingness to be defeated. It is a dogmatic fortitude to fulfill what one intended regardless of outer appearances. According to Dyer (2013), the physical universe and everything in it is a vibrating machine. Dyer (2013) further contended, that the act of creation itself, bringing non-being into physical-being happens through the raising of vibrational frequencies (Dyer, 2013). When the person has aligned their **thought, images** in their mind, their **feelings** and are in pursuit of their desire in their physical reality, they will easily match their intent's frequency and it will materialize in their physical world. King (2011, p. 17) explained that "there is positively an abundant supply omnipresent, but the demand for it must be made before the Law of the Universe permits it to come into the expression and use of the individual." The demand is made through aligned **thoughts, images, feelings** and the **resolve** to **act** in the **physical world** in a manner that will manifest the intent in the person's reality. King (2011, p. 17) further asserted that, "it cannot fail to come forth into expression, no matter what it is, as long as it is a constructive desire, as the spiritual energy will not create anything unlike itself… and if the individual holds an unwavering determined consciousness (King, 2011) the contemplated intent will materialize at its perfect time.

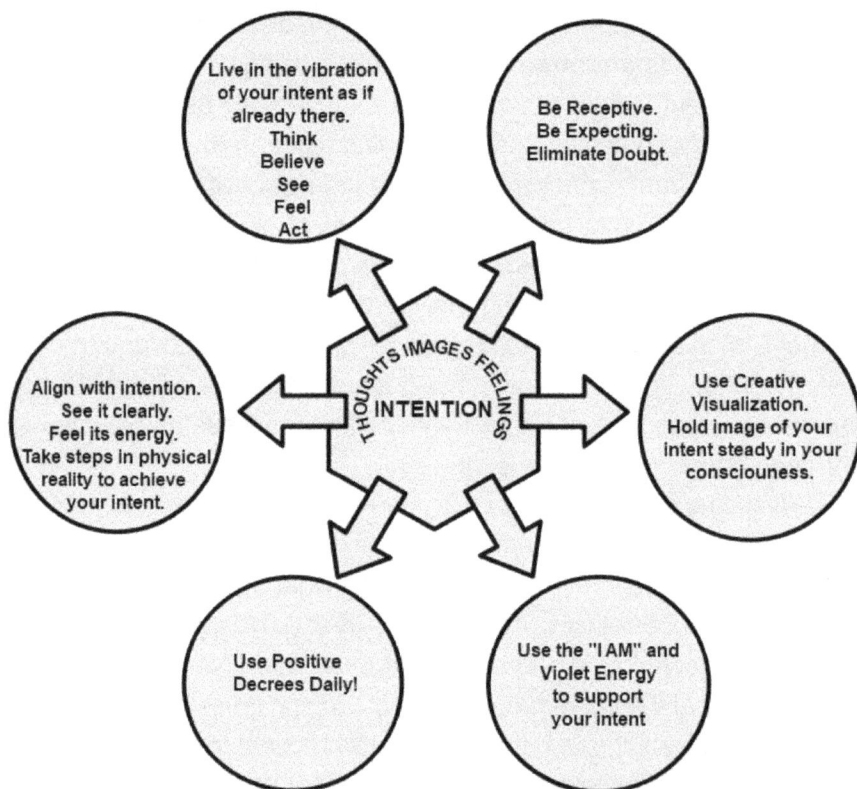

Elimination

There is nothing freer in the world than the feeling of eliminating discordant vibrations through the *violet energy* that transmutes all discords into a positive energy. By transforming negative thoughts and feelings to positive, the **Violet Flame** provides a platform for healing (Prophet, 1997). This is because the Violet Flame has the shortest wavelength which makes it the most potent energy available for human use in eliminating discord or negative karma, outside of karmic cycles. Because of its purest properties it is the closest to the Source Consciousness, which makes it the most powerful.

In the high frequencies of the **Absorption Consciousness,** only positive energy may be absorbed and retained to fill the moments of the persons' life because of its high vibrations. All **lower vibrations** are to be **eliminated,** without delay, through the use of the **Violet Flame** quickly and easily. Continuous elimination of discordant energies (intentional, or unintentional) in a person's life will ensure that their overall frequencies will remain at his or her highest potential, and allow every person to resolve situations and problems they could never handle on their own.

Everything in your life shows up as a result of the person's overall vibration. Discord is an opportunity for everyone to practice elimination to maintain or lift into higher vibrational frequencies where creation and elimination of unwanted energies occurs. Some energy is loving and supportive, some is of challenging and discordant in nature which must be eliminated so that higher energies may enter into your sphere. But in truth, energy only feels discordant when it is misaligned. If you realign the energy using your **'I AM'** presence and invoke the **Violet Flame**, discordant energy can be immediately eliminated by shattering, dissipating and consuming it. You will be free from carrying around the heaviness of its discordant baggage and your vibration will immediately increase to a higher frequency leaving you lighter, happier and peaceful.

Elimination begins with removing all energy that is misaligned in your life. This means that *all* discords must be addressed. LEP meditation with the **Violet Flame** will assist you to identify any areas of discord that must be eliminated. It is wise to remember when eliminating discordant energies that you are the creator of all that happens in your life. If you can remember that you are responsible for what you are attracting, you can eliminate much of the energy that you don't want *before* it has a chance to fully manifest.

Be on guard at all times, and should misalignment creep in relative to who you are and what you want, eliminate it at once. **Connect** to your **'I AM'** presence and **through** the spiritual energy of the **Violet Flame** eliminate all negative or discordant feelings you have relative to yourself, any other people, or situations in your life. You may not eliminate the person from your life, but you can eliminate the discordant energy relative to that person, and all your future interactions with them. Dr. Hawkins (2002) a highly regarded PhD and MD, who practiced psychiatry for decades asserts that, if you create and maintain higher vibrations, you will eliminate negativity around you. The best way to use the power of elimination is to **eliminate** all **low** vibratory negative thinking patterns and transform them to positive uplifting higher energies of positive **thoughts, images,** and **feelings** about yourself and your life which will attract like energies to you. Eliminate all misaligned energy of what is not in your best interest or your highest good, through continual assessment of what serves you and persistent positive attitude that matches your thoughts, feelings, behaviors and actions.

Elimination is a necessary ingredient for the continuation of your acceleration to higher consciousness because everyone makes mistakes at one time or another. But mistakes can be fixed if you are cognizant of them and take the effort to eliminate them from your life. For mistakes and transgressions that can't be fixed, YOU MUST MOVE ON! Surround every situation with love and forgive yourself and others, as we all make mistakes at one time or another. This is how we grow, sometimes the growth is more painful than what we think we can bear, but rest assured that you can move through it. YOU MUST MOVE THROUGH IT. Take the lesson learned from every painful and painless mistake or transgression and MOVE ON in your expanded wisdom.

The Violet Flame will help to eliminate discord through the acts of shattering, dissipating and consuming the discord through the Law of Forgiveness. Elimination is necessary to moving forward happily in life and it is vital to the continued progress of raising your personal vibrational frequencies and creating the future you want to face. The Law of Forgiveness admonishes that you cannot be forgiven for your transgressions unless you are willing to forgive others for their transgressions. The Law of Forgiveness is a special spiritual power that if used in conjunction with the Violet Flame can clear you of blockages so that you may move into higher vibrational energies.

Elimination provides a clean slate and freedom from all discords and allows you to create all constructive desires without limit. According to King (2012) individuals should look within themselves and find wherein there have been unnoticed, subtle things that are binding them. Each person should search him or herself and **eliminate** all areas of **discord** through the **use** of the **Violet Flame.** In the elimination process include all lower energies whether they appear as transgressions by you or others, baggage that has attached itself to you from lack of forgiveness, greed, selfishness, guilt, regret or in forms of worn-out personal habits, behaviors, thoughts, feelings and opinions that no longer serve your highest good, old ideas, flawed perceptions, or faulty perspectives and so on. According to King (2012) just like you pluck weeds from your garden, so should you pluck these low vibratory patterns from your consciousness," and eliminate them from your reality. "Pull them out by the roots that they have naught left by which they may grow again" (King, 2012). You will never gain victory until you stop turning back to the old negative conditions you are trying to get rid of (King, 2012).

Be cognizant! There must be a continual reminder in the consciousness to **eliminate** all **lower** forms of **energy** at their first appearance when vibrating in the higher **Absorption Consciousness,** so that they do not lower your vibration and decrease your power to attract what you need in your life. Should discordant energy appear in your life, connect with your **'I AM'** presence at once, and **invoke** the **Violet Flame**. "For it is the **'I AM'** presence that has all intelligence, power, and authority to consciously direct the energy through the outer activity of the mind" (King, 2011, p. 271), and connect to the Violet Flame so that it may give any assistance needed.

Elimination through Violet Flame

Use the **Violet Flame** often to purify any intentional or unintentional discord in your life. Violet energy is a high spiritual energy that appears as a **Violet Flame** to the human eye. The power of the violet energy has been noted by many notable energy experts, and it is always considered the closest frequency to the Source Consciousness. According to Prophet (1999) "in our physical world, the violet light has the highest frequency in the physical spectrum. Since frequency is directly proportional to energy, thus as noted before the violet light also has the most energy. That means, it has the greatest ability to change matter at the atomic level, which is why the *violet energy* is so powerful" (Prophet, 1999). Moreover, the violet energy equalizes the flow of energy between yourself and other life streams (Prophet, 1997, p. 67) which is why it is also a perfect tool to erase any karmic debt, or negative karma that may be draining your energy.

You will never progress into the realm of the highest consciousness if you do not learn to eliminate discordant energies in your energy fields. Every human being has made mistakes, errors they wish had never happened. Sometimes the mistakes are tragic, other times less so. But often energies of lower frequencies are quite painful, as the lower the vibration, the more pain and anguish is reflected in the human experience. However, knowing that you are of the Source, and your 'I AM' presence within you is that spark of God/Source Consciousness that you can call upon and direct the **Violet Flame** to **eliminate** all **discords** and release you from all bondage, should bring great comfort to many who feel that they have no control, resources or support to improve their lives, or release the baggage that is causing them much pain.

There is a reason that universally the **Violet Flame** has been called one of the most powerful vibrational frequencies available to mankind. As mentioned before that is because when called upon It heals, eliminates discords, and is powerful enough to releases old karma which increases vibrational frequencies, and allows for harmonious creations of future desires. The Violet Flame is the means by which any human being can free him/her self from his or her own human discord and imperfection (Prophet, 1997) and start creating the life and future they want to face, but it can only be done through **conscious use.**

Anything generated can be consumed. Hence, hope should never be lost because you have the power to change your reality anytime you wish, or release any painful baggage that has attached itself to you. The quickest way to restore balance if you think you made a mistake, and want to eliminate discord in your life is to call upon the **'I AM'** within you, and with an open heart and gratitude **invoke** the **Violet Flame**. **Visualize** as it **shatters, dissipates**, and **consumes** the wrong creation out of your life for the highest good of yourself and all concerned. Many people who were unable to move forward with life, who can no longer find peace in their mind or have lost all joy in their heart will find great comfort to know that no discord is too large for the **Violet Flame** to **shatter, dissipate**, and **consume**.

Consciously visualize the **Violet Flame** and call upon It through your **'I AM'** presence. Command it to eliminate all discords in your life, all wrong creations, a particular situation that you are grappling with, guilt, regret and so on. If you feel you did something wrong, adversely or inadvertently, direct the **Violet Flame** to transmute this energy and '**shatter, dissipate** and **consume**' it. Command that you are released forever from this discordant energy and so that *only good come of it,* for the highest good of yourself, and all concerned. The very act of invoking the **Violet Flame** calls upon the **Law of Forgiveness** and throws whatever wrong creation existed back to the Cosmic Law for adjustment, wherein it is adjusted outside of the individual karmic activity (King, 2012). The transmuted energy eliminates all discord for the highest good of all concerned without forming additional karma. In this way the individual can be relieved from distress and discords, and be free of them in a very short time (King, 2012).

To progress using the **Violet Flame in** creating your desires with ease, you must regularly eliminate all discordant energies in your life. The higher your frequency when you work with intent, the quicker the intended results manifest. To keep a high vibration, in which to create in, you must begin paying attention to your thoughts, pictures in your mind and feelings at all times so that you don't unintentionally unleash lower discordant energies which may cause you much strife and discord that you will have to eliminate later.

To vibrate high, there is no room for low vibrations. Remember all discordant thoughts, images and feelings whether they stem from transgressions from you or others, guilt, regret, anger, sadness and so on are of lower energies and have an impact on your overall vibration because they decrease vibrational frequencies. Every person, at one time or another has transmitted discordant energy, "all have felt discord and sent it forth in thought, feelings and spoken word" (Voice of the I AM, 1936, p. 17). People are unaware that they "are creating vibration and form, through the individual's consciousness every instant" (Voice of the I AM, 1936, p. 16), but people are human and mistakes will be made. The **Violet Flame** can rectify these mistakes by eliminating the discordant energy leaving the person free from its negative influence, and vibrating at higher mental, emotional, physical/sensory and/or spiritual frequencies, which vastly assists in their creation and manifestation activities.

It is time to be cognizant that human beings create their own reality, so **pay attention** to the **thoughts, images,** and **feeling**s that surface. If they appear in the **low** vibrations of **Lack and Survival** energies, **invoke** the **Violet Flame** and **eliminate** them immediately! Soon your **mental, emotional, physical/sensory** and **spiritual** consciousness will once again vibrate in higher harmonious energies. This occurs because the Violet Flame consumes the impure substances in all consciousness frequencies of the individual … and thereby increases the vibratory action. You will not need to worry about the details of "how" the energy eliminates, transmutes or assists you to either eliminate discord, or manifest desires, you just have to have faith and know that it is being done. "The use of the Violet consuming Flame is more valuable to you and to all mankind than all the wealth, gold and all the jewels of this planet" (Voice of the I AM, 1936, p. 20) because it heals all, eliminates discords and pain, rights wrongs, balances karma and allows complete freedom to create your new reality and the life that you so desire.

Invocation of the Violet Flame

Meditative background music is always recommended. As you begin to use the Violet Flame, you will experience feelings of joy, lightness, hope, and a newness in your life. The Violet Flame dissolves as it shatters, eliminates as it dissipates, and transmutes to higher energies, as it consumes, leaving you feeling lighter, freer, hopeful, inspired and motivated.

Quick Eliminating Discord Activity:

Begin with rhythmic breathing. Breathe in slowly for 10 counts, hold for 10 counts, release for 10 counts. (You may adjust the counts to your comfort).

- Center yourself and through your 'I AM' presence invoke the Violet Flame.
- Visualize it in your mind in all its magnificent glory, and feel the love and the power It holds. Take your time, perfect the image of the discord and place it in Its radiant shades of violet light glowing invitingly, as it awaits your command.
- As you decree verbally or mentally, whatever is more comfortable for you, keep visualizing what you specifically want to eliminate. (If it is debt, see zero balances on every statement, or large sums of money in your bank accounts. If it is a health issue, see yourself free of it, with razor focus visualize it clearly and watch it as it vanishes from your body, leaving it healthy and radiant. If it is a personal issue, see it resolved to your satisfaction and you happy and smiling. Leave the HOW to the Violet Energy to eliminate all discord in a way that

will eliminate it from your life by using only the highest energies possible. And never try to RUSH the process. Sometimes the Violet Flame works immediately. Other times, depending on the energies that must be aligned, it takes much more time and effort, with many meditations to draw what you wish to you. But each time with the image of discord firmly placed in the Violet Flame Decree:

Through the power of my 'I AM' presence, I invoke the Violet Flame to Shatter, Dissipate, and Consume this wrong creation of *(state the discord, or you can keep it general by commanding that the Violet Flame shatter, dissipate, and consume all creations that do not serve you, or you did not serve well)* and see to it that it never disturbs my world again, for the highest good of myself and all concerned. I thank the (name the discord) for its role in my life and what I have learned from it. Namaste to All. I am grateful to the Violet Flame for Its assistance. (*See the discord consumed within the Flames, and feel completely free from its grip). Do **not rush the process**, in perfect relaxation stay in the moment and send the discord loving energy, and watch as it slowly vanishes in the violet flames. When the discord completely disappears, feel lighter as the heavy baggage is gone from your life forever.* BE EXPECTANT of the results.

Conclude with breathing exercises: (You may adjust the counts to your comfort).

- *Breathe in for 10 counts*
- *Hold for 10 counts*
- *Release for 10 counts.*

Insulation

Insulation in the form of the **Electronic Circle** is an added armor of protection to ward off attacks from lower energies because it forms a barrier between you and negative energy. A conscious focus of thoughts, and mental images of an Electronic Circle placed around you provides you with protective spiritual energy and it will make it harder for discordant energy to affect you because the energy starts and ends at the same point forming a complete protective loop around you. You can visualize the protective energy around you any way you desire, but one of the best ways, since all human beings consist of the same electronic energy, is to envision yourself in an invisible, impenetrable **Electronic Circle** of protection. This will fortify you and negative energy will not be able to penetrate as easily as if you were without protection.

The **Electronic Circle** of protective energy does not attract, but repels lower forms of energy because it keeps you secure in your higher vibration within its protection. Thus, once you have eliminated all discordant and misaligned energy through the use of the Violet Flame, it is time to **insulate** yourself against all future onslaughts. "In everything you do the amount of success depends on the amount of energy you put into it" (White, 1965, p.27). If you are persistent in always being diligent and visualize yourself existing in your Electronic Circle of protection, no matter where you are or what you are doing, you will always be protected, and will always have a greater chance to remain in higher energies. The more you practice working with it, the more you will feel its energy.

Protection from discordant energies should always be utilized. Insulating from incoming lower forms of energy is beneficial to the person who is maintaining a high vibration because it protects them from outside influences which can cause discord, lower their frequency which always stifles creativity and the ability to create, and disturbs the peace of mind of individuals residing in those vibrations. People who are unprotected can be susceptible to many lower forms of energy that can appear in their life through external and internal energies, which can greatly affect their ability to eliminate discords or create desires. External energies may come from perceived negative or unwanted situations, institutions, people and any external factors. Internal energies may manifest in confusion, sadness, anger or internal turmoil, depression and so on. In either case, not being **protected** by the **Electronic Circle**, increases the chances of lower energies entering your **mental, emotional, physical/sensory** and **spiritual** fields, and can create great discord in the person's life, and seriously affect their frequency vibrations, thus cause distress in their entire life and lived experiences.

Electronic Circle

One of the best ways to insulate yourself against discordant energy is to build a **Electronic Circle** around you consciously. Think of It as an electric circle of divinely charged energy. See It as a powerful light blinding, and repelling all discordant energies, allowing only positive, high vibrations to enter your world. Feel Its protective presence around you. Visualize It, as It surrounds you, until It is completely closed, impenetrable. Always remain in your impermeable Electronic Circle, and know that nothing can ever penetrate it. Within It, you are completely protected from all discordant, lower vibrations.

To start building your Electronic Circle around you begin with breathing techniques. Visualize yourself in the middle of the Electronic Circle as your physical body floats within it. Feel the energy surrounding your physical body while you breathe slowly in and out. Build the Electronic Circle of protection with the energies of your own breath. While you breath an energy pattern will be build around you and the energy will encircle you completely in a tight impenetrable field that will repulse all discordant energies that try to evade your mental, emotional, physical/sensory or spiritual place warding off all negative attacks. You will know when the Electronic Circle is fully surrounding you because you will feel complete security. You will not be bothered by events or situations that normally would stress, upset you or cause anxiety.

Live, communicate, and make all decisions from that protected space because the more you do, the more the Electronic Circle expands, insulating you from all lower forms of energy. King (2012) instructs that you speak to each other within what he calls the "magic circle" for no matter where you are this protective circle can protect you, and that the more you use it the more it expands and is ever widening according to the sincerity and intensity with which the attention is held. King (2012) further admonishes that at first it does require sincere earnest guard but with discipline you will gain full control of it soon enough. When you insulate yourself, you command that all outer forces conform to your will, and bounce off the Electronic Circle, for you will not give them the energy to take root. King (2012) admonishes that you never really deal with people who are trying to penetrate your circle with negativity and lower your vibrations, but that you are always dealing with a force (energy) that you must control. Meaning that all discord is really just energy in the guise of people and situations that you must manage. So impersonally, manage and control that energy from within your Electronic Circle of protection, and you will remain unaffected by the discordant energy.

Project self-confidence. Do not allow discordant energy the opportunity to decrease your vibrational frequencies as a result of their negative influence. See discordant people and situations as impersonal energy that you must regulate. Operate from a place of optimism and control in the knowledge that you are within your Electronic Circle and will not allow their discords to influence your peace. By keeping your thoughts strong and your feelings impersonal, you will be insulated against being affected or influenced negatively. The best way to remain happy and safe in your Electronic Circle, especially in the throes of unexpected discordant energy, is to maintain a happy disposition, and work with all negative energy trying to penetrate your shield of protection in harmonious ways. Soon the discordant energy will be transmuted to higher vibrations providing you with much better results. In the end, you will remain unaffected by the storm.

The **Electronic Circle** that you consciously build around you, **expands** continuously with your **awareness.** The more the **Electronic Circle** expands, the more you are protected. But always be on guard that your attention does not dwell on negative conditions, as lower vibrations will always try to find a way to penetrate the insulation. Anything you think about expands, so help yourself by keeping your thoughts positive and reinforce them with affirmations and images of yourself. See and feel yourself protected within the **Electronic Circle** against any negativity or discord. Lower influences, in particular, if not managed properly and eliminated on site can cause great damage to peoples' overall vibrational frequencies, and wreak havoc in their world by bringing negative conditions into their lives.

Discordant energy is everywhere. It is very powerful and can penetrate your **Electronic Circle** which will not only drain energy very quickly and create stress in your life, but lower vibrational frequencies which will automatically begin to attract lower energies, and begin to chip away at the strength of your protection. If you are not in a good place, and unable to protect yourself from discordant energies you continuously attract lower energies to you and will not vibrate high enough to eliminate discord from your life or bring your desires into your physical reality. This may spiral downward very quickly and diminish any progress that you make and may even drag you back into the lowest energies of the Lack and Survival Consciousness field.

Be on guard! It only takes a moment to visualize the **Electronic Circle** around you every morning. To live a happy life, and create your desires, you must insulate against all discordant thoughts and low emotional energies before they find a home in your consciousness and dwell there permanently. But should discordant energies find you in a weak moment, unprotected, and try to find a home within your consciousness **eliminate them** at once by the use of the **Violet Flame** and **insulate** with the **Electronic Circle** of spiritual protection immediately!

Connection Consciousness

In the Connection Consciousness you will find your life lived in bliss. In the peak energies of the **Connection Consciousness, faith** turns into **knowing,** and **knowing** turns into living the **reality** you always wished to live. When you live in the **Connection Consciousness** you unmistakably feel the presence of God, the Source Consciousness within yourself, within everyone, and everywhere. There is nowhere that God the Source Consciousness isn't.

You are able to shut out all discordant energies, and consistently keep your energy flowing in the upward direction. You are of the mind-set that *only good comes to you,* no matter in what form it shows up. Even when discordant energy shows up you are of the mindset that if it showed up, it must somehow be good for you, whether to make you stronger, force you to experience new things, new feelings, pro-pel you towards new directions, people, career changes, or to make you grow through forgiving yourself, being determined or simply to practice controlling and managing energy and finding a way to use it to your greatest benefit.

You fully understand that good or bad are just words and as such they do not exist in your physical reality. Everything is only energy that you will respond to and not react. You will skillfully manage all discord and use it to your advantage. Moreover, you understand that man is the only creator of disharmony. "The human element, or the outer sphere of mankind is the only element in Creation that deliberately creates disharmony and consciously misuses the energy of the God sustaining it" (King, 2012, p. 8). According to King (2012) you cannot create disharmony and NOT experience its discordant effects. King (2012) further asserts that freedom in every way stands at your door, if you will keep your personality harmonized, and refuse to accept disharmonious energies from the atmosphere. "It is you who must always take your mind in hand and tell it how to behave" (King, 2012, p. 293). You are fully aware that it is and always has been up to you. It is and always has been your choice to create the future you want to face, and to live the life you want with abundance, joy and peach. It is always your choice whether you will remain strong living in the bliss of the Connection Consciousness or whether you will slip back into lower energies and have to extend much effort to regain previous higher frequencies.

In the **Connection Consciousness** you have moved from **faith** to **knowing.** You are innately aware that you have the power to achieve anything you desire because you see evidence of it everywhere in your physical **reality**. You have also gained command and regulation of energy to not only eliminate and create your wishes, but insulate yourself from future onslaught of any negativity that tries to invade your world. You have mastered all the other fields of consciousness which include, **Lack and Survival, Dedication,** and **Absorption.** You have established a close and loving relationship with your '**I AM**' consciousness and work in unity to **invoke** the **Violet Flame** to easily **eliminate** discords or **manifest** desires. You now live in the higher consciousness of the Source energy with a knowing that there are no limits, restrictions or lack. There is only your choice of where you wish to vibrate. Your vibration will match your reality.

The outer is aligned with the inner higher self. One of the biggest advantages in living in the Connection Consciousness is that little things or even big things don't frustrate, anger or even bother you. You look at everything and everyone with patience and fully understand that you never deal with people, for each person is nothing more than a bundle of energy in the guise of a physical body. Knowing this, life is easier to handle. Thoughts that enter the mind are in harmony with the Source Consciousness which means that you will not overreact, but will simply respond. You see every discordant vibration as energy that needs to be managed, thus the focus is always on the positive using these opportunities to master these energies so that they may somehow benefit you and keep you in your peak frequency.

You smile because you know that even perceived bad things were not bad at all, but an advantage for you. Discords were only opportunity to grow and expand your consciousness and gain even more power. You understand the limitless power you have at your disposal and know that as King (2012) contended that the acceptance of the limitless presence and activity of God, manifest in your outer experience is the miracle working power that has long been waiting to pour forth **Its** great abundance into your use" (King, 2012), but first **It** had to wait for you to connect to **It** through raising your vibrational frequency. The Source Consciousness will never rush you to connect yourself to **Itself**. It is your choice, your free will, whether you wish to acknowledge the presence of the Source and claim your power by raising your vibrational frequencies, to reach the Connection Consciousness and benefit from the **Source Consciousness'** abundant resources.

Living in a Higher Consciousness

In his book, *The Essential Wayne Dyer Collection,* Dr. Dyer (2013) wrote that there is a level of awareness available to you that you are probably unfamiliar with, and it extends upwards and transcends the ordinary level of consciousness. He further contended that at this higher plane of existence, the fulfillment of wishes is not only probable but it's guaranteed... at this level, your wishes can indeed be fulfilled (Dyer, 2013). It is from this level of a higher consciousness, when the individuals align themselves with the Source, having gone through the limiting energies of the **cause** and **effect** life in **Lack and Survival** field of consciousness, learned the necessity of controlling **thoughts, images**, and **feelings** in the **Dedication** energy, and mastered the powers of **contemplation, intention, elimination and insulation** in the **Absorption Consciousness** until finally reaching the **Connection Consciousness,** that every person understands that nothing is impossible for them. Free from discordant energies, an abundant, healthy, joyful life is sustainable at this peak vibration for ALL human beings on the planet.

When living in the peak vibrations of the **Connection Consciousness**, the innate changes that take place within people are quite remarkable. There is not only a shift that occurs and places the individuals into higher frequencies in all of the consciousness of mental, emotional, physical/sensory and spiritual frequencies that vastly expands power, wisdom and awareness, but a noticeable change transpires in their physical appearance. In the **Connection Consciousness** the person becomes a vibrant being that lives in his or her highest consciousness, joyful, peaceful, beaming with great health, prosperity, success and radiance.

It is innately understood that life is a gift, temporary and valuable. Living in a higher consciousness there is a tremendous mind-shift from your old belief systems and limiting thought patterns of who you are, where you come from, and what you deserve. Dyer (2013) contended that if you want to elevate your life, and become a manifester, then you have to change what you've believed to be true about yourself that has landed you where you are. In the **Connection Consciousness** there are no illusions, there is only the new reality that was born of faith, and was replaced by knowing. All doubt is banished. When you banish all doubt in favor of knowing you will create freely, without limitation. And just as Henry David Thoreau suggested, "you will meet with a success unexpected in common hours." Thoreau was convinced that "the universe will begin to conspire with you to fulfill your wishes. This is the law of co-creation."

Moving from Faith to Knowing To Reality

Ben Stein contended that 'faith is not believing that God can, it is knowing that He will.' Others have said that 'faith is not about everything turning out okay. Faith is about being okay, no matter how things turn out.' In order to move out of the low dense energy fields, faith requires you to have a personal relationship with God, and trust the Source Consciousness, the energy of all that IS.

Faith is the foundation of prayer. When one has faith, one expects to receive God's abundance and the answer to their prayers. Faith is trust, hope and belief. 'Faith is what brings the things God has provided for us from the spiritual realm into the physical realm' (Heb. 11:1). Just as when you create your reality using the **LEP Frequency**

Tool of consciousness your **expectancy** that your desires will manifest are also **based in faith.**

When you arrive in the peak **Connection Consciousness** frequency you move from **faith** to **knowing**. Your control of energy and power is at its highest potential. You still have your full support system of **faith** which is your **belief,** in the other fields of consciousness at varying degrees, from Lack and Survival, Dedication, and Absorption, but the **knowing** in the Connection Consciousness changes you forever. Life becomes vibrant and clear, and a brand-new **reality** emerges. All confusion and doubt disappear. Your world is how you wished it to be, and although modifications in life are always a given because people change their mind, or something they thought they wanted is not what they wanted at all. All these issues, in the high vibrations of the **Connection Consciousness,** are easily resolved, solved or fixed in the highest form of energy of the **Source Consciousness** which is love.

In the peak Connection Consciousness when you truly feel God your power is limitless. You feel love and the glory of God/Source and as Dr. Hawkins (2002, p. 15) shared from personal experience "everything and everyone in the world was luminous and exquisitely beautiful. All living things became radiant and expressed this radiance in stillness and splendor.... Profound changes of perception came without warning in improbable circumstances." Life is bliss.

PART 3
MECHANISMS

6

Mechanisms

The Mechanisms

Activating the 4 Fields of Consciousness Frequencies

Within the **LEP Frequency Tool** of consciousness the Mechanism is the through. The through means via, the way in which the readers will work with energy to get desired results. The **Mechanisms** of the **LEP Frequency Tool** include the **4 Consciousness Frequencies** of the *mental, emotional, physical/sensory, and spiritual* energies that operate within the human consciousness fields of *Lack and Survival, Dedication, Absorption,* and *Connection* in which people exist and move in their daily life.

The **4 Consciousness Frequencies** of the *mental, emotional, physical/sensory, and spiritual* energies are integral to people's overall vibration. They are vital because they determine the current placement and lived experiences in one of the energy fields of *Lack and Survival, Dedication, Absorption, or Connection Consciousness.* The combined vibrational frequency of the *mental, emotional, physical/sensory* and *spiritual* energy is the individuals' vibrational signature. It determines how they live, how much power is available for their use to create desires, or eliminate any unwanted discords in their life, and will affect their spiritual placement after death. The higher the combined frequency, the greater the power and ability to live and create the life they desire and the speed in which that life manifests for them, and the higher the frequency designation in the spiritual realm.

Human beings are both the receiver and transmitter of energy. Every input and output, in any of the **4 Consciousness Frequencies** of the *mental, emotional, physical/sensory,* and *spiritual* will activate the *Laws of Vibrations and Attraction*, and draw "like" energy to you, expand consciousness in that field, and enhance its characteristics. However, to move up in overall frequency, an alignment between all consciousness frequencies must be achieved. The **mental consciousness frequency** operates within the realms of **thoughts** and **images.** The **emotional consciousness frequency** contains the energies of **emotions** and **feelings.** The **physical** and **sensory consciousness frequency** includes **physical action** and the **body** and all the **sensory systems** of *sight, hearing, smell, taste, touch,* and the *sixth sense* (aka, ESP, or intuition). **The spiritual consciousness frequency** is comprised of **spiritual energies** of the Source Consciousness, and includes *personal connection to the Source Consciousness/God, faith, trust in the Source, and individual beliefs.* (To assess your personal frequency in each energy field, complete the corresponding assessments located within this book (mental (A6), emotional (A7), physical/sensory (A8), and spiritual (A9).

Mental Frequency

Wherever your consciousness resides, there you are. Thus, do not let your attention linger on any thoughts that do not serve you. This is true in the **Lack and Survival, Dedication, Absorption** and **Connection Consciousness** energy fields, but is especially true for the dense **Lack and Survival** primal energies of basic **'cause and effect,'** because these energies are most painful to experience, and reframe. Mental frequencies within the **Lack and Survival** consciousness are **low**, as usually the person is not in the best frame of mind, and the world looks bleak, and often hopeless from their perspective. Positive perceptions in the form of thoughts take much longer to take root as it takes time and often enormous effort for the person to gain confidence and awareness that they have all the power that they need to transform into a better life, if only, they became aware of that fact and chose to act.

Dedication Consciousness vibrates at **moderate** speed. It allows for greater mental control and management of thoughts and images that are planted in the mind. The **high** mental frequency within the **Absorption Consciousness** offers a sustainable mental clarity and freedom to **contemplate** anything desired, with the skill of **intention** to manifest it in the person's physical reality. The **Absorption Consciousness eliminates** any discordant energies, and mentally **insulates** against any future onslaught, should they try to reappear. The **Connection Consciousness** vibrates at **peak** mental frequencies. These peak mental vibrations are achieved through **faith,** trust and the mental strength of **knowing,** which allow for immense power and ability to direct energy to transform any constructive desire into physical reality to those who vibrate in that peak mental frequency.

Resilient mental energy is crucial to either increasing and/or maintaining high overall frequencies. Do not let your attention rest on anything discordant, or anything that drains your mental energy! **Thoughts** quickly turn to **images. Images** activate **feelings.** If you are unguarded, before you realize what is happening, your vibrational frequencies have decreased and a happy mental state has turned into sadness, anger or frustration, decreasing not only your mental frequency but your overall vibration and sending you into frequencies you don't want to face, along with squashing all abilities and power that you need to create desires or eliminate discord.

Keep your mental vibration high by always thinking harmonious thoughts. If you DO NOT GOVERN YOUR THOUGHTS in a matter of minutes, or even seconds, you can lower your vibrational frequency, and decrease the power to attract what you wish in life. It is very important to hold fast to a positive mental outlook in all things, regardless of the outer influences. Yes, sometimes that is challenging, and painful but it must be done. Outer influences are deceiving and there is good in everything, and everyone.

Perceptions are fluid, and things are not as they seem. Reality shifts based on thoughts. Keep your mental vibrations high for that is the secret to retaining your mental vibrational frequency, have peace in your life and maintain your power to create. In order to create quickly and easily, the person's mental frequency must remain steady at its highest vibration, and not fluctuate from low to high, for this will affect the speed of which manifestations form from the consciousness mental mind to physical realities.

Vibration is impersonal and does not understand the difference between happy or sad. Vibrational frequency just is and responds to like accordingly. An unhappy mental state draws to it the same type of vibrations which will only intensify the mental discord through images and feelings. When an individual has understood, "that whatsoever he connects himself with through this attention, he becomes a part of it to the degree of the intensity with which his attention is fixed, he will see the importance of keeping his attention off the seemingly destructive angles of human experience, no matter what they are" (King, 2011, p. 93).

Do not permit yourself to have a negative thought of any kind. This will only draw like energies into your mental frequencies and decrease your power by lowering your vibrations, which will rob you of optimism, change your general outlook, and negatively affect your lived experiences. Should discordant thoughts creep in, simply redirect them to something pleasant, or eliminate them completely by taking a firm stand and command them to leave you at once!

Mental Frequency in the Lack and Survival Consciousness

The Lack and Survival energies focus on awareness. Awareness is necessary before you can leave the low and dense energies of

Lack and Survival. You must be aware of your current vibrational frequency and that you have the power to change your world before you can proceed to the next consciousness state of Dedication.

Do you live in the Lack and Survival Consciousness? Take the Lack and Survival assessment included in this book and find out, as mental frequencies are key determinants of how quickly you can change your life by rising out of dense energies of misery in the Lack and Survival energies into a world where creation of desires is guaranteed. Mental frequencies must be monitored at all times, as the general energy in the Lack and Survival Consciousness usually fills the mind with thoughts and images of sadness, depression, worry, and anxiousness over roles and responsibilities, for the most part created through external economic, or self-inflicted internal perspectives, or a general outlook of misery and lack.

Life in the Lack and Survival Consciousness feels mentally heavy, and crippling. People that move in these low and dense energies are mentally fatigued, often engulfed in a cloud of problems, not living passionately but enduring each day. Their mind is filled with images of failed expectations, or mistakes, regret, guilt or stress, which only affirms this low energy's emergence in their future. On this mental plane of existence, the perception is that everything is happening to them. They think that all the effects that are appearing in their lives are the cause of others. Things are done to them, and they take little responsibly for the role that they might have had in their life that caused this energy to appear.

A defeatist attitude will only bring more defeat. Many people play the victim, or think they are victims of circumstance, where all the power comes from somewhere other than themselves. They are easily swayed by the opinion of others, or outside influences, and are not mentally strong enough to take a stand. They feel abandoned by God or think they are undeserving or incapable of making life changes. Some think they have to beg God for assistance. Others still have given up completely, they think they are powerless and have limited or no control over their life and never will, so why bother trying.

In the **Lack and Survival** mental plane the person moves in an automatic rhythm. In this low energy people are largely unobservant, unaware, and often not caring of the small joys and positive energy that surrounds them every day. The **low energy** comes in many forms, such as mental stress over financial affairs, or lack of love or support. Some people may feel like they lack a purpose or meaning in life, that perfect relationship, career, better health, or they are just conditioned to depression and a sorry state of life, and so on but it always brings with it the heavy energy of lack and survival. Mentally perceiving life as constant "survival of the fittest" is draining. The only way to move out of the low energy is to align yourself with harmonious thoughts and images, even at the smallest level.

In every discord you will find a rainbow when you look deep enough. You deserve so much better! If you make a concerted effort to leave these energies, you will move out of these low-density fields into a higher vibration. Changing mental frequencies may seem difficult at first, but "fortunately, beliefs that are consistent with the flow of the universal truth manifest more easily than those that go against the grain" (Stubbs, 1999, p.41). Thus, if you remain in a harmonious mental energy, regardless of the discordant storms that may rage around you, especially in the densest of frequencies in the primal *cause and effect* **Lack and Survival** energies, soon you will be lifted above the storm to a higher consciousness, with the powers of creation now more available to you.

Do you see yourself existing in the **Lack and Survival** energies? People are the **cause** of all their **effects**, and they do not need to beg, as God has given them the power to create what they will for themselves. Anyone can completely change the effects of their causes in their life, by changing their thoughts and mental pictures about it. **Raising** your **thoughts,** and **images** in your mind by only focusing on harmonious energies is the quickest and easiest way to **move out** of the low **Lack and Survival** energies to a higher vibration, where creating and manifesting the life you wish to live can be achieved.

Mental strength is self-sustained. But it can quickly drop in frequency when one is off guard, and/or does not keep the required faith that you do have the power to change anything you desire. It is wise to keep mental disharmony from you, as much as possible, by not accepting any thoughts of discordant nature, no matter how the outer influences may try to affect you, or what they may bring into your life. You have the ability to change mental structures from a lower to higher frequency simply by changing your thoughts, from lower to higher forms.

Even simple things like changing your mental attitude from 'I can't do this' to 'I can do anything' brings you into higher vibrations and accessibility to the power of creation. Thinking that 'only good comes to you' will change the *cause and effect* of the lower energies, and generate an expanded consciousness because you have changed the mental frequency from an undeserving attitude to one of 'I deserve good things to come to me' then decree it to the world. This will elevate your vibrations from low to high within the **Lack and Survival** field and propel you into higher mental frequency of an expanded consciousness. When you change your mental structure to positivity, you will change your behavior and actions which will produce much higher and quicker tangible results for you because you are now attracting higher frequencies. Look for verification of this in your life when you begin using your mental consciousness by changing mental patterns from negative to positive, as often witnessing tangible improvements quickly lifts the person out of denser energies into a higher energy field of existence.

In the **Lack, and Survival Consciousness** there is a consistent undercurrent of mental sadness. This is because of negative programming, negative lived experiences, and the absence of exposure to awareness that you have the power to change your life at any time and experience what life could be. If you are classically conditioned not to expect good things to come to you it will decrease the potential of living in high vibrations, which will keep you trapped in the lack and survival energies and only bring about more sadness, and often depression. Even when maintaining a mental attitude of "being above water," there is a consistent and persistent angst of fear and anxiety that all is not well. A mental attitude of your personal power must exist in the mind for you to move further.

Harmonious thoughts raise vibrational frequencies wherever they land. If you take the assessment in this book and find yourself living in the mental energies of **Lack and Survival Consciousness,** do not fret or despair. Because positive energies counteract negative ones, mentally aligning yourself with higher frequencies, of higher thoughts about yourself and your future opens the door to expanding your mental consciousness, and allows for infinite possibilities to enter your life. Find and use your mental strength to think only the highest uplifting thoughts, so that you may easily rise in frequencies. Let go of all things that are limiting or inhibiting you, in any way. Release old mental resentments, grievances and so on. Forgive all and move on, and from this point forward as White (1965 p. 57) directed, "carefully guard your thought chambers."

Harmonious thoughts that immediately replace discordant thoughts form a higher frequency and better overall mental structure, and change the **effects** of the **causes** to a higher vibration. White (1965, p. 50) asserted that "all created life is the same substance that is powered by thought." Thus, thought is where we begin. In order to leave the dense vibrations of the **Lack and Survival Consciousness,** you must **raise** your mental consciousness through the adjustment of your **thoughts** and the **images** held in your mind, to harmonious frequencies. The *Law of Vibration and the Law of Attraction* will ricochet higher vibrations to you, which will raise your mental consciousness frequency, and help increase your vibration to the next frequency of the Dedication Consciousness.

Mental Frequency in Dedication Consciousness

Dedication Consciousness moves past the awareness that must be realized in the low Lack and Survival energies. You are now aware that you have the power to change your life and have dedicated to altering the negative patterns of your thoughts and images in the mind to positive. In the Dedication Consciousness people can control and direct the energy to where they wish it to go through their dedication of regulating and managing their mental consciousness through thoughts, and images.

The **Dedication Consciousness** is a **moderate** energy field that has the ability to **frame** or **reframe thoughtform**s and **images** to attract higher frequencies to itself. It is the beginning of the creation of desires process because of the availability of the power that is now accessible to anyone who wishes to work with energy. But it requires steady discipline. Have you mentally reached the Dedication Consciousness and mastered control of your thoughts and images that are placed in your mind? Take the Dedication Consciousness assessment in this book and find out.

In the **Dedication Consciousness,** personality begins to play less of a role. The ego is slowly replaced by higher controlled harmonious thoughts, which are supported by higher harmonious images. This sets up the foundation to begin working with energies for manifestation purposes. Because controlling thoughtforms which trigger images in the mind weeds out toxic energies, it gives you the confidence of the power you hold over your mental processes. This allows you to retain a clearer vision of the harmonious things you should be thinking about and bathes you with a sense of gratitude to the Source Consciousness for making this power available for your use. Thoughts of gratefulness to the Source/God always raises vibrational frequencies and further advances the ability of the individual to use mental energy to create desires in the consciousness and materialize them in the physical world.

Mental dedication to increasing vibrational frequencies in keeping thoughts under control and in harmony is essential to the manifestation process because **thoughts** will trigger **images**, and images will activate **feelings.** The combined mental and emotional energies will produce desired results in tangible realities when backed by feelings

and action. However, in order for this to occur, a harmonious alignment of thoughts and images must first take place. This means that
a concerted and disciplined effort must occur on a mental level. All
discordant thoughts and images must be reframed to their highest
harmonious vibration in order to tap into higher frequencies, and use
those vibrations to begin the mental process of creation.

The reframing of thoughts is a mental frequency technique that
assists you to look harmoniously at perspectives which trigger harmonious images. By refashioning your mental frequency to a positive
perspective, you not only alleviate stress and anxiety in your life but
you raise yourself to a higher frequency where all things are probable.
Reframing not only changes perceptions but changes the experiences
in your physical life. It is through a strong foundation of the application
and control of the mental frequencies of thoughts and images that you
will ensure your ability to control emotions because thoughts trigger
images and images active feelings. An alignment of all 3 thoughts,
images in the mind and feelings raise vibrational frequencies to where
unlimited power is available for your use.

Mental Frequency in Absorption Consciousness

The **Absorption Consciousness** includes the mental energies
of **contemplation**, **intention, elimination**, and **insulation.** Mental
frequencies of thoughts and images in the mind in the **Dedication
Consciousness** must be consistently cultivated, if they are to become
strong enough to rise into the high **Absorption Consciousness**
energy where manifestation of desires or elimination of discord takes
center stage. The more mental energy that is exerted, and partnered
with behavior and actions of the person towards achieving any intention, the quicker the intention will appear in their life.

Contemplation and intention are focused mental energies In the
Absorption Consciousness it is important to keep your mental frequency as high as possible through positive thought and expectation
that your desires will manifest at their perfect time. As you mentally

contemplate what it is that you desire remember that you must be specific. Use imagery, and through contemplation crystallize your desire in all its glory and detail. Do not rush the process of contemplation as it is an instrument of the deeper mind and thought. Allow it the space and time to roam and muse until what you want is imprinted in your mind exactly as you wish it.

Contemplation is an important mental energy in the manifestation process. Dyer (2013) contended that in your own personal life, your willingness to contemplate as a person who is capable of attracting into your life what you want, having the relationships that you want, or being able to have abundance is vital. All you have to do is start the process of manifestation by willing to contemplate the presence of your desires in your life. Do you find yourself at the Absorption Consciousness phase? Have you mastered the mental processes established in the Dedication Consciousness? Are ready to contemplate your desire and send out the intent for its manifestation in your life? Take the Absorption Consciousness assessment located in this book and find out.

It is always wise to remember that when you vibrate at your highest potential, it is the best time to mentally contemplate anything and everything you wish to appear in your life. Mentally, arrange it exactly how you wish it. Play and imagine freely. Imagination is pure thought with a picture associated with it (McNight, 2005). The very act of contemplating, and using clear imagery, brings you closer to its energy. Clear **imagery** is very important as you begin the mental process of **contemplation,** and move into the energy of intention, which directs the energy of your **'intent'** to where you wish it to go.

After you have mentally contemplated and sent out the intention the power of **intention** will continue the manifestation of your mental desires and attract them into your physical reality. But you must do your part and actively pursue your intention in your physical world. Be bold! Seek and explore every opportunity that will bring you closer to seeing your intent in your physical world. When you send your intent to the universe, and diligently support its through your actions and behavior in your life, it will manifest for you at much greater speed.

But all readers must remember that intent is not just sent once. It is a continuous directed thought, with an imprinted image in the mind that generates energy. The contemplated thought that sent out the intention must be backed by physical action so that it can appear in the person's life when the conditions are ripe. Holding mental frequencies high, and not allowing any limiting thoughts to interfere, but continuing to send strong mental intentions for what is expected is also very important to speedy manifestation.

A strong mental expectant attitude is the right attitude in the cultivation of **intention** through **contemplation** energies. For once you have mentally **contemplated** your desire, **visualized** it and sent out the **intention,** you must mentally continue to create a space in your mind from which you experience that desire. This means having mastered the Dedication Consciousness of controlling thoughts and images in your mind, you must continually be aware of your thinking patterns because that is what mastering something means, and not allowing doubt to shatter your expectations for this weakens the intention. Do not let your intent waiver or the mental picture of your desire fade, regardless of the opposition, outer influences, or any interference from others.

Once you have contemplated and are firm in your intention, your mental picture of your *intent* must always be held steady, and your expectation of the results high. This will position you to receive whatever is desired with great speed. However, "if you doubt your ability to create the life you intend, then you're refusing the power of intention" (Dyer, 2013. p. 37). Thus, moving to higher frequencies and creating your desires will be stifled, and delayed until such a time when you are ready.

Elimination and insulation work in unison with your **'I AM'** presence and the **Violet Flame**. You may contemplate and send out the intent to eliminate any discord from your life or insulate yourself against incoming negative energies but you will need to work through your 'I AM' presence to invoke the 'Violet Flame' to *shatter, dissipate* and *consume* all wrong creations in your life, or a specific discord.

Mentally, contemplate and send out the intention in the same manner that you would to create any desire, but you must call upon your 'I AM' presence and 'Violet Flame' when you wish to eliminate discord or insulate yourself against incoming discordant energy. Further, you must support the intent with feelings of expectancy. Say verbally or in your mind, "through my mighty '**I AM**', I invoke the **Violet Flame** to *shatter, dissipate* and *consume* this discord (or all discords) from my life and ensure that it never touches my world again. Support the statement with images of the discord disappearing and feelings of belief that the discord is now eliminated from your life.

When insulating mentally call upon the **Electronic Circle,** and command that it protects you. Visualize the energy surrounding you in an impenetrable way in whatever color you choose, and support the image with a certainty that you are now protected. Do not let doubt that it is not working ever enter the mind. If you are steadfast in your stand that you have the power to achieve all you desire you can use your mental consciousness to create at will, be free of any discord, or gain protection by insulating yourself against discordant energies that try to penetrate your peace of mind.

Mental Frequency in Connection Consciousness

Mental frequency in the **Connection Consciousness** is of **peak** energy. Connection Consciousness transmutes the high energy of **faith,** and trust to the peak energies of innate **knowing**. When mentally vibrating in the Connection Consciousness you always have whatever is necessary to succeed because of your vastly expanded consciousness. You have the full mental knowledge that you are a part of the Source Consciousness and that you have all the powers of the Source by applying the universal laws of vibrational frequency. In the mental frequencies of the Connection Consciousness people become much more relaxed, cloaked in a mental knowing that they cannot fail. Thoughts and images in the mind are filled with a vibrancy and confidence never experienced before.

Living in the Connection Consciousness, you have mastered all mental control and can easily wield the power of contemplation, intention, elimination and insulation. The power of precipitation comes easily to you. Thus, what you wish is within your grasp. You can bring any thoughtforms of desires from your consciousness into your physical reality with little effort. Discords will be a thing of the past, eliminated on sight because **faith** has been replaced by a **'knowing'** within you, and the knowing produces great power at your disposal to create your ideal reality. You are mentally strong and realize that you never needed to rush anything, worry about anything or stress over anything. All your desires arrive at their own perfect time. All worry can quickly be eliminated and peace of mind effortlessly restored.

People continuously living in the mental **Connection Consciousness** vibrate at such peak frequency that they seem to possess and exhibit god-like qualities. They seem to have incredible luck. In actually, they are just vibrating at a peak frequency and have gained the skill of creating any constructive desire because of their expanded mental consciousness, and can easily bring whatever they need into their physical reality. They exhibit incredible peace and the energy of vibrancy within and all around them. Everyone in their life knows such people, they look just like every other human being, but everyone senses that they are different somehow. They exude joy and love, regardless of circumstances or outer influences. They are much slower to anger and live in a harmonious connection with the field of intent, with an unwavering belief in themselves and in the eternal power of Spirit. It always seems that great things are happening to them. Great things are happening because they draw that energy to themselves as a result of living in peak vibrational frequencies.

The Bible tells us that human beings were made "in the image of God." This means we too are creators, and can mentally manifest what we wish in our lives. The Source Consciousness gives us free will, and the tools, such as **consciousness** and other resources such as the **LEP Frequency Tool** to help humanity create whatever they wish in joy, health, prosperity and peace. In the **Connection**

Consciousness, you have complete mental control and a clear mental understanding that anything that appears in your life that is uncomfortable, unnerving, unjust and so on is just discordant energy that must be managed. Knowing that you have the power to create anything desired or surmount anything and to turn it around and use it for your good should give peace, invigorate your mind and rejuvenate your soul. This includes even the most painful experience in your life.

The knowing that your mental consciousness is the most powerful tool on earth, and that you had this tool all along you just did not know how to use it to your greatest advantage is one of the biggest growths in your spiritual progress that is experienced when vibrating mentally at this peak frequency. In the **Connection Consciousness**, you are completely detached from taking things personally, and see all life as an opportunity to create and discords simply as energy to be managed and controlled. This "innate knowing" of who you really are and how much power your really have should give great relief to all.

Emotional Frequency

Feelings are sparked by emotions through **thoughts**, and **images.** Your emotional energy interacts with your physical because emotions are felt in the body, and emotions directly affect the state of the physical body but it is a separate energy (Stubbs, 1999). Emotions are extremely important to the life of the human being because of the way they affect and influence every person, in every consciousness field of **Lack and Survival, Dedication, Absorption**, and **Connection** energies. Because emotions involve every consciousness field, they play a significant role in the manifestation process and direct how much power is available to people to create desires or eliminate discordant energy.

In the **low Lack and Survival** fields, and its primal **'cause and effect'** energies, emotions are routinely out of control, causing various discords which include, anxiety, anger, regret, guilt, depression and the like. To qualify any feeling and raise it to a higher vibration, change your feeling towards the discordant energy to one of harmony. Do not worry about justification. Forgive and release all discordant energy. I am not asking you to forget anything, or change your mind if you think a wrong has been done to you, or you wronged someone, only to forgive and release it. Holding on to discord whether you feel you are justified or not will only hurt you by depleting your power and your ability to create manifestations. When you release negative feelings all discordant or destructive energy will be transmuted to harmonious and constructive energy because you are operating in the highest emotional frequencies of feeling 'good,' which can only be achieved in higher energies.

Your personal vibration will register that peace and respond with sending vibrations of peace in return which will automatically raise your emotional frequency. It is wise to remember that within the **Emotional Frequency** whatever feeling holds your attention will intensify. Depending on your feelings, your emotional vibration will either increase or decrease affecting your overall frequencies, and ultimately your ability to use and direct the energy to manifest your desires.

Emotional frequency within the moderate energies of the **Dedication Frequencies** includes emotional maturity and **controlling** and **managing** your **feelings.** Because **thoughts** activate **images**, **images** activate **feelings**, and **feelings** activate **realizations of intent** controlling feelings is of utmost importance. If feelings are controlled and aligned with thoughts and images in the mind, things that were once only in the conscious mind can manifest in physical realities.

The energies of **contemplation, intention, elimination**, and **insulation** within the **high Absorption Consciousness** will advance the crafting of your manifestation skills. Once you have mastered how to **control** your **emotions** in the **Dedication Consciousnesses** you can align yourself with your desires and quickly bring them into your reality using the mechanisms in Absorption Consciousness of contemplation, intention, elimination and insulation. Emotions in the

Connection Consciousness respond to **conscious emotional response,** and never overreaction. At this energy field there is no need to qualify the emotionally charged energy because the person already exists in peak-quality functioning emotional frequency. The persons' consciousness and emotional vibrational frequency are perfectly aligned, and can neutralize discordant emotional energy through consistent, stable and harmonious emotional reactions.

Emotional Frequency in the Lack and Survival Consciousness

Feelings run rampant in the Lack and Survival Consciousness field. Emotions are uncontrolled and usually manifest in unintended discordant **effects** which result in unintended **causes,** usually to your great dissatisfaction because they vibrate at lower energies. You will excel in creating your life, through the universal laws put in place for your use, when you can control and manage your feelings.

Emotion is a vibration created by the individuals' focus of attention. Emotion combined with momentum magnifies the persons experience within any emotional vibratory frequency through feelings. The more attention on the emotion, the more intense the feeling. In emotionally immature people uncontrolled feelings cause much grief because of the low **cause** and **effect** energies that are found in the Lack and Survival fields. Consequently, it is vital that for those who exist in the **Lack and Survival** energy fields that all emotions are controlled at their first appearance. To get a grasp on controlling run away feelings they must be viewed impersonally, from the vantage of 'this feeling is only energy to be managed and controlled which I can do by controlling my emotions and changing my feelings toward the situation," and then do it!

Do not allow discordant emotions to dwell! This will immediately lower your vibrational frequencies and bring more of the 'like' cause and effect energies to your lived experience. Change the **thought,** change the **image,** which will activate a change of the **feeling** releasing you from the clutches of low energies.

Unmonitored emotions will stifle any feeling of happiness, peace or joy and keep you trapped in lower energies. Emotional frequencies within the Lack and Survival Consciousness create vice-like feelings that can hold the individual's captive and not allow any acceleration into a higher consciousness. People unconsciously create their emotional environment through the primal 'cause and effect' energy. Within this realm, heavy discord, anxiety, depression, sadness, guilt, regret, and anger reign, often in uncontrollable fields of scattered energy creating violent outbursts, loss of temper, heated verbal exchanges and the life, with often unfortunate results. These lower, denser emotions according to Hawkins, (2002) are rarely manifested as pure states in an individual, meaning that in the Lack and Survival fields emotional frequencies will not just show up as anger, but with combined emotions, such as sadness, guilt and so on. Hence, it is of utmost importance to increase frequencies through the harmonious alignment, of thoughts, and images which will trigger harmonious feelings.

If feelings are not controlled, the low vibratory energy, which the person moves in often produces a lack of emotional stability, and ability to process many of life's emotional discords. This inability to process low energies in the Lack and Survival field often results in tears, depression, anger, anxiety, living in constant emotional stress, and cements the person's vibrations in very low slow-moving frequencies, which stills their ability and power to create and manifest. It leaves them drained and feeling hopeless.

Discordant emotional energy, disguised as various feelings, is a powerful force to overcome. But you can and must do it! The **Lack and Survival** energies are the most challenging, but if this is where you find yourself, this is where you start! No worries though, for the growth and learning may be slow at first, as you try to bring your emotional consciousness frequencies under control, but understanding that you must do it, if you wish to change your life, should be motivation enough!

Emotional energies in the Lack and Survival plane are ruled by the ego. They are so intense because they poke at the ego. The ego is a fighter and does not tolerate being mastered well and will always strike back. The ego has great strength and is a worthy opponent. The cloudiness of the low **'cause and effect'** energy is magnified by the ego because very often the ego, sensing that it's losing its emotional power over the person, limits and alters emotional perceptions to suit its needs, which immediately lowers the individuals' vibrational frequencies. The ego will go through great lengths to protect itself, but you are stronger and the ego knows it, it just hopes that you don't

To begin lifting yourself out of the emotional energy of the Lack and Survival dense energies take the 'ego' out of the equation and **focus** on maintaining **harmonious feelings.** Taking a stand, and challenging the ego is integral to your success. The ego carries a false sense of power that manifests itself through illusory belief systems and concepts (McNight, 2013). You must be diligent, stand strong and be aware of any low emotions that try to stir within you and change them at once!

You hold the power. You are the ruler and master of your ego. Deliberately fix your attention on it and command it to cease interfering in your life for it will limit you and erode your life if you do not temper it. The ego does not understand or is aware of its immature emotional properties so it will fight hard to have its way with you and keep you in these low energies. It is part of your soul's blueprint or it would not exist, and it does have its uses. This is why the ego must be tempered and not annihilated. But the ego can become incessant at trying to control you in every moment. It does not understand energy or the bigger picture. You cannot and must not allow it to take the lead in your life and make decisions from this low emotional plane.

When the ego tries to evade your emotional space push it out with feelings of control. Feel good about the decisions you are making that come from higher emotional maturity and not a place of personal selfishness or greed. The act of feeling good will instantly temper the discordant energy of the ego and raise your vibration.

If you find yourself in a situation in which you cannot control your emotions, or find a positive way to handle the energy of the discord that will change your feeling, move away from it immediately! It is perfectly acceptable to turn your back on any discordant emotion that may bring you into lower, denser energy fields. It is the only way to leave the Lack and Survival energies and lift your vibrations to the Dedication Consciousness so that your upward shift to power may begin.

Emotional Frequency in Dedication Consciousness

In the **Dedication Consciousness**, the use of feelings to direct energy to manifest desires is prominent. Feelings are a major support system to thoughts and images in the manifestation process. This is because in the Dedication Consciousness **thoughts** activate **images**, **images** activate **feelings**, and **feelings** activate manifestation of desires because they motivate and inspire a "can do attitude" of physical action. Just as feelings have the power to influence thoughts, 'emotions themselves can function as frames, directing information, processing and affecting belief systems, and information accessibility, as well as subsequent judgments' (Nabi, 2003). Emotions often ignite various feelings, and energy systems, such as belief automatically which also helps in the manifestation process.

The instant you change a feeling, you change all the energy surrounding it, and regain control of the energy to your highest advantage. Thoughts, images and feelings in the Dedication Consciousness are processed from a much higher emotional maturity than in the Lack and Survival phase because the people moving the Dedication Consciousness have an awareness and the understanding that they have the power to use energy to create the life and future they want to live and face. Their dedication to the process of working with their mental and emotional energy domains increases their vibrational frequency, and brings higher outcomes to their life. The very attempt at controlling mental and emotional consciousness domains in every situation raises vibrations which triggers emotional peace and control.

Emotions are either positive, or negative. By changing the polarity of emotion, through raising the mental vibrations of the energy of emotion, we can increase its frequency levels and transform it to a higher vibration (Zukav & Francis, 2002). We do this through the control of our thoughts and feelings. According to Zukav and Francis (2002 p. 35), human beings' emotions arise from an energy system, rather than interactions with people or things, "emotions are currents of energy that run through you. They are more than consequences of chemical interactions, hormones, and excesses, or deficiencies of neurotransmitters." Emotions are built into our human molecular structure, but are mutable, meaning that with each intention, emotions can be changed, as easily as changing a feeling.

Emotions are more than the physical experiences that occur in various parts of your body. Emotions are subjective and rooted in perception. Emotions arise from memories and reactions to people's lived experiences and meaning that is assigned to each thought, and image in the mind which activate the feeling. This information is stored in the human brain, but often, the memory is not accurate, as people remember information in subjective ways. The truth is often muddled from the perception of the beholder, but the emotions respond with feelings of the flawed perception, which in many cases may not be the actual truth, which is why controlling emotions becomes even more enormously important.

Human beings are very emotional beings and with each extension of emotion they are constantly creating new feelings that can be used to form new meaning. The meaning of the feeling is used to either increase or decrease their vibrations. The more important the meaning, the more intense is the feeling. In the Dedication Consciousness the dedication is focused on controlling the emotions so that the attention is placed on regulating the emotional response, and not react emotionally to situations.

Respond and not react. Always remember that if you do not dedicate yourself to controlling your emotions, they will control you and will decrease your vibrational frequencies rendering you powerless to create any desires or eliminate any discord that has attached itself to you in your life. Controlling your emotions will give you the self-confidence and an overall positive sense of self because you will not overreact to situations which will cause you even more strife. Use your emotions to uplift you. Feel good about yourself and about your new found power and that power will serve you well.

Emotional Frequency in Absorption Consciousness

Supportive emotions are necessary when using vibrational frequencies to create desires. **Emotional frequency** in the **Absorption Consciousness** operate in the energies of *contemplation, intention, elimination* and *insulation*. Once you have mastered control of your feelings in the Dedication Consciousness you are elevated to the Absorption Consciousness where you can use feelings to assist you to create desires in the consciousness and bring them into your physical reality through contemplation and intention.

Contemplation, either in a form of daydreaming, imagining, meditation or just playful thinking is necessary for creation. But it is through the supporting feeling of expectation during the art of contemplation and intention that cements the picture of the desire in the heart so it can manifest in the person's reality. Feeling is the energy that activates the manifestation of desires from the consciousness to form in physical realities because authentic feelings offer an illusory sense of expectancy.

The best way to utilize the power of contemplation through regular meditation is to not only see but feel the intended desire during contemplative movements. During meditation contemplation crystalizes your needs, and details your intended desires. Crystallization in thought and supportive feelings vastly increases the speed of intentions into the physical world. When contemplating be clear, visualize and feel as if the desire has already arrived. It is only through a born thought in the consciousness that the image can be formed and sent out in feeling, so that the intent can materialize in physical realities. During contemplation the attention is held on any visualizations of the desire which is supported by your feeling, relative to it, long enough for it to be imprinted in your heart. Dedicating time to contemplation, using positive feelings to support any mental images also serves your well-being, as a happier emotional life charged with expectancy of good things to come will attract 'like' energies to you. Thus, always direct your thoughts to hold only the most positive feelings when you contemplate your intended desires. But not through sheer force of will, but through the higher energies with feelings of gratitude to the Source Consciousness for giving you its boundless power to create and live your dreams.

Every conscious experience has a feeling attached to it. Contemplation clarifies the intent through thoughts and images, but the emotional frequency of feelings needed to support the energy of intent to manifest it into physical form is the push needed to bring it into the person's physical reality. The determinant of the force of the energy that is used in bringing wishes from the consciousness, into your physical manifestation largely rests with the emotional frequency of the person. Once a desire in the consciousness has been formed through contemplation, it is sent with pure intent in thought and image and most importantly supported by a strong feeling of expectancy that it will manifest in its perfect time.

After the desire has been contemplated, crystalized and sup- ported with feeling, it is time for the intent to be sent to the universe in an expectant manner. Feel how it will be when it arrives. Aligning emo- tion to your intention is crucial to the manifestation process for inten- tion, without a strong feeling in back of it, will not produce or greatly impede results. This occurs because the energy of intent is read and responds accordingly to the frequency it receives. Thus, keeping your emotional frequency aligned with the image of your desire assists in the manifestation process because it keeps the intention energy strong and expectant. Fluctuating between low and high emotional frequencies will only delay your progress. You can't feel confident with full expectancy that your intent will materialize one moment, and hopeless the next. This type of emotional energy fluctuation greatly decreases the speed of the intended manifestations, or delays them indefinitely.

Emotional energy is the core of intention manifestation. This is because emotion is the charge that once contemplated has the power to bring your intentions into your life if you aligned yourself with it through the feeling of expectancy. Meaning that you fully expect it to come into your life, and then took the necessary physical steps to make it happen. For the very thought of intending is a command to the universe and once supported with expectant feelings activates the Law of Vibration and Attraction.

The Absorption Consciousness not only contains the higher powers of creation through contemplation and intention, it also contains the energies of elimination and insulation. The Absorption Consciousness' unmatched ability to eliminate all discordant feelings from the personal emotional energy of people and balance karma is unsurpassed. This is achieved by keeping emotions harmonious regardless of outer influences, and using the "I AM' presence and the Violet Energy to eliminate all feelings that do not serve you, and decrease your vibrational frequency.

To eliminate any discord, call upon your '**I AM'** presence and invoke the **Violet Flame** to *shatter, dissipate* and *consume* a specific emotional discord that is troubling you or all emotional discords that may have inadvertently attached to you and are now causing you strife. Remember when you are working with the violet energies you must not only call upon the Violet Flame to help you but feel your connection to your mighty "I AM" presence. Moreover, feel the power of the Violet Flame as you eliminate negative energy from your emotional body. See the discords whatever they may be, whether it is a past transgression or mistake that is causing you pain, a situation or a person in the brilliantly glowing Violet Flame and watch it disappear from your life forever. Feel it dissolving from your energy fields leaving you lighter, peaceful and freer. For details on how to use the Violet Flame, see Supplement S2.

To stay in the high vibration of the Absorption Consciousness it is also necessary to protect your emotional frequency by using the **Electronic Circle.** Surround yourself with the energy of the Electronic

Circle and add an extra layer of energy around your heart in whatever color you wish. Do this every morning before you start your day, or throughout the day, as you see fit. See yourself protected within the Electronic Circle by whatever energy color you are drawn to at the moment, and feel the energy of protection encasing you in its power and know deep within your heart that nothing can hurt you, unless you allow it.

In the emotional frequency within the Absorption energy field, you have mastered how to use your feelings to contemplate and send out the intention, and learned how to eliminate any discordant feelings that have attached itself to you. You have also learned how to protect yourself giving you the emotional strength to insulate yourself against any discordant energy that tries to enter your life by using the Electronic Circle of energy. Be warned, however, that often even when eliminated, discordant energies try to reappear in your emotional world. Masterfully handle these unwanted feelings. If you insulate yourself regularly against discord, this will stop future emotional discordant energy from entering your emotional consciousness and you will remain in peace, calm and always at the ready to create your life as you see fit. Discordant emotional energies will no longer disrupt your word and bring you pain or emotional trauma.

Emotional Frequency in Connection Consciousness

Emotional frequency in the **Connection Consciousness** is experienced as a **complete balance** of **feelings.** Emotions **connected** to the Source Consciousness bring about feelings of patience, kindness, compassion, love, joy and peace and a general feeling of happiness and well-being. You feel good about yourself and you are in full control of your emotions and regulate your feelings with ease.

In this peak emotional consciousness, you radiate happiness. "Love, joy and laughter keep the endorphins in your brain working (McNight, 2005). McNight (2005) contends that these are the chemicals that give off a "high" without the ingestion of mind – altering drugs, drinking or smoking various substances. When the emotions of love and joy radiate through the body, it's like a pinball game when the ball hits all the right points, and sets of the 'winner' lights that make the machine seem almost to float off the floor. This is what the feel-good endorphins do to our bodies and minds (McNight, 2005, p. 70), and this is what it feels like for any person that lives in the Connection Consciousness.

Emotional frequency in the Connection Consciousness cultivates a positive existence where life's emotional storms cannot not shake you. Very slow to anger, you fully understand and can control emotional internal dynamics. This means that you are not making emotional decisions based on the ego, greed, judgments, criticism, flawed impressions or selfish reasons, but are able to detach your emotions and use them to respond with feelings that stem from a more loving, caring and collective manner.

You will automatically respond and not emotionally react when you are living in the Connection Consciousness to every person or situation. Even if you do not agree with the "energy" that is entering your emotional frequencies, your emotional response will be of a mature nature cloaked in higher vibrational frequencies resulting in controlled feelings. You will not succumb to bouts of emotional drama because you have learned to recognize emotions for what they are, which is just energy to be controlled, managed and directed. With great ease, a person living in the Connection Consciousness will be able to take only the highest vibrations from any emotional energy interaction and leave the rest behind.

You have full awareness and understanding that emotional energy, even though it may present itself in intense ways, when triggered by feelings, is really impersonal. "Every emotion is designed to inform you about how you are processing energy in your energy systems, so that you can choose to continue the same way or change," (Zukav & Francis, 2002 p.190). The acts, people, or situations are just disguised emotional energy that is assisting you to see where you are vibrating, and if modifications are needed. In the Connection

Consciousness, emotional vibrations are at peak frequencies and easily pass the emotional drama test that is often associated with feelings. In peak vibration, the person is free from lower emotional vibrational frequencies and can resonate at the harmonic emotional vibrational frequency with unlimited power to create with balance and congruence.

Physical/Sensory Frequency

It is interesting to note that many sages describe the Source Consciousness in terms of sound, visions, touch, scents, and essence. These coincide with the 5 sensory senses in the human system of see, hear, taste, smell, and touch. Sensory systems have often been seen as the seat of knowledge, and labeled under the notion of embodied cognition, which is the belief that people are motivated, and find meaning through bodily senses, and sensory lived experiences.

Many people believe that all of life is a sensory experience housed in the physical body. Sensory information does include the physical body and all that it encompasses, such as its maintenance, nutrition, exercise, illness, wellness, physical attraction and the like. Sensations provide information from the environment through the body, and the 5 senses so that people can act on that information and live their life accordingly.

The body, which is a finely tuned sensory system also provides information relative to time, place and space. The physical body is our vehicle on the earth plane and works in unison with our thoughts, images in the mind, and feelings. For it is this unison that completes the manifestation process. You can think and place the image of your desire in your mind, and support is with feeling but unless you take physical action to complete the manifestation process, for the most part it will remain in the conscious mind until the physical body acts on that intent and helps to bring the desire into your physical reality. King (2012) described the physical body as a garment which you the self-conscious thinking and experiencing individual wear. But it is a garment of most importance because it contains the consciousness awareness of the senses, which human beings use to perceive their world and the power they hold to create. It is also the vehicle that vastly assists in the manifestation process through physical effort.

Sensory and physical frequencies differ in functions in each of the vibrational consciousness fields of **Lack** and **Survival, Dedication, Absorption** and **Connection Consciousness**. Each consciousness holds varying degrees of frequencies that match, and reflect in physical manifestations the sensory interpretations of the person's life. In each consciousness field the body determines what will or will not manifest because the body will or will not physically act to get the desired results.

However, the physical body is not real or permanent, as only those things that are real do not change. The physical body on the earth plane is an illusion that disappears once the person dies. The human body is a mass of energy vibrating in the dense frequencies of the physical environment which is why it is temporary. While it is true that the body is a temporary vehicle for humans to move around in to accomplish their daily tasks and responsibilities, it is also so much more than that. "The body is a tool of consciousness through the intervention of mind, its prime value is that of communication" (Hawkins, 2002, p. 94) and conscious movement to not only live our life but create what is wished and bring it into physical realities. We move our consciousness, which is housed in our minds, around from place to place, in the physical vehicle provided us by the Source Consciousness. Information gathered from the body's sensory systems forms quick general assessments, that allow people to easily function as human beings because they can read their environments, and thus know what they need or don't need to appear in their life.

The body serves the human being until the person dies. But during its time on the earth plane the body must be well cared for to fulfill its duties so that it can provide human beings the best life possible. Thus, changing personal habits to improve physical well-being is a must for the serious individual who is on the quest of raising their vibration. Regular communication with the body and paying attention to all sensory senses is also recommended, as most people live in a basic cause and effect environment of lack and survival without realizing it, and do not pay attention to these highly important bodily functions. Most people, particularly in the low Lack and Survival Consciousness read their surrounding and make choices based on that quick sensory assessment so they can react. But they are often wrong, or miss the entire point of the experience, as their quick assessment does not offer the individual an authentic representation of what is before them.

The world perceived through the sensory experiences in the **Lack of Survival** energies is clouded in dense energy. Life, by people living in this low vibration, is seen through low energy sensory experiences of existing or enduring rather than living. The person can be awake, fully functional and responsible, but not see the beauty of the environment that is around them, or live in the sensory moment of life. Others may desire something better but do not use the action of their bodies to attain what they wish due to lack of motivation, inspiration, self-confidence that can be achieved or just cycle in overwhelming energies of fatigue which is so common in the Lack and Survival energy fields.

In higher frequencies of the **Dedication, Absorption,** and **Connection Consciousness** the world is in its full color, flavor and texture in varying degrees. In simplistic terms it is the difference of eating food to survive, or you can really taste the delicious food and appreciate the flavor, texture and aroma. In the higher consciousness, a person is in full control of sensory energy in all of the 5 senses of seeing, hearing, touching, tasting, and smelling. With each rise in consciousness field of Dedication, Absorption or Connection, the person's reality will become more vibrantly alive, and sensory experiences will intensify. The colors will be more vivid, the smells more potent, the touch more sensitive and so on. You will be able to use these 5 sharpened sensory abilities, to not only have a healthier functioning body, and see the world in a brand-new vivacious light, but be able to describe your intent more vividly, and graphically as you contemplate. The clearer the intent that is sent, the faster the results will arrive to your specifications.

The mind and emotions play an important role in the vibrational frequency of the body. It is not important what others think and feel. Do not live in the vibrations of others for your guidance when it comes your physical body, or your life in general. Live fully in your own reality, in your own vibrations because by tuning into yourself you will receive the guidance that you need to become real people (McNight, 2013) and will cherish not only your body but be in control and respectful of your own decision process when it comes to your body and your physical world.

When you listen and tune into your body you can perceive the roots of your own being and how you can use the physical body to raise your vibrational frequencies. In the manifestation process the person's diet and physically tending to the body by giving it every-thing it needs, which includes nutritious foods and exercise, along with the feelings they have about the body are monumental factors in how quickly the person moves to a higher consciousness. Diet becomes important at all consciousness fields of **Lack and Survival, Dedication Absorption,** and **Connection,** but especially in the **Lack of Survival Consciousness** fields because of the dense energy of that environment, which clouds judgment, and has a focus on the neg-ative which often triggers negative body image. As it must, because Lack and Survival inhabitants live in low discordant vibrations and low vibrations can only attract low frequencies. Thus, keeping your body healthy is a key factor in raising, and maintaining your vibrational fre-quencies and the best way to elevate its vibrations is to start with the food that is consumed and regular exercise, and listening to the body's messages.

Since what you eat can elevates consciousness, the opposite is also true. What you eat can decrease your overall consciousness vibrational frequency. This is because your body is a separate being in and of itself but it is part of a larger system of you. It gets used to certain habits and food that you digest, but this does not mean that your body will not have adverse effects from the energy of the food you are consuming. Food that is not natural and artificial ingredients will lower your frequency which will results in discomfort, illness and just an overall of 'not feeling' well because 'artificial ingredients that enhance a food's tase and appearance are often detrimental to the energy system' (McNight, 2013) within your body. This adverse energy will also affect motivation and physical action on the part of the person.

When you are eating natural foods, you are eating live food because they still have the vital life energy source still in them and your cells crave the live elements for substance (McNight, 2013). McNight (2013) contents that the life force within the foods you eat responds to the life force within you. This is so important because it is possible to change your energy frequency by consciously working on filling your body with live foods to reach a higher vibrational frequency.

According to McNight, (2013) many of the diseases that are a part of the modern life come through foods that have artificial man-made ingredients. When this balance of natural versus artificial food is thrown off, important vitamins are often destroyed and the artificial ingredients throw the energy balance off within the body leaving the body deprived of the very vitamins it needs and disease sets in (McNight, 2013). Disease sets in when the body is out of balance because it is starved for its natural sources of energy (McNight, 2013). McNight (2013) admonishes that every person should always seek the natural flow of energy, natural foods, and natural thoughts. "Stay away from the artificial, that which is not in tune with your energies – food and thought wise. This includes humans. Do not let artificial human have control of your life. Anything that is artificial is not in touch with its own energies" (McNight, 2013, p.148).

Foods that are especially good for the system are fresh juices, especially citrus, fruits and vegetables because they have the most of what the body needs for proper energy, but fruits and vegetables must not be eaten together at the same time period because they can create an imbalance (McNight, 2013). In today's world it is vital that fruits and vegetables be washed carefully because of the number of pesticides and sprays that are commonly used by crop growers.

At all costs avoid dyed food and be careful of portion sizes. People who eat from an emotional level are especially susceptible of overloading their systems. This is because they try to overcompensate emotional deprivation. McNight (2013) asserts that people should eat from a mental level. In this way they have control over the amount and type of food is ingested. McNight (2013) further contends that when the emotions are in control, then the body is often abused because the body will automatically crave foods that it is used to.

Change is not easy for the body because of the habits it acquired by eating the wrong foods. To switch habits creates a withdrawal that is not easy for the body and triggers cravings. To begin to create new habits begin with a cleansing with periods of fasting allowing the body to get in touch with its own energies and boost its vibrational frequency. Eat green, leafy vegetables or yellow vegetables as they are suited for physical cleanings (McNight, 2013). McNight (2013 p. 149) contends that, "you will find that all live vegetables have a purifying effect on the body; the more live vegetables and fruits that you eat, the better." When the body is cleansed of the wrong food vibrations, it craves only food that is in-tune with it which will increase your vibrational frequency.

Check food labels carefully, research and ensure that everything you are eating is good for you.

Energy cannot be destroyed! In particular avoid red meat! Animal products effect the digestive system in an adverse manner. Meat products are heavier in vibration and put a great strain on the digestive system, as opposed to non-meat natural products because the body is not spending most of its energy digesting these products (McNight, 2013). Non-meat, natural products are lighter in vibration thus gives the body more energy and raises its vibrational frequency.

Every time you eat something you are eating and digesting the energy of that something for that energy melds with your molecular structure and becomes one. King (2012 p. 232)) contends that "the reason that flesh food does not belong in the human body is because there is a certain animal quality in the natural structure of flesh and this automatically acts from its own trained environment of activity" and affects the human being in an adverse way. Thus, anything that is absorbed by the body you become and feel, either consciously through illness or subconsciously through an unexplained change of mood, anxiety, sadness, fear or depression.

Everything has a vibration and affects your mental, emotional, physical and spiritual energies! Animals have slower-vibratory levels. According to McNight, (2013) humans who vibrate in lower frequencies are strongly attracted to the flesh of animals because of the like-attracts-like principle. In essence, they are attracted to red meat because of the consciousness level on which they are functioning internally (McNight, 2013). McNight (2013, p. 150) contends that people, "who load their system with red meat or pork are vibrating very strongly in the lower levels of their earth-consciousness, unlike those who prefer fish and fowl which are higher in vibrations and higher source of energy." People whose diet consists of fruits, vegetables or fish function in much higher vibratory frequency than those who eat meat.

If you do eat meat, be extremely concerned how the animals you are eating were treated before they were slaughtered, and ended up on your plate. Thus, you may be eating contaminated energy, low vibratory energy from animals who have suffered immensely before they were slaughtered. Animals who were filled with fear, which you are digesting and uniting with your cellular structure will change your molecular structure. Fear is energy that cannot be destroyed but can be digested and cause internal effects on the mental and emotional consciousness of the person who has ingested the energy.

Contaminated energy, when united with your energy will contaminate you and result in lowering your vibrations. Consistent exposure to contaminated food will have harmful long – term results on the body, which may appear in different forms, such as stomach aches, not feeling good, headaches, or even a change of mood to fear, anxiety, depression, sadness, anger and the like, and greatly affect your overall health, and the manifestation process. In basic terms "if you keep the lower-vibratory animal food within you, which are also heavily laden with the emotional levels of these animals, it will be more difficult for your energy levels to shift into finer vibratory levels" (McNight, 2013, p. 150). This means that you will continue to move in decreased vibrational frequency which will have an effect on the power you can generate and the speed of manifestations you wish to create. It will also affect the way you are feeling in every way.

If you must eat meat, simple things, like eating cage free eggs, or not eating meat from mass produced factory farms, and purchasing your food from companies, groups, and organizations that participate in and promote animal well-being, can make a huge difference in your overall health and long-term longevity. (If possible, always buy from local suppliers, family farms, produce stands etc.) Those who can drop meat products altogether are rewarded with the perfect flow of their own systems and are able to lose dependence on meat products and greatly raise their vibrational frequency. The same hold true for dropping dependence or penchant for alcohol and drugs as these can also greatly decrease vibrational frequency and reduce consciousness levels which has a huge impact and affect on the powers to create. Alcohol, drugs, and meat can be lethal to anyone on the road to raising their vibrational frequencies.

A word on fasting. Occasional fasting is very important to the physical body because it allows the organs to regenerate down to the smallest cell (McNight, 2013). According to McKnight (2013) during fasting the energies burst forth from each cell in a way that's different than normal because food creates an outward flow of energy from the physical body. When food is not taken in, all the energies are inverted and the cleansing process occurs which gives people a chance to get into attunements with their bodies (McNight, 2013). Further, McNight (2013) explains that fasting also is a regeneration function and a vital aspect not only of healing but of the prolongation of physical life.

Science supports the theory that high vibrational frequencies have an immense impact on physical well-being and health, which includes food, diet, exercise and so on. For example, if you want to be healthy and free of disease, keep your vibrational frequency at 62-72 MHz, and you will be free of illness and disease (Tanio, 1992). Bruce Tanio built the first frequency monitor which measured different frequency levels. The findings indicated that, if a person keeps their body at 62 MHz illness, and disease will not materialize. By raising the frequency, disease, viruses, fungi, bacteria and so on cannot survive.

TANIO FREQUENCIES CHART

Bruce Tanio Results
Healthy human frequency: 62-72 MHz
Colds and Flu start at: 57-60 MHz
Disease starts at: 58 MHz
Candida overgrowth starts at: 55 MHz
Receptive to Cancer at: 42 MHz
Death begins at: 25 MHz

Physical/Sensory Frequencies in Lack and Survival Consciousness

The **physical/sensory frequencies** within the **Lack and Survival Consciousness** vibrate in **low** energies. Physical and sensory vibrations in low energies dull the senses when perceiving the world, and may be evident in illness, pain, or discomfort within the body itself. The physical body has been created to act in the lower rate of vibration and is the natural vehicle provided (King, 2011 p. 147). Thus, it is up to us to use our free will and raise the physical body's frequency to shift out of the dense energies into higher lighter vibrations.

Life was not meant to be as struggle. Within the **Lack and Survival Consciousness** many people experience a dullness in their general sensory systems and in the 5 senses of, sight, hearing, smell, taste, and touch. Since living in the Lack and Survival **cause** and **effect** energies is highly reactive, the senses serve as basic functionality instruments in perceiving the world, and using the senses for mere survival, rather than pleasure. Living in lack and survival energy fields does not allow the person to experience the vibrancy the 5 senses can elicit or how much pleasure the physical body can give us or the unending things it can accomplish through action, if motivated. This result of these dense vibrations puts people in the position of missing all the beautiful details of life, color, and flavor that the various environments, and settings can offer. It limits motivation, inspiration and action that must be taken to attain a better life and live out people's dreams and hopes for their future.

So much joy is missed out on when experiencing the human sensory system in the Lack and Survival energies. People's eyes are opened, their senses are functioning, but yet, as Frederick Franck asserted, "once the art of seeing is lost, meaning is lost, and all life seems ever more meaningless. They know not what they do, for they do not see what they look at." When they do look, all they see is an illusion of **lack, limitation** and **survival** in their physical world, and do not notice the everyday beauty of life. They do not understand how much potential to accomplish great things are within their grasp, for they make no effort and take no action.

The **Lack and Survival Consciousness** can hold people captive all their life because the energy systems continually produce physical sensations that people get classically conditioned to. Consequently, they see life from a skewed view of **lack** in their world. For example, if people are accustomed to seeing their physical world as lacking, their sensory interpretation will reflect that belief.

Physical sensations are tangible, thus seen as evidence. Evidence does not require faith; thus, it is an easy concept to buy into. However, evidence is not always as it appears to be. In many of his lectures, Dr. Dyer explained that, "if you change the way you look at something, what you look at changes." Thus, sensory evidence is subjective. This is because seeing depends on perception. If you are seeing from a higher vibration it will elicits positive responses, such as seeing with "appreciative eyes." Seeing from appreciate eyes inspires action and sees beauty where none was present before the change in perception. It is a wonderful way to discover things that you did not even pay attention to before and see them in new light. Things that you missed before seeing with appreciative eyes could be used toward your advantage.

Use your senses to their highest potential from a positive skew so that you are motivated, and inspired. It is the job of each person to raise their personal vibration to a higher perspective so that there is a new appreciation for everyone and everything, and that physical action that can reward you be taken. Things you thought of as ugly could take on a unique beauty, and the appreciation of that beauty will increase your vibrational frequency. As you move throughout your day observe information pouring through your sensory system, and experience everything around you in newer higher vibrations. Do not hurry or prejudge anything, but instead take time to really experience life through your body, and your senses. By the end of the day, you will notice that your senses of seeing, hearing, tasting, smelling, and touching were enhanced. You will also find that your body has many more messages for you as you move through your day. Listen to its messages. If there is misalignment in your physical energy your body will feel it and assist you to locate what needs adjustment.

Physical action must be taken to raise vibrational frequencies and create desires. When dealing with physical aspects of life such as food, shelter, clothing, physical appearance, or wished for body capabilities, the **low** energies of the **Lack and Survival Consciousness** can be deceiving, and reflect peoples' egoistic perceptions of how they think their physical life should be, or what their body should look like, what they should be able to afford and so on. They critically, and judgmentally glance over their physical existence from the "have not" mentality and are not understanding the causes of their lack. They only see limitations and imperfections in their body, and in their physical life not realizing a change of perception and action is all that is needed to move from ugly to beautiful, or experience life in a new way.

The dense energies of **Lack and Survival** is ruled, mostly by the ego. This low energy does not allow people to see the magnificent perfect unique beings that they are in their physical form, or how much they can accomplish if they only changed their perception, and took action to fulfill their dreams. With the ego in control some people are unable to appreciate their body for how it looks, what it does for them, and some are not too concerned about taking care of it because they have accepted and attitude of self-loathing. The conditioning to lower physical energies, often bring lackluster or painful sensations in the body. These affects are produced when energy drops, or they continuously exist in very low vibrations for prolonged period of time. This can produce illness, depression, and other physical effects, including headaches, overwhelming fatigue, nausea and feeling of fatigue and lack of motivation to put forth any effort to improve their lives, which will vastly dull their sensory experiences.

The better the health and the self-image of the individual, the higher their vibrational physical/sensory frequency. Thus, it is easier to shift out of the Lack and Survival fields. If people are accepting of themselves, and are in good physical condition, there is a higher alignment with their physical body, which is vibrating with better health, and the person can access higher energies of manifestation that are available for their use. Increasing your physical well-being, and your sensory vibrations, and moving away from the greyness of life to experiencing the higher energies of new colors, sounds, flavors and textures and better health, should motivate everyone to continue to keep working toward elevating their vibrational frequencies. Being fully cognizant that you are responsible for your body in the way you maintain it, present it the world, and how you use your sensory system will offer every person richer life experience and help them rise out of low energy into higher frequencies.

There is good and beauty in everything. See it! Hear it! Touch It! Smell it! Taste it! If you wish to move out of the Lack and Survival

Consciousness into higher energies, live life in a higher sensory frequency by not judging yourself harshly and being aware and appreciate what is around you. Look closer, and see the beauty that was always there before you. Or let your nostrils fill with the aroma and flowery scents surrounding you. Savor the flavor of a delicious meal, and treat food not as just nutrition to satisfy hunger but as an exploration of the senses. The positive energy flow from the pleasure received by the senses will increase your frequency and attract more of the same energy to you and elevate you to a higher vibration. And act! Stay motivated and act to achieve your desires. Use your physical body as your well-run vehicle to act in your best interest and shift to the higher frequencies of the Dedication Consciousness so that you may finally start creating the life that you deserve and the future you want to face by feeling better, and accepting yourself as a beautiful, perfect human being.

Physical/Sensory Frequencies within Dedication Consciousness

The energy of the **Dedication Consciousness** field allows for better physical health and sensory experiences. Physical/sensory frequencies in the **Dedication Consciousness** are of **moderate** energies and frame sensory information by consciously controlling thoughts, images and feelings, and using their senses to interpret, identify and describe information from true perceptions. This allows for a much better self-image and richer life experiences, and places the individuals in a higher vibratory state, in which they can perceive their environment in better light. This enables better physical responses to situations because they can frame incoming information in truer perceptions, and have the ability to physically act to bring desires that are only in the consciousness into physical realties.

Physical experiences depend on effort and action. People moving in the Dedication Consciousness are much more motivated to physical action because they have aligned their thoughts, images in their mind and feelings. They understand that the body and its senses are no longer just an information gathering systems for humanity. But that body is their vehicle of action, and it must be well maintained in order for it to accomplish goals and meet responsibilities through the commands of their thoughts, images and feelings. Thus, the body must be fed proper food, have regular exercise, and rest. Be diligent to keep it healthy, beautiful and free from disease, and harm. Additionally, since **thoughts, images, and feelings have an effect on the physical body, and** its overall **health,** it is important that people continue to be cognizant of the incoming sensory information because how the data was collected and processed determines the richness of the person's physical experiences and his or her overall vibrational frequency which holds their power to create manifestations.

In the Dedication Consciousness, at first, individuals marvel at seeing and hearing things they never saw or heard before, even though they saw and heard them numerous times before. They just never took the times to stop and experience it. They marvel at the simplistic beauty that surrounds them every day. Everything is seen in new light because they are no longer too preoccupied with the stresses of the lower energies to fail to notice. All the senses become vibrant, and they receive the messages that the body sends. Touch becomes sensual and meaningful, and new smells fill the nostrils in ways they never have before. The senses are processed in a uniquely potent and alive manner, thus affecting every person in a more intense and appreciative way. Not only do individuals in the Dedication Consciousness focus on ensuring the body is well maintained so it can act with great speed when needed, they use the senses to have a more colorful and richer life experience in their thoughts, images in the mind and feelings.

People living in the Dedication Consciousness value their physical body. They are cognizant that without a functioning body, physical action is impossible to achieve their desires. They fully understand the manifestation process and know the value of using their thoughts for manifestation which trigger images in the mind. They know that these images activate their feelings, and feelings motivate physical action until the desire is manifested in their physical reality. In the Dedication Consciousness people appreciate what the body does for them. They see beauty in themselves, and others. Their bodies appear more relaxed and they are more accepting, less judgmental about their appearance and the appearance of others.

A word of warning, be aware! Even though in the Dedication Consciousness you have mastered thoughts and images in the mind, a picture of a lower desire may be placed before you and cause you to physically act in a way that does not serve you or others around you. King (2012) admonished that thought is the molder of form but in order to master the thought you must also master the outer activity which is physical action that stems from thoughtforms.

Stay vigilant and do not allow any destructive influences to make you act in a way that is to your detriment or disadvantage which will always lower your vibrational frequency.

Physical/Sensory Frequencies within Absorption Consciousness

Physical/sensory frequencies within the **high Absorption Consciousness** encompasses being mindful of energies of **contemplation, intention, elimination, and insulation**. When you are healthy and feeling good, you are vibrating in higher energies which increase your contemplation, intention, elimination and insulation consciousness fields. This means that you can contemplate your desires with greater clarity, and send your intent with sharper precision because you are feeling well. People that fully use their sensory system in contemplation can better describe their intention because they are using all 5 senses of sight, smell, touch, hearing, and tasting to crystalize their desire. Hence usually will find themselves rewarded with much quicker progress and great strides. The clearer, and more graphic and richer the contemplation of the desire, the stronger the intent becomes, and the more inspired the person is to follow through with physical action to ensure that the intent materializes in their physical world. Thus, a well-functioning body and using the sensory system to detail the intent will vastly aid the creation process and motivate the person to act to achieve whatever it is that they have intended in the consciousness and bring it forth into their world.

Senses can also assist in the elimination of discords, and insulation against negative energy that tries to attach itself to you. Use your senses, and in a voice, loud and strong demand that any and all discord is eliminated from your energy fields at once! Command through your I AM presence and invoke the Violet Flame to *shatter, dissipate* and *consume* all discordant creations and so that you are free of them forever. Stand in unwavering conviction that the Violet Flame will eliminate all your physical discord, so that you will once more have full dominion over your body.

You can also do permanent work on your body and eliminate discordant energy through repairing and perfecting it through the electron. According to King, (2012) the electron is a focus of perfect energy that can be called upon but first you must consciously give quality and the permanency of that quality to the atomic structure. This can be accomplished through using your sensory commands, such as voice. King (2012) contends you can direct the body using your voice, and command it, "get to work and see that every particle of my body's structure is replaced with God's perfection." King (2012) directs that if there is any ailment in the body that one wished to eliminate a person may also speak to a specific organ that is causing distress and command, "now you get into perfect normal activity and see that you maintain it!"

You have internal help to heal the body and keep it running in perfect order. King (2012) further contends that during the time that life is maintained within the form, there are innumerable little workers called phagocytes, (which are cells that protect the body), whose duty it is to rebuild the atomic structure of the form and maintain the body in perfect order. When the body is feeling illness or discord it is because these phagocytes are thrown into other than their natural activity or work. King (2012 p. 231) suggests using the following directive because he affirms that the consciousness is the absolute master of every activity of the body and can mold it into perfect activity and form, thus to eliminate any physical ailments that may be creeping in call upon the phagocytes, by using the senses, your voice, "see that my body is supple, perfect in form, and beautiful, that my hair, eyes, and every part of me glows with the Light of the Inner Activity."

In addition to phagocytes use the violet energies for any deep seething health issue or to keep it working in perfect order. Working with the Violet Flame or speaking to the body to eliminate discomfort assists in its healthy maintenance. But to maintain that health and assist your body to run in perfect order do not allow any destructive energies in the form of suggestions or low vibrational frequencies to enter its energy fields through any destructive personal actions. Take care of your body, use good hygiene, be careful of the foods you eat, get medical check-ups, exercise and protect it from all disturbances.

Train yourself to imprint an image of your body healthy in your mind, and to ward of any discordant energies that may want to attach itself to it hold yourself within the Electronic Circle. With unwavering consciousness do not allow discordant energies to intrude and have you act in any way that will diminish your circle of protection. Build the Electronic Circle around your body consciously each day and assist it by not getting into any predicaments that may harm or hurt it in any way. Fix your consciousness on earnest thoughts that you will protect it and make it happen. If you keep a conscious guard over your physical body you will sustain it and keep it free from dis-ease.

Physical/Sensory Frequency in the Connection Consciousness

In the **Connection Consciousness,** you feel in well, and are in perfect health. The sensory systems operate in precise fashion. There is a present innate knowing that your sensory systems are very powerful. People moving in the Connection Consciousness take the time to be present every moment of the day. Your eyes appreciate what they see, your ears are attentive, your sense of smell and touch are significantly heightened, and you are careful to listen to all messages sent by, and through the body. "Our bodies communicate to us clearly and specifically, if we are willing to listen to them" (Gawain).

In this energy you use all your sensory systems in perfect operation. The energy in-turn blesses and returns powerful sensory vibrations to you, and increases your overall vibrations.

Moreover, you will automatically begin using your sensory systems to lift the energy of every person you come in contact with. Your eyes will look for ways to help someone, and you will respond positively in the form of assistance and physical action when you hear of another's plight. You compliment others, use your vision and see everything and everyone how God would.

The higher the frequency, the greater the overall health of the individual. Often, in the **Connection Consciousness,** the body will drastically change, and the person will look and feel better because the overall well-being of the person has increased. All of life is a sensory experience provided by and through the Source Consciousness. In the Connection Consciousness the human brain effortlessly organizes all the information that it receives from the sensory systems through the body. In this way human beings can make sense of it, and physically act on it according to their highest vibratory potential. In this peak consciousness, the brain easily filters out the unimportant and irrelevant information provided by the physical body and the sensory system and never reacts or overreacts, but responds through harmonious perceptions, and positive action.

Spiritual Frequency

All energy is spiritual. The speed of its vibrations determines its frequency. When we emit high frequency energy into the world by expressing love, and performing acts of kindness, and have compassion in our hearts our spiritual energy vibrates much higher, and brings us greater rewards. By being mindful that every human being creates the energy he or she emits, allows for the opportunity to quickly improve results, so they may raise the person into a higher vibration. They raise into a higher vibration because of the newfound understanding that every **thought, image** and **feeling** has enormous impact on the spiritual life and the lived experiences of every soul because their thoughts, images and feelings create physical realities.

The lived experience of every soul is determined by the overall vibrational frequency living on the earth plane. So, if you don't like your life, change it! There is no one to blame, no one to point the finger at, just redirect your thoughts, and images and align them with your highest feeling of a particular matter, or need in your life and you will succeed. Do not be dissuaded or think that you cannot do it. For undoubtedly you can! You are of spirit and since all energy is spiritual you always had the power to create anything that you wished, you just needed the awareness that you can, and understanding of how to do it. If you are reading these words now, you are now aware that you can, and have the **LEP Frequency Tool** of consciousness to help you do it.

Spiritual energies are the life force that exist in all living matter. They may seem supernatural, but they are in fact, the most natural and consistent thing in the universe. Spiritual energy that vibrates in high frequencies creates harmony, success and well-being. In contrast, spiritual energy can also live in lower vibrations and create discord, stress, and strife. It is all in the vibration. In low frequency you will find lack in high frequency you will find abundance. Thus spiritual energy is felt at different levels because of the frequency in each level. In the **Lack and Survival** consciousness fields, which vibrates at the lowest frequency, the energy is **low** and dense. The lack and burdens of the mental, emotional and physical world are enormous. It takes great strength to elevate to the next **moderate** consciousness of **Dedication,** where control over **thoughts, images** and **feelings** are gained.

The **Absorption Consciousness** vibrates in high spiritual energies, and includes the powerful energies of **contemplation, intention, elimination**, and **insulation**. Within these energies is Spirit in action. The Absorption Consciousness energies bring to life, what was before only in the person's consciousness into the physical world because it elicits action. Using spiritual frequencies at the highest vibration in the Absorption Consciousness brings manifestations into physical realities very quickly.

The **Connection Consciousness** vibrates at **peak** spiritual frequency, and is the closest to the Source Consciousness vibration. Within this peak frequency, unlimited spiritual power is available for every constructive desire. Living in the elevated spiritual knowing 'that once you match the desire of your expectation all constructive desires will manifest' life becomes joy. "You are no longer at the mercy of the world, but rather affected only by what your mind believes" (Hawkins, 2002, p. 19), thus you can create anything using the high spiritual energies of the Source Consciousness, with great speed. If you can think it and support it with unwavering images, and strong feelings which trigger action, you can achieve it. It is that simple.

Spiritual Frequency in Lack and Survival Consciousness

The **low** spiritual frequency in the **'cause and effect'** energy of the **Lack and Survival Consciousness** is much slower. It gives the illusion of an imperfect world full of pain, lack, and sorrow. Faith, and hope are at its lowest vibrations and the link to the Source Consciousness/God is very weak. Feeling of abandonment, desertion and rejection reign. The people caught in low spiritual energies, often blame others for their 'lot' in life, God, nature, or just plain bad luck. They carry with them an energy and an enormous lack of connection to God/Source Consciousness that is mixed with feeling of being unloved, overlooked, neglected or unsupported by the universal energies.

When living in the Lack and Survival energies, the only place to go is up. Raising your spiritual frequency by affirming your faith in your connection to the Source Consciousness not only strengthens faith but restores hope. A connection to God, the Source of All That Is moves you away from the egos' interpretation of reality, which clouds your accomplishments, focuses on pride, what and how much you don't have, and all the perceived wrongs, lack and sorrow in your life.

In reality there is no such thing as lack. But when vibrating low in spiritual vibrations, perceptual distortions run rampant, and lack is perceived everywhere which causes the effects of depressive feelings of not being supported and loved by the Source Consciousness, who has unlimited abundance available for your use, and is just waiting for you to make the effort and return to It so that It may unleash the love and abundance you seek. With the return of hope and spiritual faith, they will **rise** quickly above the **Lack and Survival Consciousness** because they will feel love, and confidence that there is someone watching over them, and wants to bestow all It has on them. But unless the person makes the effort to reconnect to that energy of pure love, even the Source Consciousness cannot help.

Human beings are evolutionary, with an evolving conscious-ness. Evolving out of low energies expands your consciousness, and allows greater flow of spiritual energy to surge to you. Evolving not only restores faith which gives assurance of support and good things to come, but rebuilds hope. It strengthens belief and inspires positive feelings of worthiness to receive all that is desired.

Moving out of the **Lack and Survival** spiritual energies into higher frequencies requires changing your perception from lack, and work-ing from a higher spiritual frequency of faith and hope. This requires removing the egocentric temptations that foster envy, anger, vindic-tiveness, jealousy, greed, selfishness and competition and evolving to live in a higher vibration of love, kindness and compassion, which are the purest energies of Spirit. The ego is not a part of your soul/spirit body because in the Spirit world there is no need for it, as there is no conflict and only love exists. Hence, it is important to note that the personality survives the death of the physical body, but the ego does not (McNight, 2005). Release the ego as the controller and work in unison with it but as you the controller and the determiner in all deci-sions in your life. Spirit sits in wait for all those cycling in lower ener-gies to realize that they are loved but must make the effort and rise in frequencies of expectations and awareness that they have all the power within themselves that they need. They do not need to depend on the ego to make decisions for them. They do not need to beg, or plead with God, the Source of ALL THAT Is, they just need to take control and act with faith to create the world they wish to live and the future they want to face.

There is purpose in everything and the **Lack and Survival Consciousness** provides an opportunity for mankind to experience lower energies of life. This is so that people can grow and increase their vibrations and enjoy a higher way of life. Without Lack and Survival energy, people would not understand the difference that vibrational frequencies can make in their life, and that all the power they need to create they have in their possession because they are of the Source Consciousness. It cannot be any other way because they are a part of God and have access to the same energy to manifest as God/Source has. Knowing that life is not just a world of cause and effects that are random, and that low energies exist to help humanity grow provides an opportunity for people to strive for greater things.

You always have direct access to the Source Consciousness/ God. The knowledge that people always have a link to the Source, and thus have all the power they need to live happy and prosperous lives should ease the worry of many and bring comfort to those who are still stuck in these low energies. This awareness is a chance for all people to learn to elevate, manage, and direct spiritual energy from lower to higher frequency, and increase their power and the ability to create the life desired, and at the same time retain their higher frequency when they die. In other words, it gives humanity a chance to use their free will and create their dreams based on their specifications on the earth plane, and simultaneously improve their placement in the spiritual realm after death.

Free will gives us the freedom to live our life to the blueprint that we choose. Every person is created in Gods', the Source Consciousness' image, and thus is forever connected at their core to this energy of All That Is (McNight, 2005). McNight (2005) maintains that the Source

Consciousness/God is the ultimate creator. Bu because of free will which is the mechanism that allows people to spiritually grow and is the reason for their manifestation of the planet earth, people are creators of their own destinies. "That is the nature of free will that God gave to us when we were sculpted out of the Pure Essence of the God Energy (McNight, 2005, p.33). Consequently, to rise in higher spiritual frequency begins with our free will and our thoughts. The will and the very thought that you are ready for higher spiritual frequencies to enter your life deepens faith, restores hope and sends the signal to the universe that you are ready for *only good to come to you.* The energy of the Source Consciousness will respond with support. Don't delay! If you are moving in Lack and Survival energies send thoughts of readiness and expectations and assistance will flow to you without fail.

Spiritual Frequency in Dedication Consciousness

Spiritual frequency in the moderate vibrations of the **Dedication Consciousness** elevates the energies of **thoughts, images** and **feelings** and assists to frame them for their best possible outcomes. When our mental and emotional energy fields are of the highest spiritual connection, we have achieved harmony between spirit and body and as such our frequency increases along with our power to create. Living your life takes on a new meaning because it is also tied to the belief that we are supported by the Source Consciousness from whom all power flows. Thus, it is more than just controlling your thoughts, the images in your mind, and your feelings. It is taking full responsibility for doing it, understanding where the power comes from, and believing and trusting that because of the new found spiritual faith, and your effort to change your life, rewards are sure to follow.

Thoughts are a living substance. Thoughts and images are part of the energetic fields of creation. Through thoughts, the images in the mind and feelings of the spiritual connection to the Source Consciousness, if used backed with a strong feelings and belief in the power of creation, wonders and miracles occur. The energy of the belief in the Source Consciousness/God, and that you are fully supported by this energy, is emitted through your thoughts, images and feelings when you are creating your life. This energy is received by the Source Consciousness and returned at the corresponding frequency. The stronger the mental and emotional energies, the deeper the belief. The deeper the belief the stronger the link to the Source Consciousness, and the greater the power that will be received.

Do not question the mechanics of how the energy of Source Consciousness works. Just have the spiritual faith that this is the way it works because it has been proven by scientists, scholars, philosophers, spiritual leaders and various experts and masters in energy. Your job is to always remember that all things with God are possible. McNight, (2005) contents that doubt causes your energetic transmitters and receptors to shut down, having the faith and trust in the process is what keeps them clear. McNight (2005) further asserts that doubts are thoughts alive and electric in nature. When you concentrate on your doubts they will expand and stagnate other energies, and just thinking about them gives them power (McNight, 2005). Have confidence in yourself and the process and you will quickly rise out of the Lack and Survival energies, master the Dedication Consciousness and move into a new vibrant world of creating your life the way you wish in the Absorption Consciousness, until you can reach the peak frequency of the Connection Consciousness where marvels await.

Spiritual Frequency in Absorption Consciousness

The **Absorption Consciousness** houses the **Spiritual frequencies** of *contemplation, intention, elimination* and *insulation,* which are your powers of creation of your life well lived. In this high frequency resonance between these energy fields happens. Resonance occurs when an energy field such as contemplation easily transfers its energy to the field of intention. At the quantum mechanical level, the entire universe is made up of spiritual energy that responds to the power of contemplation and intention, and once resonance occurs manifestations follow.

Contemplating your desired outcome activates the spiritual energy of intent. When the person has deep spiritual faith and trust in the Source Consciousness employing the energy of contemplation and intention allows them to create whatever constructive manifestation is desired in the conscious mind and with swift outcomes manifest it into their physical reality. Being at your highest spiritual energy potential, means that you are deeply connected to the Source Consciousness and are consciously linked to your **'I AM'** presence, which increases your power and ability, to direct energy and produce the life that you want to live in your physical realm and build the future you want to face.

Most people are likely familiar with the phrase, "as God intended." Since you are of the Source, you create as the Source in the frequency that you exist in, as God. This means that what you intend must also come into fruition when you use the powers of contemplation and intention because you are creating using the same energy as God/Source Consciousness. You are both of the same energy, as is everything else. You are not separated from each other, but live within the same energy. The higher your vibration the more energy/power you have at your disposal. But you create in the same way the Source Consciousness creates and are using the same power, only at different frequency levels. Your frequency level determines how fast manifestation in your life occur.

Spiritual alignment with the Source Consciousness is necessary because it determines the speed in which you will see your desires manifest in your physical reality. Living in high Spiritual frequencies means always contemplating from a pure heart in alignment with the Source Consciousness. Otherwise, intentions become ego-centric, and operate from lower energy levels which will delay manifestations or stifle them permanently. When intentions become ego-centric, they greatly lose their potency. Even if after a time should the desire manifest, you will not enjoy the end result. Additionally, remembering your connection with the Source Consciousness and showing a grateful attitude, brings you closer to this highest of all energies and will speed up the manifestation process.

When using the spiritual energies of contemplation, and intention patience must be demonstrated. Contemplative energy must resonate with your intention; thus, your thoughts must be aligned with images in your mind, and backed by strong feelings. The intention must be clear with an expectation that nurtures belief in your power and the Source/God, and eliminates all doubt that what you have intended, will manifest. Time should not concern you, as your manifestations will occur in their perfect time.

Working with the high spiritual energies in the Absorption Consciousness field individuals must have inner peace and rise above discords. Always take a stand and not to accept anything negative but focus only on creating what you desire with full expectancy that it will materialize in its perfect time. As Apostle Paul contended, "If we live by the Spirit, let us also be guided by the Spirit" (Gal 5: 25). This means that your desire, to manifest, must be of constructive nature, as the Source Consciousness will not assist you to create anything that is unlike itself. Spend much time in contemplation to ensure that your intended desire not only meets your perfect needs but that it has constructive qualities.

Your desires must always be of harmonious energy, and through the use of constructive contemplative energies and the power of your authentic intent it will manifest. No one should feel distressed over outer conditions, when within a few moments of contemplation, a person can redirect the energy, and set forth a new intention to change any situation, and bring harmony into their world. The more proficient you are at connecting to the Source Consciousness, and the more efficient you are at using your energy fields of contemplation and intention to create your desires, the quicker the results will manifest in your physical world.

The Absorption Consciousness also includes the energy of elimination of discords, and insulating from incoming discordant energies. When eliminating and discordant energy in your life, regardless of how painful, the '**I AM**' presence must be called upon and the energy of the **Violet Flame** must be invoked, as collaboratively they can remove any negative aspect from your life forever. Holding a strong spiritual belief that the Violet Flame has the ability to cleanse you will greatly assist you in removing all negative energy and cleanse you. The violet energy promotes healing, freedom and can accelerate your spiritual development because it also deals with spiritual growth.

Many physical diseases form from discordant mental and emotional states which may not only affect your physical wellbeing but your auric field. When you use the Violet Flame for elimination purposes you must have a strong spiritual belief in Its power. The belief activates the energy so that it can release all negative conditions from your life by transmuting the negative energy for good because energy cannot be destroyed. It can only change form; thus, it must be transmuted. The reason that deep spiritual faith is needed in the elimination of discordant energy process is because often when eliminating discord or insulating against incoming discordant energy doubt surfaces and interrupts the process.

Whenever you feel the need, use the Violet Flame to eliminate all discordant energy from your life, and surround yourself with the Electronic Circle of protection. Do not give discord or any disturbance power by focusing your attention on it. Your attention should always be on its elimination from your energy fields. The words, 'I can't or have not' should forever be wiped out of your vocabulary, for you can achieve all your goals, and can have what you desire, and can eliminate everything that you don't want in your life. Anything and everything that is holding you back or causing you pain, or stress can be eliminated through the Violet Flame. Any rebellion within the consciousness that you cannot do something or eliminate a discord no matter how painful, should be put down as a great offense to the Source Consciousness who is granting you the ability to use the power that is being bestowed upon you. (For specific instructions on how to eliminate with the Violet Flame see the supplement section.

If you are vibrating at the **Absorption Consciousness** frequency your vibration is a powerful spiritual alchemy. The ability to **contemplate** and send out your desires through the energy of **intent** will bring manifestations into your life that will be seen as pure miracles. The energy of elimination through the use of your **'I AM'** presence and the violet energy, in particular the **Violet Flame** will allow you to purify your energy fields, remove discordant energy from your life forever, and balance karma, outside of karmic activity. Insulation through the **Electronic Circle** will protect you from disturbances that try to evade your life, and offer you sustaining peace.

Spiritual Frequency in Connection Consciousness

In the **Connection Consciousness**, the Newtonian linear sequence of 'cause and effect' energies of the Lack and Survival Consciousness have been replaced by **peak** Spiritual frequencies. In this dimension the truth is clear. Once lifted out of the dense fields of Lack and Survival Consciousness, and the Dedication and Absorption Consciousness energies have been mastered, the individuals now have command of full power of the Source Consciousness. They fully understand that 'to think that the physical world is real is erroneous thinking, and to think that the spiritual world is unreal, is equally erroneous' (McNight, 2013). The flawed thinking occurs because living in the dense dimension such as earth, things of the spirit are unclear, but when we perceive them from the soul body mode, it is like seeing face to face (McNight, 2013). For some people this maybe be difficult to believe because humanity has been taught to believe in science, of things that can be seen or measured, and what a person cannot see or touch is not real (McNight,, 2013). This is flawed thinking, just because you cannot see or physically measure something it does not mean it is not real. In the Connection Consciousness this flawed thinking has been corrected, and the truth is not only revealed but by those in this peak frequency it is lived every day.

McNight (2005) contends that the appreciation of the part that the ego plays in human lives is a vital part of the energy of the physical body. This is because the physical world is so intense the ego acts as a shield or protector for the human personality that is innate within people. "It is like a reflector of fear, hatred, insecurity and all the emotions that dissipate with the astral body when the soul body enters another realm. It reflects these emotions back to the world as it checks thought ID's." Even though the ego lives in lower energies it is not a negative emotion but "an energy that is stronger than any emotion, functioning like a parental protector of the human personality" (McNight, 2005). Thus, it does have its uses but it cannot run free for it can cause much stress and damage. In the peak energy of Connection Consciousness, the ego's purpose is fully understood, and even appreciated because of the acknowledgment that God would not give people something that was not useful, but the individuals who vibrate in this peak frequency are completely free from its clutch. The ego is completely tempered and controlled and lives within the person in a concerted manner.

In the **Connection Consciousness people live from the inside out**. They live through their Spirit first and not the logical mind, selfishness, greed, personality or ego. Doing what is right, and not what is right for them keeps them in a peak vibration and offers much greater rewards, not only in the physical world but assures top placement in the afterlife.

In the Spiritual realization of the Connection Consciousness you fully know, that if you **caused** it, you can **change** it, thereby changing its **effects.** In this energy there is an understanding that nothing is happening to you. You have only experienced the energy that you have created and had to live its effects because energy sent, always returns to its source. In living from the inside out that energy that is returned is harmonious and of the highest frequency because the intent was always positive, thus benefits are great and results sometimes immediate.

In the **Connection Consciousness, faith** has been replaced by **knowing,** and knowing has been replaced by the new reality the person lives and moves in. In the **Connection Consciousness** all Spiritual energy is calm, steady, and only of the purest, harmonious vibrations. You have eliminated all doubt and fear, forgave yourself and others for all transgressions. You are with a strong spiritual connection to God the Source Consciousness and nothing can keep you from moving forward in the attainment of anything you desire. It is a fixed consciousness that you are free of all baggage or attachments that can weigh you down and have an inner knowing with absolute certainty that you can create your life and your manifestations, and that you had this power all along.

You only see the ONENESS of life. Hawkins (2002 p.12) asserts that when in high vibratory states "the world is illuminated by the clarity of Oneness which expresses Itself in all things revealed in their immeasurable beauty and perfection." There is no spiritual separation from the Source or anyone else, regardless of peoples' religion or belief systems. In this energy field you are distinctly aware that all people are only separated by vibrational fields within various spiritual frequencies.

You are living a life of bliss. Nothing is denied you. You show reverence for all life, and create your reality from a source of inner well-being. All problems, scarcities, and challenges go away because the Source operates in a state of happiness (Dyer, 2015). Moreover, in the peak energies of the Connection Consciousness you have an expanded understanding of your purpose on the earth plane. Your purpose on this planet is of a larger scope than just creating the life that you want to live, and to create the future you want to face. Life as a spirit is about knowing and growing (McNight, 2005). Growing so that your well lived life can elevate your frequency and placement in the spiritual realm until you can get back into the awareness of the pure presence of the Source Consciousness. McNight (2005 p.31) affirms that "God's presence is a part of our innate being, and is always within us in the form of Spirit, the True reality."

7

Afterlife Progression And Karma

"If death were the end of everything, then life indeed would be meaningless."

~Michael Newton

Soul Placement After Death

Death is merely a word that describes a concept not fully understood by most of humanity. Death is just another earthly experience. Death, in itself, is not a reality, but can be best described as an experience with a transformation point from the physical to the etheric-substance whose systems are at a stopping point (McNight, 2013). McNight (2013) further explains that death is a process of transformation which takes place as a shifting of base energies from the physical home base into the energy of the etheric body. Newton (2000) in agreement with McNight, (2005) proffered that there is no such thing as "death" death is just a transition of energy from one form to another. After this transition (death) the soul will go into the dimension of its highest vibratory level achieved on the earth plane. Placement after death will never occur in a higher vibration than the overall frequency of the soul when that person was alive. The soul of the person simply arrives in the vibrational frequency of the dimension level to which they evolved to at the end of their life.

Death may be a mystery to some folks. But to those living in higher vibrations death is not a mystery at all, but a normal progression from one energy system to another. Thus, death is not the end, but a well-choreographed transition between the conscious and the unconscious energy fields which exemplify the concept of death (Newton, 2009). As souls, "we do not die but merely shed the bodily form" (Newton, 2009, p. 292), and after physical death, souls' journey back home with space reserved for their own colony (Newton, 2009) meaning the energy that matches their vibrational frequency. The colony is a representation of other spirits vibrating at similar fields of consciousness awareness levels.

According to Newton (2009), as a result of forces of reincarnation, we are all products of our past physical lives on earth as well as our spiritual soul experiences between lives. Newton (2000 p. 1) who was also a pioneer in the practice of hypnosis regression, proclaimed that, "if death were the end of everything about us, life indeed would be meaningless." But it is not meaningless. It is the greatest gift to human kind from the Source Consciousness, and the way in which the Source can expand Its consciousness. It knows Itself through us, and our experiences because we are all **one** energy. We are just separated by our vibrational frequency until we can evolve and reach the pure frequency of the Source Consciousness. Thus, the Source experiences Itself through us, while giving us free will and unlimited power to create any constructive desire and simultaneously increase our vibrational frequency until our merge with pure Source Consciousness energy is complete.

Soul placement after death is determined by our performance on the earth plane. In simpler terms when you die you are attracted to that which you are most like when you drop your physical body (McNight, 2005). The human body is dropped but the Spirit lives on. Thus, energy did not die but only changed form. Dr. Michael Newton, a renowned psychiatrist, and an expert in the life after death phenomenon, in his various interviews, and books explained that energy is just the vibrational force that your spirit is evolving in at any given time, place or space. Dr. Newton described death and soul placements after death in the spiritual realms asserting that every soul has a specific energy field pattern which reflects an immortal blueprint of its character, and when we die our soul vibration will lift us to the plane that is most compatible to our vibration.

Placement after death is really a consciousness energy state with knowledge, and awareness, as key players. You were born with the vibrational frequency you established in the past. The way you think, feel, act and live your life will either increase, or decrease your vibrational frequency in this lifetime, and that frequency will carry over into the spiritual realm after death. According to Newton (2000) everyone has a designated place in the spiritual world. That place is determined by the person's consciousness (vibrational) frequency when they die because soul placement is determined by the soul's *overall* vibrational frequency.

Your overall frequency which is the culmination of your mental, emotional, physical/sensory and spiritual consciousness, while you are alive, is the same as the frequency you will be placed in after your death. McNight (2013 p. 62) explained that "your life (vibratory rate) in the body is the same as your life out of the body or death." Your soul/spirit are electromagnetic and upon physical death you will move into where the density of your energy (frequency) automatically places you (McNight, 2005). This happens because "when you die, you have built into your physical, soul and spirit bodies an automatic placement system that moves you to the realm that has your same vibratory rate" (McNight, 2005, p.83). The spiritual realms are states of being and are related to the energy centers within us which manifest at varying degrees of vibration (McNight, 2005). Hence, when someone dies, they are instantly placed in the same energy center (realm) in which they vibrate. This means that individuals who are vibrating high in all 4 consciousness frequencies of mental, emotional, physical and spiritual consciousness frequencies will retain that collective frequency in the spiritual realms and be placed accordingly in the etheric realm of the corresponding frequency.

It is undisputed that spiritual energy exists at many different vibrational frequencies. Jesus Christ said that, "there are many mansions in my Father's house." He meant many different vibrational consciousness dwellings. Each energy field consists of a specific vibration that matches the consciousness frequency of the spirits who dwells in that vibration. Your designated space within the spiritual plane depends on your soul's vibrational frequency, and performance while on earth. The higher the vibration, the higher the consciousness and placement. Thus, it behooves all human kind to increase their vibrational frequencies in this embodiment through, love, kindness, patience, and compassion avoiding all judgments and criticism. These efforts will pay off not only in the current lifetime through a better life because you will vibrate at higher frequency, but a higher soul placement in the afterlife.

To understand the full power of energy is to understand and accept that reincarnation does exist. Not only that it exists, but is the operating force in your existence which includes your spiritual identity. Your physical life is nothing more than a well-planned exercise. Each lifetime is one of many life streams that provides you the opportunities to raise your vibration so that you can exist on higher planes in the spiritual world until you can completely merge in the pure energy of the Source/God. Many experts describe the earth as a school, and that is, in part, correct. Once you master its conditions fully, you will vibrate too high to require the need to increase your vibrations through human means, thus you will graduate outside of this dense environment, and no longer reincarnate.

Always remember that happiness is a choice, and not dependent on anything outside of you. You create your own problems and you create your own peace. Either way, the Source experiences a part of Itself. The Source Consciousness can experience Itself through you, positively or negatively. The choice is yours. But all energy will always come home to roost because frequencies only attract *like* energies, and thus your energy in this lifetime will only give you what you put out. What you put out will be the frequency that determines your spiritual placement after death.

Unequivocally, you will return to the Source Consciousness at the end of your life, and your vibrational frequency will determine your placement. However, according to McNight (2013) if a soul after death cannot move into the etheric realms because they do not realize that their dead, they get locked in a time warp of emotionally charged energy and it takes a higher consciousness of vibration to release them. McNight (2013) further explained that other souls are locked in low mental or emotional vibrations as a result of certain earth level attachments such as addictions, anger and the like, or various concepts or beliefs that confine them to the earth plane of existence. These souls cannot be placed in the spiritual realms after death and stay at this earth-level consciousness until they are able to release themselves from the thoughtforms and emotions that confine them. The souls who are locked in the physical realm of vibration after death are considered earth-bound souls or ghosts as a result of their attachments to the earth plane (McNight, 2013).

Human lives are opportunities to experience life in physical form in the happiest way possible. This is true because you are the determiner of your happiness. Express yourself through your desires, passion and inspiration and make every effort to raise your vibrations so you can attain higher frequencies more quickly and raise your spiritual placement until you can fully join with the Source Consciousness' essence once more. Because we live in a world of slower vibratory levels, we cannot perceive the energies of God in fullness, and we cannot be fully back in God's presence until our energy levels are rarified and match the purity of God (McNight, 2005 p. 31). This is why it is so important to raise our vibrational frequencies to their highest point BEFORE we die so placement in the spiritual realm can be elevated. "If people would just live in light, love and joy energy as much as possible while on the earth plane, the vibration created would offer incredible benefits for everyone involved (McNight, 2005, p. 90).

Karma and Vibrations

Everything that you do creates an effect somewhere. That is true. But the vast majority of humanity think karma must be equaled person to person. This is untrue. Although sometimes karma may be equaled in that manner, there are many times karma does not need to be balanced in that way (King, 2012). Generally, karma is not for binding people to each other to equal wrongs between the two individuals (King, 2012). Karma is not about individual to individual, but energy to energy. Thus, each action of a certain vibration will bring about that same vibration, (the returning energy is karma in action) but it may not be from the same person, situation, or issue, and it could be in another time, place, or setting. Again, to reinforce, the vibration does not have to come from the person of original karmic debt. The energy of karma can come from any low vibrating energy that matches the frequency in which you sent it, and it will affect you at the same degree, thus balancing the karma.

The energy sent out is always swirling and intensifies before it reconnects to its host to balance the karmic vibration. When the **Violet Flame** is used to remove any discords, baggage or discomfort, it is most often used outside of the karmic debt because it is consumed under the Law of Forgiveness, which means it is done outside of karmic activity. Thus, freedom and healing from all wrong creations that are plaguing any individual is at hand. Discords, mental or emotional disturbances, regrets, guilt and the like can be released, and healing with fresh beginnings will replace the uncomfortable and often painful energy. Always eliminate discord with a forgiving heart to you and everyone else, regardless of circumstances, as forgiveness is a requirement if you want to be released from the karmic obligation. Additionally, forgiveness, "is a necessary step in the evolution of your consciousness" (Newton, 2009, p. 82) in order to raise your vibrational frequencies.

Forgiveness will also free you by releasing the energy of karma when you use the violet energies. Invoke the **Violet Flame** often to remove any negative karma that has attached itself to you, or you unintentionally picked up through your mental, emotional activity or your actions. See supplements (S10) for how to remove karmic debt. The personal choices you make in life are very relevant because in the end it is your overall vibrations that you carry with you to the after-life which determines your placement in the spiritual world. If you have a lot of negative karma that must be worked out your vibrational frequency will be decreased. Energy doesn't care who you are, how much money you have, who you are married to, what job you have, what foods you like, or where you live. It only is concerned with what vibrations are sent so it can balance the energy.

No one ever gets away with anything. Karmic energy that has not had a chance to be equaled in the current embodiment will be adjusted in the next life or through many reincarnations. Karmic cycles guide the evolution of your soul. They do not pass judgement, nor are they involved in any personal equalizations or righting of perceived or authentic wrongs. The job of karma is to balance energies in a completely impersonal way, and this can come from any source.

Karma that is unequaled and causing distress to the person can be eliminated by the person before it had a chance to automatically balance the energy itself, through the collaboration of your 'I AM' presence and the Violet Flame (Supplement S9) which activates the Law of Forgiveness. According to King (2012, p. 14), the person can "…dissipate and consume wrong creations through the Law of Forgiveness which throws it back to the Cosmic Law for adjustment, wherein it is adjusted outside of the individual karmic activity." King (2012) further clarified that all-consuming is but a reordering of the balancing of the atomic activity, and that the electronic activity is always permanently balanced within itself. All discord is but a loss of balance of a particular element or atom. It is only when the electron becomes clothed in a disturbing quality that discord is possible (King, 2012) and karma is generated.

Karma involves the sum of our deeds from this lifetime and all our past lives if it has not had a chance to balance itself. To balance all karma from all lifetimes, see Supplement (S10). Free will is caught in the events of cause and effect (Newton, 2009, p. 226), and just as you have an opportunity to advance with each lifetime, you also have the danger of slipping back into lower vibrational frequencies and generate more negative karma. Thus, it is also important to remember that we don't always move forward in our karmic development (Newton, 2009, p. 234) as sometimes the inability to handle a harsh life, or various issues such as addictions, can interfere with advancement to higher vibrational frequency. It may also decrease the person's vibrational fields, and create new karmic debts that must be repaid; thus, it keeps the person locked in lower vibrations. But it is important to remember that karma is not a punishment or reward system; it is a system of balance.

In order to limit the creation of new negative karma, you have to vibrate high. This means that many times, you have to take the high road, be the example, and do what is right, not what is right for you. Come from a place of love and service, and love and service will return to you, for the universe will respond to your vibration. Leo Tolstoy once said *"Everyone thinks of changing the world, but no one thinks of changing himself."* In other words, in order to benefit from good karma and increase your vibrational frequencies, instead of creating bad karma, you have to change the way you live by changing your thoughts, images in the mind, and feelings which trigger action and behavior.

You must vibrate high with every **thought, image** and **feeling** and follow up with positive **action**. Be of the mindset that "**only good comes to you**," and you only send good, regardless of the outer forces or outer expressions. Should you make a mistake, and not manage the energy correctly, immediately call upon the 'I AM' presence, invoke the Violet Flame which will work with the Law of Forgiveness to shatter, dissipate and consume the wrong creations in your life, outside of karmic debt, for the highest good of all concerned! (Supplement S9 and S10). Always thank your 'I AM' presence and the Violet Flame, for its assistance. Gratitude instantly increases energy.

8

Tying it All Together

Life is **determined** by vibrational frequencies. The collective vibrational speed of the **mental, emotional, physical/sensory** and **spiritual consciousness** will determine the overall frequency of each person. This book introduced the big picture and produced evidence that everything and everyone is vibration, and as such holds the same powers to either eliminate discord in their life, or create any reality they wish. Within these pages the readers received full instructions on how to use the **LEP Frequency Tool** of consciousness to broaden their life experiences and fully become a conscious vibrating being on a continuous quest to increase their vibrational frequencies, and create the life they wish to live, the future they want to face, and assure a higher energy placement for themselves in the afterlife. Moreover, the readers learned how to eliminate discord in their life, karmic debt, and insulate themselves against incoming discordant energy,

The **Prep** assisted the readers to prepare their **mental, and inner** energy fields to receive and maintain higher energies. **Thoughts, images**, and **feelings** must always be of the highest vibrations because they are what directs behavior, **actions,** and life choices, which determines lived experiences and frequency placements. The **Means** helped the readers identify in which consciousness field of **Lack and Survival, Dedication, Absorption** or **Connection** they live, and *how* to raise their consciousness vibrations to a higher frequency. The **Mechanisms** provided the readers the *through, the action needed,* to activate and raise the consciousness of the

mental, emotional, physical/sensory and **spiritual** energy fields so that they may vibrate at their highest potential, and have full use of the unlimited powers of the Source Consciousness, that they can use to either create whatever is desired, or eliminate all discords from their life.

The book also includes **Assessments and Supplements** that assist the readers to identify their personal vibrational frequencies in various target areas, and aid in the proficiency of working with high frequency energy. Assessments evaluate vibrations and personal frequency levels at the current moment and should be used at regular intervals. Vibrations can drop very quickly if **thoughts, images** and **feelings** are not monitored. **Supplements** which include various exercises for meditation, healing, releasing karma, creating specific manifestations, and so on could be used within the **Prep** process, or independently.

Ending with personal reflections, the book offers some insightful knowledge gained throughout the writing process. As so often is true, the writer experiences every word that is written, and can substantiate the effectiveness of the words and advice. Such is the case with this book.

If you put these words into practice, you will find that the benefits gained from using the knowledge and the power, herewith contained, is beyond compare. The **LEP Frequency Tool** of consciousness is completely aligned with the activity of the **Source Consciousness,** and allies itself intimately with the '**I AM**' presence of each individual, and the healing energies of the **Violet Flame** to ensure that any constructive desire manifests, and any discord is eliminated. Any reader who is serious about progressing to higher levels of frequency to live the life in which they wish to live, must make a commitment to using the **LEP Frequency Tool** of consciouenss and then **do it!**

You cannot passively wait for the right conditions of life to appear in your life, you must make them happen. Align your thoughts, images, and feelings, and follow through with your actions. You will attract what you desire because you are aligning yourself with the Laws of Vibration and Attraction. It is certain beyond all doubt, that science, and the many masters and sages are indeed, correct. We all have the power to create our own world because we are all energy, and energy is all there is. There is no one to blame. There is only lack of effort, should your life not be what you wish. Louise Hay, who was, and continues to be, such an inspiration to me and many others, shared a belief that I also hold dear, and in which I wish to end this chapter because it is so fitting, "no person, place, or thing has any power over me, for I am the only thinker in my mind. I create my own reality and everyone in it" (Louise Hay). Rise high for victory is yours! Namaste.

9

Personal Reflections

In working with the energies, I found the biggest hurdle to be myself. The problem as it appeared did not have to do with the power of the 'I AM' or the effectiveness of the Violet Flame or that the LEP Frequency Tool of consciousness did not work. On the contrary, it works too well. As my strong, clear intentions were manifested, instead of joy, many times, I felt anxiety, and mental stress, proceeded by feelings of confusion. My desires were appearing, but were not bringing me the fulfillment and happiness I hoped to receive.

It took an excessively long time to arrive at the moment of clarity. The problem was with the accuracy of the intention. It was deciphering what I really needed, not what I thought I wanted. Using the **LEP Frequency Tool** of consciousness, it was evidently clear that, my intentions will always materialize. If I am connected to the frequency of my desires through my thoughts, images in my mind, my feelings, and my actions to reach them, then they must come! And they did. What I thought I wanted appeared in my life, often, within a few hours or days, but when it appeared exactly as I intended, it did not bring with it the accompanying results of fulfillment, happiness or joy. Thus, I learned very quickly that nothing will squash manifestations or delay your desires appearing in your physical world, faster, than misaligned intent, and focusing on the wants and not on the needs.

If you are diligent in using the **LEP Frequency Tool** of consciousness and your desires are still not manifesting, review your intent.

Either your intent is misaligned, you have not sent out your intent properly, or you are simply not pursuing your intent in the physical world when opportunities arise. Thus, it continues to only be formed in your consciousness. If your intentions are materializing but are not brining you the joy and fulfillment you sought, begin again with contemplation, you are most likely focusing on the wants and not the needs. To realign, restart the process with contemplation again, and ensure that your intent is truly aligned with who you are and what you need in your life. Again, be careful with wants, and focus on the needs.

Look beyond the ego and listen to your heart as it is your true guiding system. By being mindful of your needs you will set yourself up for success. Take your time! Once you have contemplated and are clear on your intent, keep it focused, and imprint it on your mind and heart. Back the desire with a supportive feeling, so that it takes root. Use your spiritual energy and believe with an expectant attitude. Do not let doubt enter your energy fields! Hold the picture of your intent steady continuously, and feel the expectant results while you pursue every opportunity on the physical plane to ensure its materialization in your tangible life. Stand firm in your determination. Do not be daunted, intimidated, influenced by others, or be swayed from your intention! Only you know what you really need. Stand firm and do not let the picture of your desire fade!

I was also unprepared as to how quickly manifestations occurred once I seriously began to use the **LEP Frequency Tool**. In my own experience, my world completely transformed, and at times chaos ensued. I was shocked at my world falling apart, until I remembered the Chaos Principle that was once shared by Rosalind McNight, "When everything falls apart, it is coming together at a higher level." All my relationships went through a major overhaul. I lost old friendships, and even time-tested loving relationships, my passion for my career as a successful college professor no longer brought me joy, I felt tired and moody and it seemed as if nothing in my life was going right. But just as quickly as it all had fallen apart; it swiftly came together at a much higher level. Yes, I lost friendships, and loved ones, but quickly gained new ones. People who were much more compatible with who I was as a person begin appearing in my life.

Much to the surprise of many in my social circle, I retired early from my professorship position, a career I enjoyed and never thought of leaving because it no longer brough the fulfillment it once did. With great passion in my heart, I changed direction and have dedicated my life to "service." I have dedicated myself to writing books and conducting workshops and seminars on how to teach people to use the **LEP Frequency Tool** of consciousness to bring about positive manifestations in their life. I have found my own happiness and fulfillment in teaching others how to raise their personal vibrational frequency, and delight in watching them create their new lives – filled with harmony and abundance.

The changes in my life came so quickly and furiously that it is important to emphasize to the readers that you must take them in stride. If drastic changes are happening, thus it is for your own good, regardless of outer appearances. If you are working with the **LEP Frequency Tool** of consciousness *'only good can come to you'* and your life will also be transformed. The newer version of you is always more powerful because you have an expansion of consciousness which changes the way you think and feel, thus changing you as a person, how you act, the way you live, and what shows up in your life.

Be warned! Your higher vibration will affect others, especially those that know you well. The energy emanating from you will be of higher quality, thus they may no longer be able to relate to. you. However, your world will now open up, bristling with opportunities because with the higher vibrations you will attract new people, and new situations that are much more aligned with the new you. You, in turn, will increase your vibrations and expand your world by being around them.

It is not difficult to understand that changes in your own life affect others. If you are in a relationship and your partner is vibrating at lower energies, one can see how this can quickly become a problem. Your partner eventually must meet you at the higher frequency. If not, the relationship will be fraught with peril, and often end. Whether your partner or anyone else is in line with who you need to be, and how you need to live your life to be happy, ultimately should not be road block. Not using the gift of energy creation that was freely given by the Source Consciousness so that you can create what you need, or eliminate what you don't want in your life, will leave you unfulfilled, miserable and your relationships will suffer anyway. Thus, it is wise to spend increased time in meditation and truthful contemplation of what you need and how you want to live. Be understanding of others opinions but always follow your own path.

I have found that when you follow your own journey you learn to continuously operate from your highest energy fields. You are aligning yourself with higher frequencies of the Source Consciousness, higher thoughts, ideas, images in the mind, and feelings. You become vibrantly alive, and creative juices start flowing motivating you and inspiring you to act. People become more cooperative, and life flows in joyous energy. You always think from an expanded level of consciousness and connect with higher frequencies which are integral to forming physical manifestations in your lived experience.

The Lived Experience Phenomenon of a human being is a blank canvas waiting for its owner to begin its work. There is no use sitting around thinking you can't do it, feeling sorry for yourself or your lot in life, living in regret, guilt and so on. Such behavior is never productive it will never bring happiness, joy or peace. It only lowers energy, and it MUST be nipped at first opportunity.

Well-being, love, prosperity, abundance, new career opportunities, and so on are here for you. This is your journey. It is always up to you, as to what and how much you will manifest. But be prepared, it will come. Thus, be sure of what you need to be fulfilled, and how you want your life to look. The surest safeguard is, if you want **only good to come to you** and your life, be clear with your intention and always come from a place of good. You have all the tools you need, in the form of your **consciousness** and the **LEP Frequency Tool** to guide you to create the life you wish to live, and the future you want to face, but you alone must provide the effort and the discipline required to **raise** yourself to vibrational **frequencies** beyond your expectations.

On a last note, relative to time for activities, it is with a deliberate omission that I do not provide set times for the exercises or activities in either the Assessment or Supplements. You may complete them when you wish, and take as little or as much time as you desire. Through my various workshops, I have found that what people need, prefer or the time they can afford to donate to exercises and activities varies because of their many responsibilities. Thus, I leave time allocations to the readers. You decide how much time you should spend in creating your life. For example, my time spent in meditation with the Violet Flame varies depending on my schedule but is included daily, usually in the morning, and right before bedtime. When time is of the essence, sometimes a short connection accompanied by quick decree to send out the intent will suffice. If you seriously spend time in meditation using the Violet Flame (Supplement S3) and include it in your daily regimen, "in a few weeks or months, you will feel such freedom and ease in your bodies, such clearness in your minds and such victory in your affairs, that you will no longer wish to do anything but continue Its use" (Voice of I AM, 1936, p. 23). Be blessed on your journey. It is now up to you. Namaste.

10

Time For Action

LEP ASSESSMENTS AND SUPPLEMENTS

The Assessments and Supplements in this book were deliberately kept basic so that each reader can customize each resource for their own specific needs. Assessments should not be viewed as a performance measure, but as an identifier of vibrational frequencies within the persons' energy fields. Assessments should be taken periodically to ensure that you are maintaining and living in high vibrational frequencies. The assessments were designed as a ranking system so that you can identify low frequencies within your energy fields.

The Supplements permit a broader spectrum for learning and practice. Be honest in your answers and you will gather relevant information about yourself and what you need to do in order to reach what you desire, or find what you are seeking. The Supplements will greatly enhance and complete your experience when working with vibrational frequencies. Use them frequently and get the full benefit.

ASSESSMENTS

LEP PREP ASSESSMENT MENTAL AND EMOTIONAL (A1)

DIRECTIONS: Read each question carefully. If you answered '**YES**' to all the questions you are well prepared. If you answered '**NO**' to any question, that area needs immediate adjustment and modification before you can proceed further.

MENTAL PREPARATION

QUESTION YOUR THOUGHTS! – *Query and check-in with your thoughts!*
- Do you regularly check-in with your thoughts?
- Do you question the thoughts in your mind?
- Do you consider yourself mentally healthy and strong?
- Are your thoughts aligned with a highest version of you?
- Do your think from your highest mental frequency?
- Do you automatically question any thought that does not serve you?
- Can you easily eradicate discordant thoughts, fear and mental anxiety from your mind?
- Are you mentally ready and confident that you can control your thoughts?
- Are you strong in your mental convictions and not easily influenced?
- Do you think you are powerful, valuable, deserving and can achieve all your desires?

CHALLENGE YOUR THOUGHTS! – *Test the voice in your head!*
- Do you challenge all thoughts that don't uplift you or are not in your self-interest?
- Do you challenge negative self-talk?

- Do you stand at the ready to challenge any thoughts that upset you or lower your confidence?
- Do you challenge impulsive or recurring thoughts when they try to influence you negatively?
- Do you challenge your thoughts when others try to force their opinion on you or influence you?
- Do you challenge your thoughts when they try to stop you from forgiving yourself and others?

GOVERN YOUR THOUGHTS! – *Control and Regulate your thoughts!*

- Do you govern your thoughts? Do you think before you speak?
- Do you manage your thoughts by being in charge and controlling them?
- Do you govern your ego intelligence (voice in your head)?
- Do you discipline your thoughts? Allowing only the highest thoughts and banish the rest?
- Do you block intruding thoughts that do not serve you?
- Are you able to block thoughts of your past mistakes, regret, fear, and anxiety?
- Are you mentally able to forgive yourself and others for past misdeeds, whether intentional or not?
- Do you direct the energy consciously to where you wish it to go by governing your thoughts?
- Do you stand at the ready to consistently govern your thoughts from all discordant energy?
- Have you fully stopped replaying the same discordant thoughts in your mind over and over?
- Have you have mentally forgiven yourself for and no longer relive past transgressions in your mind?
- Do you govern your thoughts when they continue to bring you pain, discomfort, fear and anxiety?

EMOTIONAL – INNER PREPARATION

QUESTION YOUR EMOTIONS – *Query and check-in with your emotions!*

- Do you question your emotions? Why are you allowing yourself to feel this way?
- Do you regularly check-in with your emotions?
- Do you regularly question how and why you feel the way that you do?
- Do you question discordant feelings when they crop up?
- Do you consider yourself emotionally healthy and strong?
- Are your feelings about yourself of the highest order and reflect the highest version of you?
- Do you emotionally react from your highest emotional frequency?
- Do you automatically question any feeling that does not serve you?
- Can you easily eradicate discordant feelings, fear and emotional anxiety from your mind?
- Are you emotionally ready and confident that you can control your feelings?
- Are you strong in your emotional convictions and not easily influenced?
- Do you have high self-esteem and feel that you are valuable, and deserving?
- Are you happy? Do you feel powerful and confident that you can achieve your desires?

CHALLENGE YOUR EMOTIONS! – *Regulate your emotions!*

- Do you feel you can easily control your emotions?
- Do you challenge emotional discords and negative perceptions?
- Do you challenge negative influences from outer expressions?
- Do you challenge disappointing feelings, or lack of self-worth?

- Do you take a stand and challenge your emotional ego?
- Do you challenge any emotion or feelings that does not serve you?
- Do you challenge disturbing feelings when they show up?
- Do you challenge any feeling that limits you and your ability to create?

GOVERN YOUR EMOTIONS! – *Control your emotions!*

- Do you easily govern your feelings?
- Do you discipline and monitor your feelings?
- Do you block intruding feelings of past mistakes, regret or guilt?
- Do you control disturbing emotional triggers from outer influences?
- Do you govern your feelings so that you react from your highest emotional vibration?
- Do you generally respond and not react to discordant emotional situations?
- Do govern your emotional ego?
- Do you emotionally release disturbing feelings and forgive yourself and others for all past misdeeds whether they were intentional or unintentional?
- Do you emotionally control your temper, and react with compassion, and kindness?
- Do you give yourself permission to feel happy?
- Are you able to emotionally release all discordant feelings and regain harmony in your heart?

LEP LACK AND SURVIVAL ASSESSMENT (A2)

How do you live?

DIRECTIONS: If you agree with the examples of the statements below in each category of *Thoughts, Images* and *Feelings,* place a check by the appropriate bullet. Each check represents **LOW** vibrational energy (Lack and Survival Consciousness) that must be corrected. If you placed a check near any bullet STOP, reread the statement and immediately reverse that thought, image and/or feeling by paraphrasing statements in positive terms. By reversing the thought, image and/or feeling on the spot you will release the discordant energy attached to it, and replace it with much higher vibrations raising your frequency. When you can place a check by each bullet you are ready to move out of the Lack and Survival energy field of consciousness and into the higher manifestation energies of expanded consciousness.

Example: **'My thoughts usually drift toward pessimism, rather than optimism." — "My thoughts drift toward optimism, rather than pessimism."**

THOUGHTS

- My thoughts are usually framed in limitation, lack and survival. I relive past mistakes over and over.
- My thoughts are usually focused on what I don't have instead of being grateful for what I do have.
- I spend too much time thinking about what people think of me.
- I don't think of myself as happy. My thoughts often turn to sadness, fear, anger, and anxiety.
- My thoughts tend to attract lower denser energies of pessimism first rather than optimism.
- I often think that I am without any real power to change things, and life just happens to me.
- My mental self-talks tend to be generally negative in nature, critical, and judgmental of myself, others.

- My thoughts often reflect low self-esteem and self-worth, and a general sense of numbness.

IMAGES

- The images in my head reflect lack and limitation rather than what I really want, and how I want to live.
- I see myself as someone who carries baggage, anger, guilt, regret and/or resentment.
- When I look at the world, I often see unhappiness, and sadness before joy.
- I tend to visualize things going wrong in my life rather than right, and a general sense of worry.
- My mental pictures are often rooted in past mistakes rather than future opportunities.
- The mental pictures in my mind are not clear, or I keep changing them because of my own indecision, unhappiness, lack of passion, doubt that they will materialize or outer influences by others.
- I do not see myself as a happy, successful, or joyful person.

FEELINGS

- Tears often flow in my life. I often feel depressed and anxious. Boxed in, unsupported, limited.
- I don't feel happy. I often feel like I will never have enough of anything, love, money, opportunity…
- I often feel complicit, or numb, I care about things less and less or feel like I just exist to endure.
- I anger easily, have lack of patience, and often get very emotional.
- I often feel undeserving, with low self-esteem even though I may not show it to the outside world.
- I often feel like my emotions are out of control and/or I have a hard time controlling them.
- I often feel like I don't have support, feel like a failure, and lack the ability to change my circumstances.

LEP DEDICATION ASSESSMENT (A3)

How do you live?

DIRECTIONS: If you agree with the examples of the statements below in each category of *Thoughts, Images* and *Feelings*, place a check next to the bullet. Each check represents **moderate** vibrational energy. If you are in **moderate** vibrational energy (Dedication Consciousness) you can easily work with energy to increase your frequency and begin creating your new life.

THOUGHTS

- I am dedicated to mentally use vibrational frequencies to change the process of how I live and create.
- My thoughts are not framed in limitation, lack and survival, but are rooted in expectant hope and faith.
- I have released all regrets, guilt and anxiety and no longer relive past mistakes over and over.
- My thoughts are usually focused on being grateful for what I do have, and not what I don't have.
- I care less and less as to what people think of me.
- I think of myself as happy. My thoughts do not often turn to sadness, fear, anger, and anxiety.
- My thoughts focus on optimism, not pessimism.
- I think that I am powerful and can change things, and do not allow life just to happen to me.
- My mental self-talks tend to be generally positive in nature, and not critical, or judgmental.
- My thoughts often reflect high self-esteem and self-worth, and a general sense of joy.
- I catch and reframe discordant thoughts and bring them to higher frequency.
- I can easily control and manage my thoughts.
- I am able to ignore all outer influences in my mind that don't serve me.

- I am consciously framing my thoughts to create my life to my specifications.
- My thoughts are generally of harmonious nature.

IMAGES

- Disregarding all outer influences, I do not allow images of lower vibrations to enter my experience.
- I am reframing all discordant images by looking at them from positive perspectives.
- I often spend time framing the pictures in my mind to define how I want my future to look.
- I am always careful of the pictures I put in my mind and easily control the images in my head.
- I consciously frame the images in my head to attract harmonious vibrations.
- I use imagery to support my thoughts and feelings when creating desires.
- My mental pictures are never rooted in past mistakes, guilt, regret, or fear but in future opportunities.

FEELINGS

- I am dedicated to emotionally use vibrational frequencies to change the process of how I live and create.
- I can control my feelings, and direct the emotional energy to where I want it to go.
- Through reframing and releasing discordant feelings, I have gained emotional maturity.
- My feelings always support my highest thoughts and images in my mind.
- I can reframe discordant feelings and align them with higher energies of peace and happiness.
- I feel and believe in myself and in my ability to create my reality.

- I have control over my emotions and generally exhibit self-control.
- I maintain emotional harmony within myself seeking no other approval.
- I do not spend time reliving past mistakes, and forgive all transgressions by myself and others.

LEP Absorption Assessment (A4)

How do you live?

DIRECTIONS: If you agree with the examples of the statements below in each category of **Thoughts, Images and Feelings,** place a check by each bullet. The Absorption Consciousness represents **HIGH** vibrational energy and includes the fields of contemplation, intention, elimination and insulation. If you are in **HIGH** vibratory frequency you are ready and at the right frequency to fully work with contemplation, intention, elimination, and insulation energies to manifest all that you desire, and move into even higher energies of expanded consciousness. With each new expansion your strength and power grow.

THOUGHTS

- I think of myself and know that I am a joyful, powerful individual that can create/recreate my life at will.
- I spend much time in contemplation designing, and detailing my life experience.
- I can mentally eliminate all discordant energy upon appearance from my mind.
- I send clear intent of my desires with full expectancy that they will materialize in my physical world.
- I use the Electronic Circle, when needed, to mentally insulate against discordant energy in my life.
- Through absorption of positive energy, and eliminating discordant energy I am continuously able to mentally maintain and raise my vibrational frequencies.
- My thoughts never relive past mistakes, regret, guilt or anxiety. These thoughts are processed as learning.
- I surrender all mistakes to God, and forgive myself and others at all times.
- I listen and respond with patience, kindness and love at all times.

- I am completely free. Fear is no longer a part of my mental life.

IMAGES

- The images in my mind are of high energy. Disregarding all outer influences,
- Contemplation is a regular part of my life. Using creative visualization and the energy of "wonder" I create exactly what I desire. No one can influence me, or sway me from my intention.
- I see myself, as proficient at eliminating discordant energy in my life and manifesting what I need.
- The images of my intended desires are always aligned with supportive thoughts and feelings.
- I visualize my intent in its fullest detail using all my senses, and witness its manifestation.
- I see the Violet Flame in my mind whenever I need assistance in elimination or creation of new energies.

FEELINGS

- I use my feelings as a barometer to live a joyful life, and make immediate changes upon discomfort.
- My feelings always support my thoughts and images in my mind when forming my intent.
- I use my emotions to insulate against discordant energies by not allowing them to affect me.
- I feel powerful and supported by life and God in every way, and know that it is my choice to be joyful.
- My emotions are never out of control. My heart is full of compassion and love.
- I do not resist any feelings but allow all emotions to flow through me easily without any attachments.
- My feelings are always aligned (in harmony) with my highest thoughts and images in my mind.
- I show great fortitude and discipline to ensure harmony in my emotional life.

- Anger, regret, guilt, anxiety or fear or no longer a part of my experience. I can control them easily.
- I resonate with forgiveness, compassion and kindness towards myself and others.
- Past transgressions by myself and others no longer have a hold on me.

LEP CONNECTION ASSESSMENT (A5)

DIRECTIONS: If you agree with the examples of the statements below in each category of *Thoughts, Images* and *Feelings*, place a check by each bullet. Each check represents **PEAK** vibrational energy (Connection Consciousness). If you are in PEAK vibratory frequency you masterfully work with energy to manifest all that you desire. You have complete control of mental, emotional, physical and spiritual consciousness, understand energy and the cycle of life. You live a life is bliss.

THOUGHTS

- I steadfastly believe that I can create my reality at any time. What I believe will manifest.
- I know that WE are all ONE. One energy that streams from the One Source. All is not only possible but probable when understanding, and working with energies of the Source.
- I have mastered full command of my thoughts at all times.
- I am mentally aware of how powerful I am. There is no separation between myself and God.
- I am not limited by past thinking, mistakes or transgressions. I live from a clean slate of forgiveness
- I always think well myself. I make ALL decisions from my highest consciousness.
- My thoughts are always positive and inspirational. Sadness never dwells in my mind.
- I live by mental constructs of thoughts of forgiveness, kindness, compassion and love towards all.
- I know and live in the mental consciousness of a spiritual knowing that everything and everyone is just energy that needs to be managed and I manage it well at all times.
- 'Faith' has turned to 'knowing' and knowing has turned to living the 'reality' of my choosing.
- All mental fear and worry are gone from my world. They do not exist.

IMAGES

- I always see myself in top form happy, healthy, prosperous and radiant.
- My images are always of me living in my perfect world, fully connected to the Source/God.
- My mental pictures always reflect the exact conditions and desires I wish to produce.
- I see myself in alignment with the Source Consciousness and draw on Its unlimited power.
- I see myself always living in higher energies of consciousness, and respond from that frequency.
- I am able to see the good in everything, change what I can, and accept in harmony what I can't.
- I see myself attracting everything and everyone that I need to fulfill all my desires.

FEELINGS

- I have enormous belief and confidence in myself. I feel very powerful without low moments.
- I feel like I am living my life aligned (in harmony) with my highest potential.
- I feel connected to the Source Consciousness and give great gratitude for the love and power.
- Faith has turned into internal knowing, and I now feel that I can create anything I wish.
- I feel happy and whole with profound changes within me. I have daily moments of emotional bliss.
- I am disciplined, exhibiting great emotional control under every circumstance.
- No matter what occurs in my life I know that since ONLY GOOD COMES TO ME I refuse to feel bad because this 'bad,' is just low energy of perception, leading to eventual good.

- All emotional fear and worry are gone from my world. They do not exist.
- I live in harmony in all consciousness frequencies.
- I am excited about my life and passionately live every day in my highest potential. I AM FREE.

MENTAL FREQUENCY ASSESSMENT (A6)

DIRECTIONS: Read each statement below and write the number 1, 2, 3 or 4 next to each statement. The assigned number will identify where you are vibrating in each statement. The number that repeats itself the most identifies your overall mental vibrational frequency. If the number 1 is selected in each statement you have mastered the mental level. Your job at this point is to maintain this peak energy field.

(1) Strongly Agree – Peak Consciousness Frequency
(2) Agree – High Consciousness Frequency
(3) Somewhat Agree – Moderate Frequency
(4) Do Not Agree – Low Consciousness Frequency

- My thoughts are centered on enjoying life, and not on lack and survival.
- My thoughts are disciplined at all times reflecting only highest frequencies.
- My thoughts do not wallow in past mistakes, failures, regret, guilt or fear.
- My thoughts always focus on gratitude and optimism about my life and what I do have not what I don't.
- I am fully dedicated to control thoughts so discordant energies do not enter my life.
- Mental images in my mind most often reflect happiness, joy, and satisfaction in life.
- I am confident and do not beat myself over errors in life.
- I love life. My thoughts and mental images are always harmonious.
- I am able to interpret incoming information (energy) on a mature impersonal mental level, and frame my responses appropriately.

- I contemplate in harmonious expectancy/confidence using my thoughts, images, and imagination.
- I am aligned (in harmony) with my intention, and my desires manifest accordingly.
- I have mastered the 'Violet Flame,' and I AM energy. I eliminate all discords that are causing me mental stress easily and effortlessly, and create my desires easily in my physical world.
- I live without any limitation in an expanded consciousness mental reality which is always connected to the Source Consciousness and understand the spiritual power of vibrational frequency in life.
- My thoughts are consistently of the highest order about myself and others.
- I forgive all and easily.
- I live life in a KNOWING that I am a spiritual being having a physical experience. Each day is a gift and I send out high vibrations so I am able to sustain living in a higher mental consciousness.
- I know that there is no lack. Life was not meant to be a survival. I rise out of every discordant condition.
- Love is all there is. I know it is the strongest vibration and I express love in who I am and do.
- I question, challenge, govern and guard my mental consciouenss at all times.
- With full determination I have entered into my own divinity. I am a self-generating and self-purifying.
- I no longer allow the energy of human limitation, and weakness into my world.
- I am limitless in my creation process and understand the law of precipitation. I cannot desire something that is not possible of manifestation. If I can desire it, this means it must be possible to achieve it.

- I do not subscribe to the lower energy of envy, jealousy, criticism, condemnation and/or judgments.
- Lying, ill will, manipulations no longer have a place in my life. My mental concepts, include integrity, honor, ethics, service, love, kindness and compassion.
- I think from my highest consciousness understanding that the I AM within me is the only dependable, eternal and permanent source that holds dominion and the connection to the Source/God that grants me power.
- I consciously guide all mental activity into constructive use using the highest frequencies.
- I control all outer consciousness, transcend limitation of mind and liberate myself from all discordant energy.
- I AM FREE, FOREVER FREE FROM PAST THE PAST AND ALL THAT IT INCLUDES. It's mental pain, disappointments, mistakes, failures and transgressions intentional and unintentional.

EMOTIONAL FREQUENCY ASSESSMENT (A7)

DIRECTIONS: Read each statement below and write the number 1, 2, 3 or 4 next to each statement. The assigned number will identify where you are vibrating in each statement. The number that repeats itself the most identifies your overall emotional vibrational frequency. If the number 1 is selected in each statement you have mastered the emotional level. Your job at this point is to maintain this peak energy field.

(1) Strongly Agree – Peak Consciousness Frequency
(2) Agree – High Consciousness Frequency
(3) Somewhat Agree – Moderate Frequency
(4) Do Not Agree – Low Consciousness Frequency

- My emotions are centered on enjoying life, and not on lack and survival.
- My emotions are disciplined at all times reflecting only highest frequencies.
- My feelings do not wallow in past mistakes, failures, sorrow, regret, guilt or fear.
- I no longer feel like I live in lack always trying to survive in a limited life in a limited world.
- I am fully dedicated to control my emotions and respond and not impulsively react.
- I no longer feel moody, sad, anxious or depressed about my lot in life.
- I no longer feel stuck and powerless in my situation, pain, or circumstance.
- I can easily direct my feelings where I want them to go.
- I can control my feelings.
- I use my emotions wisely, from a much higher perspective, and do not over react.
- I have emotionally matured and maintain positive, and uplifting feelings.

- I always utilize my emotions during contemplation to visualize my desires.
- I always use my feelings to support my intention.
- I eliminate all discordant emotional feelings that do not serve me or my highest good
- I am emotionally insulated from discordant feelings that do not inspire, uplift or serve me.
- My faith has been replaced by a feeling of knowing that the Source and I are of one consciousness.
- I feel an innate connection to the Violet Flame, and comfortable using the violet energy.
- I am truly happy and at peace. I am emotionally detached and insulated from all discordant feelings and emotions that do not serve me or my highest good.
- There is great compassion and love in my heart.
- I no longer hold any resentment, forgive myself and others easily
- I no longer hold or relive any discordant feelings that stem from past mistakes, misdeeds, or failures.
- I realize there are no failures only learning experiences.
- I have released all regret, guilt and all pain of the heart. The pain of the heart is now seen in an impersonal way, as opportunities for growth and soul expansion. I have fully detached from pain of the heart.
- I have mastered all emotional fields of energy. There is no more fear of any kind, this includes death.
- The energy of my emotions is fully aligned with my higher self and vibrates at my peak frequency.
- Using my emotions, I easily activate the vibrations of contemplation, intention, elimination and insulation and align them with my thoughts and mental images to create the life I want and the future I want to face.
- I do not suffer from emotional stress, sorrow, grief, worry and anxiety.

- I am full of hope and faith in my heart. I do not endure but enjoy my life.
- My emotions are always balanced and I do not react but respond to outer influences and situations.
- I am emotionally mature and no longer prone to sadness of any kind, anger, anxiety, regret, guilt, or fear.
- I regularly, question, challenge, govern, monitor and control my emotions.
- My heart is at peace. I have forgiven and hold no ill will, judgments, or criticism towards myself or others.
- I AM FREE, FOREVER FREE FROM PAST THE PAST AND ALL THAT IT INCLUDES: emotional pain, disappointments, mistakes, failures and transgressions intentional and unintentional.

PHYSICAL/SENSORY FREQUENCY ASSESSMENT (A8)

DIRECTIONS: Read each statement below and write the number 1, 2, 3 or 4 next to each statement. The assigned number will identify where you are vibrating in each statement. The number that repeats itself the most identifies your overall physical/sensory vibrational frequency. If the number 1 is selected in each statement you have mastered the sensory/physical level. Your job at this point is to maintain this peak energy field.

(1) Strongly Agree – Peak Consciousness Frequency
(2) Agree – High Consciousness Frequency
(3) Somewhat Agree – Moderate Frequency
(4) Do Not Agree – Low Consciousness Frequency

- My senses of sight, smell, taste, hearing, and touch have heightened. I use them for more than functionality, but as tools to explore my world more fully and in the manifestation process.
- My body is sacred to me. I am very healthy and feel really good.
- I am consciously aware, communicate, and listen to my body for any messages that it has for me.
- I am generally happy with my physical appearance.
- I see my physical body in its pure perfection and strengthen the spirit within it.
- I have fully changed the narrative toward my physical body. There is no judgment, only love and appreciation for this wondrous vehicle that allows me to live my life so fully and holds my spirit and assists me to achieve all my desires as I walk the earth and experience life in a new way.
- My body is very important to me I make a conscious effort to make healthy food choices. I choose "fresh" and stay away from low vibrating produce, meats and products.

- I am listening to the sensory messages from my body and heed its advice.
- I go to great lengths to take care of my body physically in every way, hygiene, doctor checkups, maintenance.
- I keep myself in the best physical shape, and free from disease by consuming the right food.
- Knowing the value of a healthy body to increase vibrational frequencies, I use physical activity to strengthen the body and keep exercise as a regular part and routine in my life.
- I am using all my senses to make better decisions and interpret incoming outer energies.
- I am fully using my senses to my highest potential, appreciate and pay attention to my surroundings.
- I use all my senses to assist me during contemplation and intention to identify and manifest my desires.
- I no longer see my body as flawed but perfect in every way.
- I am easily eliminating incoming discordant energy that may cause me bodily or sensory discomfort.
- I insulate myself through protecting my body through the use of the Electronic Circle
- I use my senses as the Source Consciousness would. I see, hear, taste, touch and smell from higher energy.
- My sensory system became vibrantly alive. Everything is appreciated, and received with a higher sense of connection and communication – every sound, sight, taste, smell and touch.
- I use my sensory system of sound, vision, taste, smell and touch to assist me to creatively visualize desires during contemplation and intention. I realize that it will take my physical body to complete the creation process, as physical action must follow every intention.\
- I am always cognizant of my breath. I am aware on a conscious level and realize how breathing properly can help me stay healthy. I know breath is an important function in the body.

I am aware of my breathing patterns because I know proper breathing releases stress, allows the body to find its own balance and provides mental clarity and improve the immune response in the physical body.

- I have become proficient using the energy of the I AM and the Violet Flame to eliminate discordant energy that is causing me sensory and/or physical discomfort.
- My body has become very sacred to me, and I treat it as so.

SPIRITUAL FREQUENCY ASSESSMENT (A9)

DIRECTIONS: Read each statement below and write the number 1, 2, 3 or 4 next to each statement. The assigned number will identify where you are vibrating in each statement. The number that repeats itself the most is identifies overall spiritual vibrational frequency. If the number 1 is selected in each statement you have mastered the spiritual level. Your job at this point is to maintain this peak energy field.

(1) Strongly Agree – Peak Consciousness Frequency
(2) Agree – High Consciousness Frequency
(3) Somewhat Agree – Moderate Frequency
(4) Do Not Agree – Low Consciousness Frequency

- My belief is strong. Spiritual energy and power available for my use is abundant.
- Because I know they are of spiritual nature I control discordant effects in my life easily.
- I am using spiritual energy to change my life. Life is no longer just an experience in survival but joy.
- My spirit is no longer restless but full of purpose, alive and inspired.
- I am in-tune with spiritual energies. I direct my thoughts, images in my mind, and feelings from a spiritual center.
- I live in my highest spiritual maturity potential and act from that place of consciousness.
- Living in higher energies of the Source, I now have the ability to control my thoughts, images and feelings.
- Through strong spiritual faith, I easily reframe meaning of energies through the lens of the Source Consciousness to respond from my highest frequency.
- I am very connected to Spirit and spiritual energies when I contemplate my desires, wants and needs.

- I am very connected to Spirit and at my highest frequency when I form and send my intentions.
- Utilizing spiritual energy, I eliminate all discords in my life through the use of the I AM energy and Violet Flame.
- Using spiritual energies and the power of the Electronic Circle, I am insulating myself from discordant energies.
- I am spiritually connected to the Source Consciousness through a KNOWING that there is no separation between us. The Source's power is my power available and ready for my use.
- Faith has turned to knowing, and knowing has turned into my reality allowing me the way in which I wish to live.
- I am in complete alignment (in harmony) with the Source Consciousness and use its unlimited power to create desires or eliminate discordant energies.
- I send love, blessings and gratitude to the Source Consciousness every day. I feel the love returned.
- I live in high spiritual frequencies, I have released all discord, mental, emotional, and physical and all baggage and attachments that no longer serve me.
- I live my life in the highest frequencies of service, forgiveness, kindness, compassion and love towards "all".
- Through strong spiritual faith, I easily reframe the meaning of incoming discordant energies and use the lens of spirit who changes my perception to see the real truth of it, and I act accordingly.
- I live in higher energies of Spirit at all times and understand that I am the architect of all my mental, emotional, physical and spiritual patterns, thus I have the ability to control the experiences of my life at all times.
- I live in my highest spiritual potential and know that I can create all my desires. Nothing outside of myself can control what I want, get, think, envision, feel or believe.
- In full understanding of its effects, I have consciously stopped generating negative karma.

- I have gained mastery and I am the conscious director of all my life experiences.
- God within me is alive. I feel God's love and power working miracles within me every day and in every way.
- Living in my highest frequency I can shatter, dissipate and consume all wrong creations and restart my life.
- I sit in silence often. I have acquired the habit to meditate and listen to my inner guidance.
- I no longer act from a human energy perception but from a spiritual perception of love, honor and integrity.
- I consider myself a loving presence commanding peace, love and harmony in my life experiences.

LEP Mental Check-in Assessment (A10)

DIRECTIONS: Answer the questions by recording **Y** for yes, and **N** for no. **YES** to all questions identifies higher frequencies. You are ready to work with Source Consciousness energies. This section checks on the pattern of your thoughts. Your answers will identify if your thoughts are harmonious and vibrating in higher frequencies or if adjustments are needed. Think about the questions carefully, before you answer. Retake the assessment often, as your general mood impacts the answers to the questions.

THOUGHTS – MENTAL CHECK IN QUESTIONS	Y/N
Are your thoughts vibrating high?	
Are you thinking happy, uplifting and inspiring thoughts?	
Do you easily monitor and control your thoughts?	
Do your thoughts convey confidence in yourself?	
Do your thoughts confirm that you have unlimited potential?	
Listen to your self-talk, is it positive?	
Do you question, challenge, and govern your thoughts?	
Have you been able to let go of all mental baggage and attachments in your life?	
Have you mentally forgiven yourself and others for past transgressions?	
Have you moved past all your mistakes and failures and not think of them again?	
Have you released your regrets, guilt, and sorrow in your life?	
Are you able to move forward and look towards the future with a positive outlook?	
Have you learned to stop focusing on the negative thoughts?	
Do you think you are a happy person?	
Are you generally thinking from an optimistic perspective?	
Do you question, challenge and govern your thoughts?	
Are you blocking all discordant thoughts that don't serve you?	

Do you consider yourself mentally strong?	
I have a strong positive mental belief system? I BELIEVE IN ME.	
Are you mentally committed to yourself and the effort it takes to create your life?	
Do you possess mental (psychological) toughness?	

LEP Emotional Check-in Assessment (A11)

DIRECTIONS: Answer the questions by recording **Y** for yes, and **N** for no. Aa **YES** to all questions identifies higher frequencies. You are ready to work with Source Consciousness energies. This section checks on the pattern of your emotions. Your answers will identify if your emotions/feelings are harmonious and vibrating in higher frequencies or if adjustments are needed. Think about the questions carefully, before you answer. Retake the assessment often, as your general mood impacts the answers to the questions.

FEELINGS – EMOTIONAL CHECK IN QUESTIONS	Y/N
Do you question, challenge and govern your feelings?	
Are your emotions vibrating high?	
Are you generally feeling happy motivated and inspired?	
Do your emotions convey confidence and high self-esteem?	
Do your feelings confirm your high self-worth and unlimited potential?	
Listen to your emotions. Do you feel great and content at this moment?	
Are your emotions generally controlled? Are you easily able to control, anxiety, anger, depression and criticism and judgments against others and of you?	
Are you able to move past all your emotional mistakes and failures and not feel the pain of them again?	
Is there forgiveness in your heart for yourself and others?	
Are you able to release your emotional regrets, guilt and pain, and negative feelings towards yourself and others?	
Are you moving forward towards the future with emotions of optimism, hope, faith and joy?	
Do you think that you are emotionally balanced and a person who possesses emotional maturity?	
Look in your heart. Are you genuinely happy?	
Do you love yourself?	

Do you feel loved? (by God, animals, yourself, others)	
Do you show kindness, understanding and patience to yourself and others?	
Do you feel supported in life? (by God, yourself, others)	
Have you left pity, self-doubt, and self, self-disappointment behind?	
Do you think you are emotionally strong?	
I have a strong emotional belief system. I BELIEVE IN ME.	
Are you emotionally committed to yourself and your efforts to create your life?	
Do you possess emotional toughness?	

THE MEANS 4 VIBRATIONAL CONSCIOUSNESS FIELDS (A12)

DIRECTIONS: Inquisitively inquire while reflecting upon each category and determine in which frequency of Lack and Survival, Dedication, Absorption, and Connection you reside.

LACK AND SURVIVAL CONSCIOUSNESS

LOW VIBRATIONAL FIELD:

- Dense energies. Living and moving in low vibrational energy. Thoughts, images and feelings are one of lack and survival. A sense of heaviness and lack of success about life. For the most part life is hard, mentally, emotionally, spiritually, and/or physically. Often, feeling like a victim, rather than victor, with small gains in life. The mentality of "things are just happening to me, and I can't seem to control them" has found a residence in my reality. Unfulfilled. Maintaining, but often feeling overwhelmed and tired, or complicit. Not seeing the fruits or rewards from or of life. Outer influences carry importance and have a way of swaying you away from what is best for you. There is an inability to manage discordant energy in general, and the world seems dark and gray instead of vibrantly alive. Pessimism trumps optimism. **Connection to the Source Consciousness is low.**

- Not understanding the causes of the effects in your life. Feeling lack of love and support in life. A feeling of hopelessness, weak faith in yourself, and Spirit. Often moody or depressed, harsh judgment and criticism of yourself and others. Inability to forgive yourself or others for your and their transgressions. Reliving past mistakes over and over, and unable to let go of regrets, guilt, sorrow in life and pain, or attachments that no longer serve you. Lack of interest, motivation and passion for and in life. Inability to see true purpose for your life, and to manage discordant energy in general. Feeling powerless the world seems dark and gray instead of vibrantly alive. Asking if going on in life is even worth it? Feelings of sadness without seeing a way out persist.

- A feeling of giving up dominates, as you run on autopilot. Often living a complicit life. You do not grow but life becomes stale, challenging, demanding and suffocating. Often lack of self-esteem, confidence in yourself, and feelings of anger, sadness, guilt, regret, anxiety, despair and fear stifle all energy and snuff out joy, and inspiration. Lack in the belief system that you have the power to change your world at any time. Spiritually lacking, numb or no longer caring about life. Suicide is sometimes considered, as the feeling of lack and survival intensify. There is no forgiveness for yourself or others, or a sense of value and worth as a deserving human being.

**Moving out of Lack and Survival energies.
Show your inner strength.**

**Be uncomfortable allow yourself to move through this field
YOU WILL come out on the other side.**

- Allow yourself to move through every thought, image and emotion. Do not hold back. Often it will be painful, it is a much-needed exercise and must be done. You will come out on the other side with full knowledge of who you are, and how you want to change yourself and what you want your future to look like on the other side. In order for you to know this you must explore where you have been. **Forgiveness,** and **Acceptance** of yourself and your misdeeds is very important. If you have trouble processing your mistakes, guilts, regrets it is important to **accept yourself** for whatever happened, and all your decisions. **Surrender** it all to the Source Consciousness/God no matter how great the perceived failures or how much pain you are in. Surrender all to the Source Consciousness, and take the position that all of what you perceive is errors on your part is just part of your expansion, development and growth. Remember people change their ways because they have come through the wisdom of failure. Expansion of the consciousness is vital to raising your frequency, use your failures to your advantage for growth and expansion. Once you surrender all that is painful to you, connect to the love of God, and use the Violet Flame to cleanse you. You will receive a new beginning, a new slate, to prove yourself and your worth again. Remember, once you surrender, you may not relive those points again. You have given them to the Source. They are no longer yours, but they are with God/Source who will transmute the negative to the positive and only good will come of it. Lack and Survival allows for new beginnings and new growth. When you do this, you will be ready for the change. The next field, the Dedication Consciousness allows the person to dedicate to this process of change, but acceptance of who you have become and how you live your life, and forgiveness for all is the energy needed to begin the change from low to higher frequency.

- If you cannot logically let go, bypass the mind and work with emotions and belief. Belief does not require an identify with the logical mind.

- Do not feel sorry for yourself or wallow in self-pity. Open yourself in honesty to full examination as an observer, detached from the all the has happened. BE AN OBSERVER. You are an observer of yourself and not a judge. This exercise is not to relive the pain; it is to assess so that you know what within you needs adjustment to put you on the road to higher energies.

DEDICATION CONSCIOUSNESS

MODERATE VIBRATIONAL FIELD: Moving into higher frequencies. Consciously leaving behind the dense energies of the lack and survival perception. Thoughts, images, and feelings are of higher inspirational energies. As you begin to sense the energy from a higher level you consciously dedicate to making the effort to change your life and new excitement forms. A sense of readiness and commitment to raising personal frequencies to manifest your desires has rooted in your mind, and heart. Feeling confident and inspired, you understand the need to control your thoughts, emotions and feelings, and not relive past mistakes or failures which will only chain you to the lower vibrations of energy. By gaining control, and directing your energy to higher vibrations of acceptance and forgiveness, life immediately becomes easier. You have the ability to shut out the inner and outer mind and create from a sense of your authentic self. You understand how to frame information for the most accurate meaning from incoming energies. Moderate gains are made, as you begin to use your mental and emotional energies to create the life you wish to live. Moderate connection to the Source Consciousness.

YOU ARE DEDICATING BECAUSE YOU KNOW YOU ARE WORTHY. IF YOU WERE NOT WORTHY OR FORGIVEN FOR YOUR PAST TRANSGRESSIONS. YOU WOULD NOT BE GIVEN A SECOND CHANCE TO REDEEM YOURSELF, EXPAND AND GROW IN LOVE, HEALTH AND SUCCESS. DEDICATE!

This is where you ask yourself.... How much did you grow when your life was easy?

MODERATE VIBRATIONAL FIELD: Hope and Faith return. Moving into higher frequencies. Consciously leaving behind the dense energies of the lack and survival perception. Thoughts, images, and feelings are of higher inspirational energies. As you begin to sense the energy from a higher level you consciously dedicate to making the effort to change your life **each day**, and take time to enjoy the new excitement as it forms. You begin to see that you have power to change every facet of your life. A sense of readiness and commitment to raising personal frequencies to manifest your desires has rooted in your mind, and heart. Feeling confident and inspired, you understand the need to control your thoughts, emotions and feelings and that they must be governed at all times. By gaining control, and directing your mental, and emotional energies to where you wish them to go life is easier and you begin to see balance and successes in your life. You become more playful and are developing a sense of wonder and joy. You have let go of past mistakes, despair criticism and judgments. The ability to release mental and emotional baggage and attachments that no longer serve you increases and you are stronger each day. As the realization is made that you have the power to begin crafting your new life, and that nothing outside of you controls what you can and cannot achieve or have in your life strengthens your dedication to the process of raising your frequency and your power greatly increases. You have dedicated to reach for higher spiritual growth and happiness and diligently use your power for constructive desires in life.

Strength and Fortitude is Needed Daily in the Dedication Consciousness

Contrast Is important in raising vibrational frequencies. All is forgiven. You understand that you must have failures for expansion. If there are no errors, there are no opportunities for growth. The Dedication consciousness is where you keep your head and emotions in the game. Very important not to return to Lack and Survival through reliving past transgressions. Do not disparage yourself over anything. To make progress in the Dedication Consciousness you must be committedly persistent and dedicated to continue remaining and striving for higher frequencies at all times.

Weakness is no longer a part of your world. With a devotion to the vibrational frequency process, you are steadfast in your desire to work with energies, and will not be dissuaded. You have learned to let go and surrender all discords to the Source Consciousness the minute it arises in your consciousness in a continuous fashion. Every discordant thought, every feeling, every image is surrendered immediately upon arrival. Should you fall and make a mistake, immediately correct the energy. You are allowed mistakes, but you also know to equal the karma you must correct the mistakes as soon as possible to continuously evolve in the love energy and remain in higher frequency.

ABSORPTION CONSCIOUSNESS

HIGH VIBRATIONAL FIELD: Higher energy. Excitement is high as you are experiencing large gains through your proficiency of contemplation, intention, elimination, and insulation. You see yourself as happy and successful. Vibrating high, all the right people and opportunities are drawn to you to help you achieve all that you intend. You enjoy your new empowerment and understanding of how the universe works. Creating your desires comes easily. Your life dramatically improves and you feel it is finally on track. You can easily eliminate discord and insulate from lower energies. Outer influences rarely get a rise out of you. You manage incoming discordant energy appropriately and in full control. A high connection to the Source is achieved, greatly expanding your consciousness and raising your overall vibrational frequency, allowing much more power available for your use and keeping you in high energy fields.

HIGH VIBRATIONAL FIELD: Higher energy. You take your time and skillfully use contemplation to detail exactly what you need in your life. You have become an expert in the power of intention and competently send your intent from your consciousness. You have confidence and the energy of expectation that it will materialize for you in your physical world in its perfect time. The practice of living inside out in thinking, seeing and feeling from high frequencies assists desires to appear in your world with great speed. You have mastered the spiritual energies of the I AM and the Violet Flame and can easily create desires or eliminate discords from your life. You have become proficient at using the Electronic Circle and can easily insulate from lower energies. Outer influences rarely get a rise out of you. Sadness, anger, depression, judgments, criticism and fear are no longer a part of your world, as these have been replaced with the energies of patience, love, understanding, kindness, strong faith in yourself, your power, and in your connection to the Source Consciousness. You manage incoming discordant energy appropriately. A high connection to the Source is achieved, greatly expanding your consciousness and raising your overall vibrational frequency, allowing much more power available for your use. Your perception has forever changed. You see yourself in a positive light and feeling good about yourself., You are passionate about life and marvel at how much you can accomplish. You have learned to absorb all energies and transmute them to the highest frequencies. Nothing is wasted. Discordant energies that life brings are now absorbed and transmuted into powerful positive vibrations because you no longer take things personally. You know that discord in terms of people or situations is just energy that must be managed and controlled. Positive energies are elevated and expanded in higher consciousness fields. You take full responsibility of your life and happiness. You understand that what is in your mind is your lived experience.

This is the stage where you are in it... to win it... You know happiness is not found outside of you. It is within you.

If you are vibrating in the Absorption Consciousness you have conqured the Dedication Consciousness and no longer need to rededicate to the process of raising your vibrational frequency daily. In the Absorption Consciouenss you have already attained all the data you need as to who you don't want to be and the kind of person you want to be and the future you want to face. You know longer revert to pass mistakes but had released them completely. You have the comprehension of understanding alignement. **Alignment means you are in harmony**. The focus is on unwavering determination to create your life and your future to your specification, taking great care not to generate new karma. You have proven your fortitude as a spiritual being who is ready to completely change your life. The moralistic and ethical dialogue with yourself is aligned with your mental, emotional, physical, and spiritual fortitude.

CONNECTION CONSCIOUSNESS
Perfected will and mindset. Good will extends to all of life.
The understanding that you and life are a team.
Living only in the energy of NOW.

PEAK VIBRATIONAL FIELD: Peak Ascension Level. You have mastered all fields of consciousness Lack and Survival, Dedication, Absorption, and Connection. You have mastered forgiveness, kindness, compassion and love. You have patience and acceptance for all things. You live in a Peak connection to the Source Consciousness, where ALL is probable. The high frequency achieved in the earthly embodiment of everyone reaching the Connection Frequency will be transferred to the spiritual world because soul placement is determined by the soul's *overall* vibrational frequency upon death. Your efforts in this world will have their just rewards in the afterlife.

PEAK VIBRATIONAL FIELD: Peak Ascension Level. You control all outer activity and manage it from an inner connection to the Source Consciousness. You can command and direct energy to eliminate discords or manifest anything you desire, in some cases, almost instantaneously. You live in pure joy, health, wealth, prosperity and worthy desires are created in perfect order and alignment (harmony). You live in the pure knowing that you are master of your own thoughts, images and feelings, and as such can create any reality you wish. Outside influences are just energy, and a non-factor except to serve you. You look at life from a broader perspective as if it is all here to assist you to grow spiritually, expand your consciousness and live passionately through your lived experiences. You fully understand that life was never meant to be a struggle. You are the creator of your happiness just as you are the creator of your misery. There is no one to blame. There is only the knowing that you can direct energy to wherever you wish it to go and YOU DO. You direct energy effortlessly. You have conquered the mental, emotional, physical/sensory and spiritual fields. Your thoughts and emotions are alive, and through these power mechanisms you realize that you can achieve all you desire and live-in peace and harmony with yourself, others and your surroundings. Nature now has a special place in your heart as you appreciate everyone and everything around you because you know that in the ONENESS of the Source you are all connected. This information strengthens and nourishes your spirit, and allows you to clearly see how you can change your world anytime. Living from the highest energy of inner knowing and power perspective allows everything to fall into place in the outer reality. Faith, hope is fully integrated with your soul. You now know that you had this power all along, and you always will – if you continue to vibrate in the peak frequency. You are living your dreams, and miracles in your life are everyday experiences. You feel truly loved and blessed, and you love and bless others unconditionally.

To stay and maintain your frequency in the Connection Consciousnes LIVE IN THE ENERGY OF LOVE.

Be generous. Give of yourself. Uplift yourself and others. You are at completion. It is the end to all suffering. You are One with the Source. You never waiver. You live in the knowing that ALL fear is an illusion. You continuously live in the stop frame of the moment where only NOW matters. You have ultimate knowledge and wisdom and full control of karmic fields. By living in the Connection Consciouenss you are looking at your life and the world lovingly thereby constantly raising your level of consciousness and your vibrational frequency immeasurably. This is because you are witnessing life with a loving eye seeing the sacredness of all existence. You are always living in higher consciouenss looking at the world from an expanded perspective. You do not allow any negative thoughts or emotions because you know that all is well. You are walking the pathway of non-duality. You know you are the Source, and the Source is you. You are devoted to each other. The physical life is a shifting illusion. Nothing is real, thus you can make the illusion anything you desire. You exist as if you are a light body living in the dense energy of the earth.

SUPPLEMENTS

LIVE IN HIGH FREQUENCY TIPS (S1)

NEVER GIVE UP ON YOURSELF OR YOUR DREAMS! USE YOUR INHERENT ENERGY TOOLS!

- **Mental Energy**
- **Emotional Energy**
- **Physical/Sensory Energy**
- **Spiritual Energy**

MENTAL
STAY MENTALLY TOUGH

- Always keep a positive mental attitude. Never allow discordant thoughts to enter your mind. Thoughts trigger images. Images create feelings. Always keep positive and uplifting images in your mind. Aligned thoughts and images affect manifestations, and your quality of life. If they are discordant, this will attract low vibrations into your world. Discord will be felt in the mind and mental attitude and will plummet your frequencies.
- Create only constructive desires through thought (without limitation). Eliminate doubt and know you can create without limitation. Consciously expand your mental capabilities.
- Disregard all discordant outer appearances. Do not take them personally but just energy that must be managed and controlled. Keep your thoughts in harmony at all times!
- Withhold judgments and criticism against yourself or others. Accept and forgive. Do not hold on to or relive past transgressions or mistakes by yourself or others. MOVE ON.
- Release all mental baggage that does not serve you, all guilt, regret, and all mental anguish. NOW
- Be mentally strong! The stronger your mental capacity the stronger your power to create.
- Disregard all discordant outer appearances for they are not a threat, but just energy that must be managed and redirected, and keep your thoughts in harmony at all times!

251

EMOTIONAL
STAY EMOTIONALLY STRONG

- Always respond with controlled emotions because emotions trigger feelings.
- Images create feelings. Always keep positive and uplifting images in your mind.
- Guard your emotions for they give create intense feelings, often unwarranted.
- Always maintain a positive emotional attitude. Exemplify emotional maturity.
- Use your emotions as a barometer for what you are thinking. If you don't like what you are feeling, change your thinking.
- Release all feelings of anger, fear, depression, guilt or regret and all emotions that do not bring you peace. NOW.
- Release all your discordant emotional attachments and baggage that does not serve you. NOW.
- Always hold the highest emotional vibrations in your heart. Come from a place of love, compassion and kindness.
- Question, Challenge and Govern your emotions at all times. Do not create emotional drama in your life! So much of what happens to you depends on you and how you feel about it. You act from your feelings. Stop! Look within and know every emotion creates decisions followed by action. Is this really what you want? Don't create your own misery.

PHYSICAL/SENSORY
BE BODY CONSCIOUS

Your body is a sensory system. Listen to it and look for the signals its sends! Take care of it!

- Eat a balanced diet. Buy organic or local vegetables.

- Do not eat mass produced farm meats! Buy only from repu-
table farms!
- Do not wear animal fur of any kind. Discordant energy is invis-
ible and easily transmitted.
- Always look your best! You will feel better!
- Learn to use your body to consciously experience the world,
and let your body teach you!
- Take your health and physical appearance seriously. You are
radiant! Shine!
- Be vigilant with your body! Get physical check-ups!
- Accept your body, cherish it and find beauty in it.
- Be aware of your breathing. Learn how to breathe properly.
- Consciously Use Your Senses! SEE, HEAR, TOUCH, TASTE,
SMELL.

SPIRITUAL
YOU ARE AN ETERNAL SPIRIT IN BODY

- BELIEVE IN THE SOURCE. BELIEVE IN YOURSELF. YOU
AND THE SOURCE ARE ONE
- MEDITATE. Get in the practice of meditation.
- Control all outer activity through inner wisdom and your higher
self.
- Work with your inner spiritual energy of the 'I AM' (God) pres-
ence in you.
- Use the Violet Flame every day to eliminate any discord in
your life or to create a constructive desire.
- Keep the link to the Source Consciousness clean at all times!
Be in constant connection with the Source Consciousness.
Talk to the Source, your spirit, your I AM presence and the
Violet energy.
- View life from a broader perspective, you are to create without
limit all constructive desires as God because you are using the

same powers of God/Source, and you are of the same energy. There is no separation.

- The closer you become to the Source, the higher you are vibrating.
- The closer you become to the Source, the greater the power that is available for your use.
- Life is about expansion of the soul. Always remember not to dwell on past mistakes or failures. No current thought can ever change one minute of the past. Forgive, accept, and move on. It is all about expansion. The failure expanded you in a positive way for if you have guilt or regret you have spiritually grown. Thank the people, situations, or what you call bad decisions or transgressions on your part, for the have made a better, loving, kind, and compassionate person. RELEASE IT ALL AND SURRENDER IT TO GOD. THE SOURCE KNOWS YOUR HEART. FOR IT IS YOU. YOU ARE FREE FOREVER FREE IF YOU ALLOW YOURSELF TO BE.

USING THE VIOLET FLAME In-Brief (S2)

Use the Violet Flame Decrees Often and DE-STRESS!

To cleanse your spiritual energy, it is recommended that you invoke the Violet Flame through your 'I AM' presence at least once a day. Twice would be ideal, especially in the morning before you begin your day to clear any discordant energy that may have attached itself to you, and at night to eliminate any discordant vibrations that you may have inadvertently picked up during the day, which can lower your vibrational frequencies.

CLEARING BEFORE DECREES

Close your eyes, and clearing your mind focus only on your breathing. Breathe in for 10 counts, hold for 10 counts, and release for 10 counts (or whatever is comfortable for you). Do this at least 3 times. When centered and balanced, feel the connection with your 'I AM' presence and visualize the Violet Flame's glorious radiance bathe you in ITS violet healing energies. See and feel all your discordant energy, all your problems, worries, anxieties and the like, melt away inside the brilliant flames leaving only a warm loving glow. Feel the Violet Flames heal your mental, emotional, sensory/physical and spiritual energy fields until you are completely cleansed, rejuvenated and free from all baggage. Take your time and let the Violet Flame restore you to higher energies by removing all that does not serve you. Feeling safe within the Violet Energy, begin the below decree or create one of your own.

DECREES (USE BELOW OR CREATE YOUR OWN) – Decrees can be in your mind as thoughtforms or voiced verbally. For greater strength verbally is recommended, as the power is doubled. You are using thoughtforms and sound.

Through my mighty 'I AM' presence, I invoke the Violet Flame to shatter, dissipate and consume all wrong creations and discordant energies from all my energy fields so that I may vibrate at my highest frequencies, thus bring all that I need to me quickly and easily,(or to free me from all discords). And so it is decreed. AND SO IT IS. With gratitude I thank the I AM presence within me, the Violet energy, the Source Consciousness and all who have provided me assistance in this endeavor, and send blessings and love. I am now free, forever free from this discordant energy, and ready to bring forth to me exactly what I desire (name the discord, and/or desire).

CONCLUSION

FOR CREATION: Using the Violet Energy and the Law of Attraction and Vibration, see and feel the desire in all its glory appear in your life. See and feel every aspect of it. How it looks. How much Its help means to you. How wonderful you feel having it. How you are using desire, and how much joy it brings you. Visualize every detail.

FOR REMOVING DISCORD: See and feel all discordant energy loosen from you and melt away within the Violet Flame, leaving only various shades of violet energy sparkling brilliantly. You are cleansed mentally, emotionally, physically and spiritually, feeling lighter, balanced and centered. You are at union with the Source Consciousness and feel completely sustained in that high vibration. This is one of the best times to begin creating, spending time in contemplation, and sending your intent to the world. Conclude with breathing exercises. Breathe in for 10 counts, hold for 10 counts and release for 10 counts (or whatever is comfortable for you). BELIEVE IN ITS POWER. Belief is vital for it is the activator of energy.

Meditations for General Abundance Decrees (S3)

Meditative background music is recommended, and should be used with meditation as it rests and relaxes the mind. Short breathing activity is recommended prior to starting any meditation to fully connect your energy to the Source Consciousness. Breathe in for 10 counts, hold for 10 counts, and release for 10 counts. (You may adjust the counts to your comfort). Breathing will balance and center you so that you may quickly connect to your 'I AM' presence so that you may invoke the Violet Flame.

1. Volet Flame meditation should be practiced in the light. You may use a candle but avoid dark rooms.
2. Be fully aware that you are a part of the Source Consciousness and it is your birthright to create the world in which you exist in. There should be no doubt in your mind relative to your power to create.
3. STILL THE OUTER MIND. Should it wander, bring it back, each time reconnecting it to your **'I AM'** presence by visualizing a bright light emanating from your heart center and connect to this energy with your thoughts, images in your mind and feelings until you and the energy are one. If you have trouble focusing begin releasing all thoughts as they arise in the stop frame of the moment, and surrender them to the Source/God. With your continued diligence as thoughts arise the mind will begin to surrender itself as your meditation unfolds. Do not identify yourself as the observed only of that which you are observing. Let go of all problems, guilt, regret, fears, unwanted attachments, and anxiety. Clear your mind remember the energy behind thought is formless, and begins itself as a thought. When you release the energy in the stop frame of every moment, you release the thought clearing your mind, and you will begin to feel the peace that is a prerequisite for fruitful meditation.
4. As you connect to your "**I AM**" presence, speak to it mentally, or verbally, whichever feels more comfortable to you

and through the energy of the 'I AM' invoke the **Violet Flame.**

5. Invoke the Violet Flame verbally or mentally commanding Its presence and visualize IT appearing before you in all its brilliant violet glory

6. Contemplate and place the image of all you need, a specific desire, or see yourself extremely happy, healthy, loved and surrounded by all your heart's desires into the dazzling Violet Flames and begin the decrees that will set the energy in motion to send out the intent and manifest the desire in your physical world. You have full confidence. NO DOUBT SHALL ENTER YOUR MIND.

7. Begin Decrees. (Use the below decree examples or create your own.)

- *"I, as my mighty 'I AM' presence invoke the power of the Violet Flame to see to it that I am extremely happy, healthy, loved and surrounded by all that I desire. See to it that I live in great abundance and prosperity and that all my needs are met quickly and easily for the highest good of myself and all concerned. And so, it is decreed." Namaste.*

- *"I, as my mighty 'I AM' presence invoke the power of the Violet Flame to see to it that I am attracting tremendous abundance and prosperity into my life and that everything I need will always appear on time for the highest good of myself and all concerned! And so, it is decreed." Namaste.*

- *"I as my mighty 'I AM' presence invoke the power of the Violet Flame to see to it that I am attracting (specifically NAME the desire ex. large sums of money, the perfect opportunity, the perfect career, the perfect relationships) easily and effortlessly every day and in every way for the highest good of myself and all concerned! And so, it is decreed."*

- *"I as my mighty 'I AM' presence invoke the power of the Violet Flame to see to it that I am always healthy and feeling good, that I do not suffer ailments of the mind, fractured emotions of the heart or dis-ease in the body for the highest good of myself and all concerned! And so, it is decreed."*

8. Do not rush the meditation. Take your time. Use your thoughts, images in the mind and feelings to boost your decrees and feel the energy you wish manifested. TRUST – DO NOT DOUBT THE PROCESS.

9. Support it with a spiritual/inner belief, a 'knowing' that it will manifest without setting any specific time for results. Thank your 'I AM' presence, which is your connection to the Source and Its power, the Violet Flame and the Source Consciousness, (and all other energies that you may not even be aware of that have come to your aid), for all their assistance to bring your desires into your physical world in their perfect time. End with the word "NAMASTE"

10. To align with your desire, and assist the Violet Energies to quickly achieve desired results follow through with your every physical action, behavior, word and deed, to manifest your desire in your physical reality. By taking every opportunity to bring that which you desire into your reality you are helping the manifestation to appear in your life on a faster track. Physical action is required whenever working with thoughts, images and feelings for manifestation.

Specific Manifestation Meditation (S4)

Meditative background music is recommended, and should be used with meditation as it rests and relaxes the mind. Short breathing activity is recommended prior to starting any meditation to fully connect your energy to the Source Consciousness. Breathe in for 10 counts, hold for 10 counts, and release for 10 counts. (Breathing counts may be adjusted for comfort). Breathing will balance and center you so that you may quickly connect to your 'I AM' presence so that you may invoke the Violet Flame.

1. Violet Flame Meditation should be practiced in the light. You many use a candle but avoid dark rooms.
2. Be fully aware that you are a part of the Source Consciousness and it is your birthright to create the world in which you exist in.
3. Take a quick assessment of your overall vibration. Are your thoughts, images in the mind, and feelings vibrating in harmony or is there discord? If they are in harmony, you are ready to meditate from your highest frequency. If there is discord you must balance your mental, emotional, physical and spiritual consciousness by replacing any anxiety, fear or doubt with thoughts and feelings of complete trust that you are connected with the Source because you are a part of the Source/God and your desires will manifest. Use your emotions and feel this connection.
4. STILL THE OUTER MIND. Should it wander, bring it back immediately and reconnect it to your 'I AM' presence by visualizing a bright light emanating from your heart center, and connect to this energy with your thoughts, images in the mind and feelings of your power until you and the energy are one.
5. As you connect to your 'I AM' presence, speak to it mentally, or verbally, whichever feels more comfortable to you and through this energy invoke the Violet Flame.

6. Invoke the Violet Flame verbally or mentally by commanding Its presence and visualize It appearing before you glowing brightly in various shades of brilliant violet colors.

7. Concentrate and visualize your desire. See it exactly the way you wish it. Use all your senses of sight, hearing, smell, taste and touch to conjure up its energies. Feel its energy and how it will feel to have it manifested. Live in this moment, and feel gratitude as if your desire is already here. Think about every aspect of it but do not place any *permanent* expectation for the time of results, as your desire will appear at its perfect time, place and space, and when it does it will be worth the wait.

8. Continue to lovingly hold the complete vision of your desired manifestation within the Violet Flame and contemplate by attentively visualizing your desire. Take your time! See your desire manifest and play out in your life in many different scenarios and forms. Contemplate and go deeper into your meditation. Do you see yourself happy with the results? Is this really what you needed? If not make modifications. If yes, do not let any doubt creep in but keep the intent strong, and release the image of your desire to the Violet Flames. When you do, the energy has been activated to be moved from the fields of consciousness into form and into your physical reality.

9. Decree with determined attention: *"**Through my 'I AM' presence and the power of the Violet Flame I command that my desire (name the desire, see it and feel it), manifest for me in its perfect time, place and space for the highest good of myself and all concerned. And so, it is decreed. I thank all the energies for the assistance and send blessings and love." Namaste.**

10. Imprint the same image of the desire that you released to the Violet Flame for manifestation in your consciousness. DO NOT LET THE PICTURE FADE! This will propel the energy forward to full manifestation in your physical life.

11. Thank the I AM presence, and the Violet Flame, the Source Consciousness and all other spiritual energy that you may not have been aware of, for blessing you with assistance and remain in the state of gratitude knowing that your desire will manifest. Gratitude is an important key in manifestation when working with higher energies. The I AM and the Violet Flame are the active Presence of the Source Consciousness, and helping you create your reality through the use of Its power. End with the word, NAMASTE

12. Meditate on your desire often, act and behave in your physical world in every way that attracts it to you. This means follow through with every physical action, behavior and deed to assist it to materialize it for you with greater speed.

Meditation for General Elimination of Discordant Energy (S5)

Meditative background music is recommended, and should be used with meditation as it rests and relaxes the mind. Short breathing activity is recommended prior to starting any meditation to fully connect your energy to the Source Consciousness. Breathe in for 10 counts, hold for 10 counts, and release for 10 counts. (Breathing counts may be adjusted for comfort). Breathing will balance and center you so that you may quickly connect to your 'I AM' presence so that you may invoke the Violet Flame.

1. Violet Flame Meditation should be practiced in the light. You many use a candle but avoid dark rooms.
2. Be fully aware that you are a part of the Source Consciousness and it is your birthright to create the world in which you exist in.
3. Take a quick assessment of your overall vibration. Are your thoughts, images in the mind, and feelings vibrating in harmony or is there discord? If they are in harmony, you are ready to meditate from your highest frequency. If there is discord you must balance your mental, emotional, physical and spiritual consciousness by replacing any anxiety, fear or doubt with thoughts and feelings of complete trust.
4. STILL THE OUTER MIND. Should it wander, bring it back immediately and reconnect it to your 'I AM' presence by visualizing a bright light emanating from your heart center, and connect to this energy with your thoughts, images in the mind and feelings of your power until you and the energy are one.
5. As you connect to your 'I AM' presence, speak to it mentally, or verbally, whichever feels more comfortable to you, and through this energy invoke the Violet Flame.
6. Invoke the Violet Flame verbally or mentally by commanding Its presence and visualize It appearing before you glowing brightly in various shades of brilliant violet energy.

7. Concentrate and visualize and feel all your discords (financial problems, debt etc.) and prepare to release them from your life forever.

8. Decree with determined attention: "***Through my 'I AM' presence I invoke the Violet Flame to shatter, dissipate and consume all wrong creations in my life (outside of karmic laws) so that I am free of all discords for the highest good of myself and all concerned. I thank them for what they have taught me, and the growth I achieved from this low energy, but now I release them into the Violet Flame for total elimination. Violet Flame see to it that they never touch my life or world again! And so, it is decreed. I thank all the energies and send blessings and love in gratefulness for their assistance." Namaste.***

9. See the discords disappear into to the Violet Flame, each one melting away until there is nothing left. Believe and know that it is gone from your energy forever and that its discordant energy will resolve itself to the highest good of yourself and it will never return to cause you strife in the manner that it did again.

10. Thank the I AM presence, and the Violet Flame for blessing you with their assistance and remain in the state of gratitude knowing that you are now forever free from its discordant clutches. Gratitude is an important key in working with the higher power and energies. NAMASTE

11. Act and behave in your physical world in a lighter way knowing that your life is swiftly changing for the better as the energy realigns. Follow through with every physical action, opportunity, behavior and deed to assist the energy as they work to clear your fields from discord.

Meditation for Elimination of Specific Discordant Energy (S6)

Meditative background music is recommended, and should be used with meditation as it rests and relaxes the mind. Short breathing activity is recommended prior to starting any meditation to fully connect your energy to the Source Consciousness. Breathe in for 10 counts, hold for 10 counts, and release for 10 counts (or whatever is comfortable for you). Breathing will balance and center you so that you may quickly connect to your 'I AM' presence so that you may invoke the Violet Flame.

1. Meditation with the Violet Flame should be practiced in the light. Avoid dark rooms.
2. Be fully aware that you are a part of the Source Consciousness and it is your birthright to create the world in which you exist in.
3. Take a quick assessment of your overall vibration. Are your thoughts and feelings vibrating in harmony or is there discord? If they are in harmony, you are ready to meditate from your highest frequency. If there is discord you must balance your thoughts and feelings by replacing any anxiety or doubt with complete trust.
4. STILL THE OUTER MIND. Should it wander, bring it back immediately and reconnect it to your 'I AM' presence by visualizing a bright light emanating from your heart center, and connect to this energy with your thoughts and feelings until you and the energy are one.
5. As you connect to your 'I AM' presence speak to it mentally, or verbally, however it feels more comfortable to you and through this energy invoke the Violet Flame to assist you.
6. Invoke the Violet Flame verbally or mentally by commanding Its presence and visualize It appearing before you in various brilliantly colored violet shades glowing brightly. Its healing energies are waiting to be commanded.

7. Mentally place the discord (problem, situation, person etc.) in the Violet Flames and visualize the flames dissolving the specific discord that is causing your stress.

8. Begin a short but powerful Decree. *"Through the power of my 'I AM' presence I invoke the Violet Flame to shatter, dissipate and consume this wrong creation (name the discord) outside of karmic laws, and eliminate it from my life forever, and see to it that it never touches my life and world again, for the highest good of myself and all concerned. And so it is decreed."*

9. Use your emotions to boost your decrees and watch as the discord completely melts away leaving only brilliantly glowing violet energy in its wake.

10. Support it with a spiritual/inner belief, a 'knowing' that the discord that caused you unhappiness in your life is now eliminated, without creating further negative karma.

11. Always thank your faithful 'I AM' presence, the Violet Flame, and the Source Consciousness from Whom your power flows, and all energies who are helping that you may not be conscious of. Show gratitude to the lessons that the discord has taught you for energy is never wasted while you release it back to the Source Consciousness, freeing you completely from its low vibrations and agonizing clutch. End with NAMASTE.

12. Breathe in for 10 counts, hold for 10 counts, and release for 10 counts.

General Healing Meditation (S7)

Meditative background music is recommended, and should be used with meditation as it rests and relaxes the mind. Short breathing activity is recommended prior to starting any meditation to fully connect your energy to the Source Consciousness. Breathe in for 10 counts, hold for 10 counts, and release for 10 counts (or whatever is comfortable for you). Breathing will balance and center you so that you may quickly connect to your 'I AM' presence so that you may invoke the Violet Flame.

1. Meditation with the Violet Flame should be practiced in the light, not in dark rooms.
2. Be fully aware that you are a part of the Source Consciousness and it is your birthright to create the world in which you exist in.
3. Take a quick assessment of your overall vibration. Are your thoughts, and feelings vibrating in harmony or is there discord? If they are in harmony, you are ready to meditate from your highest frequency. If there is discord you must balance your thoughts and feelings by replacing any anxiety or doubt with thoughts and feelings of complete trust.
4. STILL THE OUTER MIND. Should it wander, bring it back immediately and reconnect it to your 'I AM' presence by visualizing a bright light emanating from your heart center, and connect to this energy with your thoughts and feelings until you and the energy are one.
5. Close your eyes and through your 'I AM" invoke the Violet Flame and see it mentally materialize before you. Mentally enter the Violet Flame and let the violet energies wash over your, caress, shower and heal you. Take your time, really feel the energy flowing through you, within you and all around you, as the violet energy cleans and heals you completely and everything It touches. Take your time. Bathe in Its loving energy and let It move through you in perfect peace, and

joy, while it heals any and all discords in all of your mental, emotional, physical/sensory and spiritual energy fields. Feel the unconditional love and peace as the energy becomes one with you.

6. Support all mental images with your emotions, and feel the healing energy while you decree: **"Through the power of my 'I AM' presence I invoke the Violet Flame to shatter, dissipate and consume all wrong creation of any discordant energy and see to it that it is eliminated and never enters my world again. I decree that I AM in perfect health, and healed from all discordant energies that may be present in my (mental, emotional, sensory/physical and spiritual energy fields) SELECT a field of ailment. And so it is decreed." Namaste.**

7. Use your emotions to boost your decrees and feel health, energy and peace returning to your mental, emotional, and physical health.

8. Support it with a spiritual/inner belief, a 'knowing' that the discords that caused you unhappiness in your life are now eliminated and you are on the road to healing. Repeat this decree often for rejuvenation.

9. Always thank your faithful 'I AM' presence, the Violet Flame, and the Source Consciousness, and all other energies that you may not be aware of, at the end of each healing meditation. NAMASTE

10. Breathe in for 10 counts, hold for 10 counts, and release for 10 counts. (You may adjust the counts to your comfort).

Specific Healing Meditation (S8)

Meditative background music is recommended, and should be used with meditation as it rests and relaxes the mind. Short breathing activity is recommended prior to starting any meditation to fully connect your energy to the Source Consciousness. Breathe in for 10 counts, hold for 10 counts, and release for 10 counts. (You may adjust the counts to your comfort). Breathing will balance and center you so that you may quickly connect to your 'I AM' presence so that you may invoke the Violet Flame.

- Meditation with the Violet Flame should be practiced in the light. Avoid dark rooms.
- Be fully aware that you are a part of the Source Consciousness and it is your birthright to create the world in which you exist in.
- Take a quick assessment of your overall vibration. Are your thoughts, and feelings vibrating in harmony or is there discord? If they are in harmony, you are ready to meditate from your highest frequency. If there is discord you must balance your thoughts and feelings by replacing any anxiety or doubt with thoughts and feelings of complete trust.
- STILL THE OUTER MIND. Should it wander, bring it back immediately and reconnect it to your 'I AM' presence by visualizing a bright light emanating from your heart, and connect to this energy with your thoughts and feelings until you and the energy are one.
- Close your eyes and through your 'I AM" invoke the Violet Flame and see it mentally materialize before you. Mentally enter the Violet Flame and let the violet energies wash over your, caress and heal you, as you ask the Violet Flame to heal your particular discord. Take your time, really feel the energy flowing through you, within you and all around you, as the violet energy cleans and heals everything It touches. Bathe in

Its loving energy and when comfortable direct the violet flame to the area of the body that needs healing with laser focus. Visualize the violet fire annihilating the ailment, and see the affliction and all the pain associated with it dissolve in the violet blaze. Feel free of its grasp. Visualize your body healthy and you feeling vibrantly alive. (Discord can be any health condition, or any issue that is causing stress, such as a relationship that needs healing, guilt, regret etc.)

- If it is a physical ailment, envision the part that needs healing and focus like a laser beam on it and send violet beams to that area (repeat often). Envision the area as you work to eliminate the ailment, and watch as the area returns to perfect health.

- If it is a mental anguish or emotional ailment like a broken, or spiritual (dark night of the soul) envision the area and focus like a laser beam on it and send brilliant violet beams to that area interchanged with pink healing energy (repeat often). Take your time and really focus the energy.

- Support all mental images of healing with your emotions, and feel the healing energy while you confidently decree: *"Through the power of my 'I AM' presence, I invoke the Violet Flame, to shatter, dissipate and consume this wrong condition of my ailment (discord). Violet Flame I call upon you to see to it that I am healed and that this discord (name the discord) never touches my world again. I decree that I am healed from (name the discord) now and forever for the highest good of myself and all concerned. I am released and in perfect health, and peace. And so it is decreed."*

- Use your emotions to boost your decrees and feel health, energy and peace returning to you.

- Support it with a spiritual/inner belief, a 'knowing' that the ailment that caused you unhappiness in your life is now eliminated forever.

- Always thank your faithful 'I AM' presence, the Violet Flame, and the Source Consciousness, and all other energies you may not be aware of, for their assistance. NAMASTE
- Breathe in for 10 counts, hold for 10 counts, and release for 10 counts. (You may adjust the counts to your comfort).

Dissolving General Karma Meditation (S9)

Let me assure you there is a way to correct all that you have done. There is a way to release guilt, regret, failures and any all-past transgressions. You can correct all past mistakes and transmute them back into higher frequencies and raise them to the highest frequencies in all situations. With the Violet Flame you will not need to worry about "how" the energy is being corrected and lifted to higher frequencies where solutions to every problem are available, you just need to have faith and know that it is being corrected. Your job is to activate the Violet Flame through your use of your own "I AM Consciousness" so that the energy can be directed and flow freely to achieve all your constructive desires, including releasing all karma through the Law of Forgiveness outside of the karmic cycles.

Meditative background music is recommended. As you consciously remove any discordant thoughts, images and feelings from all your energy fields and begin to release all stress and tension. Breathe in for 10 counts, hold for 10 counts, and release for 10 counts (you may adjust the counts to your comfort). Breathing will balance and center you so that you may quickly connect to your 'I AM' presence.

- o Meditation with **the Violet Flame** should be practiced in the light or dim light. Avoid dark rooms.
- o Be fully aware that you are a part of the Source Consciousness and it is your birthright to create the world in which you exist in and free yourself from all baggage, and karmic laws.
- o Take a quick assessment of your overall vibration. Are your thoughts and feelings vibrating in harmony, or is there discord? If they are in harmony, you are ready to meditate from your highest frequency. If there is discord you must balance your thoughts and feelings by replacing any anxiety or doubt

with thoughts and feelings of complete trust that through the Violet Flame and invoking the Law of Forgiveness you will be released from all discordant karmic energies.

o STILL THE OUTER MIND. Should it wander, bring it back immediately and reconnect it to your 'I AM' presence by visualizing a bright light emanating from your heart, and connect to this energy with your thoughts and feelings until you and the energy are one.

o As you connect to your 'I AM' presence, speak to it mentally, or verbally, however it feels more comfortable to you, and through this energy invoke the Violet Flame to assist you.

o Invoke the Violet Flame verbally or mentally by commanding Its presence and see It appear before you glowing brightly in various shades of violet, as it awaits your command.

o Command the Violet Flame to activate the Law of Forgiveness, and eliminate all karmic debt with everyone and everything that needs this balance of energies with you, and ask It to transmute that energy for 'good,' for the highest good of yourself, and all concerned, by decreeing:

"Violet Flame shatter, dissipate and consume all wrong creations in my life, clear and release me from all my karmic debts, and see to it that only 'good' comes of them for the highest good of myself, and all concerned. Call upon the Law of Forgiveness to free me from all karmic debts that I may have intentionally or unintentionally created. Do so without delay and grant me a new beginning free of all karmic debt, attachments and debris. I forgive myself and others, and I am eternally grateful that I have been forgiven, and can now walk free, forever free, from all records of my misdeeds. And so it is decreed." **Namaste.**

o Support it with a spiritual/inner belief, a 'knowing' that you are now free of all karmic debt.

o   Always thank your faithful 'I AM' presence, the Violet Flame, and the Source Consciousness from whom your power flows. End with breathing exercises. Breathe in for 10, hold for 10 and release for 10 counts (or whatever is comfortable for you). NAMASTE.

Dissolving Specific Karma Meditation (S10)

Meditative background music is recommended. As you consciously remove any discordant thoughts, images and feelings from all your energy fields and begin to release all stress and tension, breathe in for 10 counts, hold for 10 counts, and release for 10 counts (you may adjust the counts to your comfort). Breathing will balance and center you so that you may quickly connect to your 'I AM' presence.

o Meditation with the Violet Flame should be practiced in the light. Avoid dark rooms.

o Be fully aware that you are a part of the Source Consciousness and it is your birthright to create the world in which you exist in.

o Take a quick assessment of your overall vibration. Are your thoughts and feelings vibrating in harmony, or is there discord? If they are in harmony, you are ready to meditate from your highest frequency. If there is discord you must balance your thoughts and feelings by replacing any anxiety or doubt with thoughts and feelings of complete trust.

o STILL THE OUTER MIND. Should it wander, bring it back immediately and reconnect it to your 'I AM' presence by visualizing a bright light emanating from your heart, and connect to this energy with your thoughts and feelings until you and the energy are one.

o As you connect to your 'I AM' presence, speak to it mentally, or verbally, however it feels more comfortable to you, and through this energy invoke the Violet Flame to assist you.

o Invoke the Violet Flame by commanding Its presence and see It appear before you glowing brightly in various shades of violet, as it awaits your command.

o Command the Violet Flame to eliminate the specific karmic debt that you think you need to be released from, whether the debt was caused intentionally or unintentionally, and ask the

Violet Flame to transmute that energy for 'good' for the highest good of yourself, and all concerned, by decreeing:

"Violet Flame shatter, dissipate and consume this wrong creation in my life and release me from this specific (name the debt) karmic debt, and see to it that only 'good' comes of it, for the highest good of myself, and all concerned. Call upon the Law of Forgiveness to ensure that I am totally free me from this karmic debt (be specific) that I may have intentionally or unintentionally created. Do so without delay and grant me a new beginning free of this karmic debt, its attachments and debris. I forgive myself and others, and I am eternally grateful that I have been forgiven, and can now walk free, forever free, from this record of my misdeed. And so it is decreed." Namaste.

o Do not question how the energy of the Violet Flame and the Law of Forgiveness will release you, but instead place trust in your mind and emotions and believe that it is so.

o Always thank your faithful 'I AM' presence, the Violet Flame, the Law of Forgiveness, and the Source Consciousness from whom your power flows.

o End with breathing exercises, breathe in for 10 counts, hold for 10 counts and release for 10 counts (or whatever is comfortable for you).

Love/Mate Manifestation Meditation (S11)

Meditative background music is recommended. As you consciously remove any discordant thoughts, images and feelings from all your energy fields and begin to release all stress and tension, breathe in for 10 counts, hold for 10 counts, and release for 10 counts (you may adjust the counts to your comfort). Breathing will balance and center you so that you may quickly connect to your 'I AM' presence.

- Meditation with the Violet Flame should be practiced in the light. Avoid dark rooms.
- Be fully aware that you are a part of the Source Consciousness and it is your birthright to create the world in which you exist in.
- Take a quick assessment of your overall vibration. Are your thoughts and feelings vibrating in harmony, or is there discord? If they are in harmony, you are ready to meditate from your highest frequency. If there is discord you must balance your thoughts and feelings by replacing any anxiety or doubt with thoughts and feelings of complete trust that your desires will manifest and feel how wonderful it will be when the do!
- STILL THE OUTER MIND. Should it wander, bring it back immediately and reconnect it to your 'I AM' presence by visualizing a bright light emanating from your heart center, and connect to this energy with your thoughts and feelings until you and the energy are one.
- As you connect to your 'I AM' presence speak to it mentally, or verbally, however it feels more comfortable to you, and through this energy invoke the Violet Flame to assist you.
- Invoke the Violet Flame verbally or mentally by commanding Its presence and see It appear before you glowing brightly, in brilliant shades of violet, as it awaits your command.

- Close your eyes and consciously connect to your 'I AM' so that through It you can invoke the Violet Flame and visualize your desire and see it mentally materialize before you. BE SPECIFIC!
- See yourself bathing in the loving energy of the Violet Flame. Feel the energy with your every cell and let it move through you in perfect peace, and joy and INVOKE the Violet Flame.
- Concentrate and visualize whatever kind of love you wish to appear in your life. If you wish for a perfect mate, see him or her manifesting in the Violet Flame. See him or her exactly the way you wish. Every character trait, and detail should be contemplated, including physical characteristics, mental, and emotional traits, ethical or spiritual values, whatever is important to you. Use all your senses to conjure up the perfect mate. Feel his or her energy all around you. Think about what it would feel like to touch him or her, and how, when, and where would you want it to happen, but do not place any permanent expectation for the time of results, as your desire will appear in its perfect time, place and space. Forcing energies works in reverse and delays manifestations.

  Decree: "*I as my mighty 'I AM' presence and through the power of the Violet Flame decree that I am attracting love (or my perfect mate) into my life. And that person will appear in his or her own perfect time, space and place for the highest good of myself and all concerned. He or she will have all the qualities I seek (name the qualities, and visualize as you decree). And so it is decreed.*" Namaste.
- Continue to lovingly hold the complete vision within the Violet Flame, support it with feeling, and be still in the knowledge that the spirit is working on your behalf. Be completely open and receptive to all energy and do not let doubt enter your energy fields.

- Imprint the image of your desire on your consciousness and in your heart in your highest vibration. DO NOT ALLOW THE IMAGE TO FADE. Until it appears hold the imprint on your heart. (Faith is placed in the power of the Violet Energy for physical manifestations). End with words of gratitude to your 'I AM' presence, the Violet Flame, and your Source Consciousness.

DECREE SAMPLES (S12)

Various Short Powerful Decrees for Love, Relationships, Prosperity

o "I, as my mighty 'I AM' presence and through the power of my I AM invoke the Violet Flame to see to it that my desire (name the desire, visualize it in the Violet Flame, and support it with feeling) quickly and easily manifests itself for me for the highest good of myself and all concerned! And so it is decreed. I thank all the energies for their assistance and send blessings and love. Namaste."

o "I, as my mighty 'I AM' presence and through the power of the Violet Flame decree that the Violet Flame shatter, dissipate and consume this wrong creation of my debt and that I am forever free of financial stress and debt for the highest good of myself and all concerned. And so it is decreed. I thank all the energies for their assistance and send blessings and love. Namaste."

o "I, as my mighty 'I AM' presence and through the power of the Violet Flame decree that I am attracting everything and everyone that I need in my life! And that they appear exactly on time for the highest good of myself and all concerned. And so it is decreed. I thank all the energies for their assistance and send blessings and love. Namaste."

o "I, as my mighty 'I AM' presence and through the power of the Violet Flame decree that I am attracting great wealth easily and effortlessly into my life every day and in every way!" And so it is decreed. I thank all the energies for their assistance and send blessings and love. Namaste."

o "I, as my mighty 'I AM' presence and through the power of the Violet Flame decree that I am attracting healthy relationships in my life that love, empower, and support me for the highest good of myself and all concerned! And so it is decreed. I thank all the energies for their assistance and send blessings and love. Namaste."

o "I, as my mighty 'I AM' presence and through the power of the Violet Flame decree that I am attracting love, peace and joy into my life every day and in every way! And so it is decreed. I thank all the energies for their assistance and send blessings and love. Namaste."

o "I, as my mighty 'I AM' presence and through the power of the Violet Flame decree that I am attracting opportunities into my life that I take advantage of every day and in every way!" And so it is decreed. I thank all the energies for their assistance and send blessings and love. Namaste."

o "I, as my mighty 'I AM' presence and through the power of the Violet Flame decree that I am in perfect health! Nothing other than my well-being permeates my existence. And so it is decreed. I thank all the energies for their assistance and send blessings and love. Namaste."

o "I, as my mighty 'I AM' presence and through the power of the Violet Flame decree that my life is filled with abundance and prosperity always! And that discord is immediately shattered, dissipated and consumed upon first appearance and never finds a place to root in my life. And so it is decreed. I thank all the energies for their assistance and send blessings and love." Namaste.

Only Good Comes to Me Daily Meditation (S13)

Meditative background music is recommended. As you consciously remove any discordant thoughts, images and feelings from all your energy fields and begin to release all stress and tension, breathe in for 10 counts, hold for 10 counts, and release for 10 counts (you may adjust the counts to your comfort). Breathing will balance and center you so that you may quickly connect to your 'I AM' presence.

- Meditation with the Violet Flame should be practiced in the light. Avoid dark rooms.
- Be fully aware that you are a part of the Source Consciousness and it is your birthright to create the world in which you exist in.
- Take a quick assessment of your overall vibration. Are your thoughts and feelings vibrating in harmony, or is there discord? If they are in harmony, you are ready to meditate from your highest frequency. If there is discord you must balance your thoughts and feelings by replacing any anxiety or doubt with thoughts and feelings of complete trust that whatever is ailing you – you are forgiven, you are unconditionally loved, and will always be supported by the Source/God. All is well, fear not.
- STILL THE OUTER MIND. Should it wander, bring it back immediately and reconnect it to your 'I AM' presence by visualizing a bright light emanating from your heart center, and connect to this energy with your thoughts and feelings until you and the energy are one.
- As you connect to your 'I AM' presence speak to it mentally, or verbally, however it feels more comfortable to you, and through this energy invoke the Violet Flame to assist you.
- Invoke the Violet Flame verbally or mentally by commanding Its presence and see It appear before you glowing brightly, in brilliant shades of violet, as it awaits your command.

- Close your eyes and consciously connect to your 'I AM' so that through It you can invoke the Violet Flame and send your decree.

  "Through my 'I AM' presence I invoke the Violet Flame to see to it that ONLY GOOD COMES TO ME, always and forever for my highest good and the good of all concerned. And so it is decreed. Namaste."

- Thank the Violet Flame, your 'I AM' energy and the Source Consciousness for all its assistance.

- End with a small prayer of gratitude. You must be conscious that the Violet Flame is the active Presence of Source Consciousness doing the consuming, and attracting higher energies to you so that *Only Good Comes To You,* thus helping you create your reality through the use of Its power.

- Breath in for 10 counts, hold for 10 counts and release for 10 counts, (or whatever is comfortable for you).

References

Aristotle, BrainyQuote. Retrieved from https://www.brainyquote.com/quotes/aristotle_132267

Bible, Gal. 5:25. NKJV

Carroll, L. (1997). *The journey home.* Hay House Publishing

Carroll, L. (2011). *The twelve layers of DNA.* Platinum Publishing House.

Castaneda, C. Goodreads.com Quote. Retrieved from https://www.goodreads.com/work/quotes/2713696-the-power-of-intention

Cayce, E. (2010). *The power of your mind.,* Virginia Beach, VA: A. R. E. Press.

Cayce, E. E., & Cayce, H. L. (2004). *The outer limits of Edgar Cayce's power.* New York, NY: ARE Press. (1971

Chopra, D. (1994). The seven spiritual laws of success: A practical guide to the fulfillment of your dreams. Amber Allen Publishing.

Dictionary.com (online).

Dyer, W. (2013). *The essential Wayne Dyer collection.* Hay House, Inc.

Dyer, W. (interview) http://www.soulisticyoga.co.uk/inspire/i-am-light-discovering-and-living-from-your-impersonal-self-with-dr-wayne-dyer

Dyer, (2015). Manifesting your souls' purpose with Dr. Wayne Dyer. http://www.gratitudeseeds.com/manifesting-your-souls-purpose-with-dr-wayne-dyer/

Dyer, W. (2014) I *can see clearly now.* Hay House.

Dyer, W. (2009). *The shift movie.* Hay House.

Dyer, W. QuoteFancy. Retrieved from

https://www.google.com/search?q=dyer+quotes+you+attract+what+you+are&tbm=isch&source=iu&ictx=1&fir=qUBAHXcdWHvHOM%

253A%252C92sxBUI6nkkbHM%252C_&vet=1&usg=AI4_-kTiprz
mjOz5v_UGVdEMIWuVG9ro1Q&sa=X&ved=2ahUKEwjqxq_-xsv
jAhWuuVkKHSvcDjsQ9QEwAHoECAkQBg#imgrc=qUBAHXcd
WHvHOM:&vet=1

Einstein, A. (1906). Quantum Theory.

Ellen, V. (2005). *Sacred heart yoga: Activation of the sacred seals.* Flagstaff, AZ: Light Technology Publishing.

Franck, F. The meaning of life is to see. Retrieved from https://the-awakenedeye.com/pages/seeingdrawing-as-meditation/

Gawain, S. (1978). *Creative visualization.* New World Library.

Gawain, S. BrainyQuote Retrieved from https://www.brainyquote.com/quotes/shakti_gawain_390054

Hawkins, D. (2002). *Force vs power.* Hay House, Inc.

Hay, L. Quotes. https://medium.com/the-mission/11-louise-hay-quotes-that-could-change-your-life-in-an-instant-c454262f6a6d

Hay, L. (2012). You can heal your life. Retrieved from https://www.youtube.com/results?search_query=you+can+heal+your+life+movie

Hay, L. Interview (2008).

Hay, L. Brainyquote. Goodreads.com https://www.goodreads.com/quotes/479579-no-person-place-or-thing-has-any-power-over-me

Hay, L. (2007). *You can heal your life: The Movie.* Hay House.

Hay, L. (1995). *Life! Reflections on your journey.* Hay House.

Hay, L. (1994). *101 Power thoughts.* Hay House.

Hay, L. (1984). *You can heal your life.* Hay House.

Hay, L. The nourished me. Retrieved from https://thenourishedme-blog.com/archive/2019/5/8/f6d6iw4s4qp6dcr6u34nqc0asbr9gt https://thenourishedmeblog.com/archive/2019/5/8/f6d6iw4s4qp6dcr6u34nqc0asbr9gt

Heb. 11:1 Bible. St James

Huxley, A. AZquotes.com. Retrieved from https://www.azquotes.com/quote/798018

Huxley, A. Goodreads.com retrieved from https://www.goodreads.com/quotes/8015118-for-until-this-morning-i-had-known-contemplation-only-in

King, G. R. (2012). *The ascended master instruction.* St. Germain Press, Inc.

King, G. R. (2011). *The I AM discourses.* St. Germain Press, Inc.

King, G. R. (2007). *Unveiled mysteries.* BiblioBazar

King, G. R. (1993). *The magic presence.* St Germain Press, Inc.

Mark 11:24. Bible. St. James.

Matthew 17:20. Bible. St James.

McNight, R. (2013). *Cosmic journeys: My out of body explorations with Robert A. Monroe.* Panta Rei – Crossroads Press.

McNight, R. (2005). *Soul journeys.* Hampton Roads.

Nabi, 2003. Exploring the Framing Effects of Emotion: Do Discrete Emotions Differentially Influence Information Accessibility, Information Seeking, and Policy Preference? *Communication Research 30*(2), 224–247.

Newton, M. (2000). *Journey of souls.* St. Paul, MN: Llewellyn Publications.

Newton, M. (2003). *Destiny of souls.* St. Paul, MN: Llewellyn Publications.

Newton, M. (2009). *Memories of the afterlife.* St. Paul, MN: Llewellyn Publications.

Newton, M. (2014). Interview. http://psychicfocus.blogspot.com/2014/11/q-xxxxii-michael-newtons-research-edgar.html)

Olsen, B. (2018). *Modern esoteric: Beyond our senses.* Consortium of Collective Consciousness Publishing.

Planck, M. (1959). *The new science.* Meridian Books.

Planck, M. Max Planck Wikiquote (1931, January, 25).

Proctor, B. The Law of Vibration. Retrieved from https://www.awakenthegreatnesswithin.com/the-law-of-vibration-from-bob-proctor/

Prophet, E. C. (1999). *St. Germain's prophecy for the new millennium.* Corwin Springs, MT:
Summit University Press.

Prophet, E. C. (1997). *Violet flame: To heal the body, mind & soul.* Corwin Springs, MT: Summit University Press.

Prophet, E.C. (1993). *Saint Germain on alchemy.* Corwin Springs, MT: Summit University Press.

Rumi, M. Quotes. Retrieved from https://www.energyyog a.com/quotes/rumi-quotes

Schrodinger, (1931). As quoted in *The Observer* (11 January 1931); also in *Psychic Research* (1931), Vol. 25, p. 91

Sheldrake, R. (2010-2011). The Law of Attraction: Does it grant us an evolutionary edge?

Retrieved from https://www.huffpost.com/entry/the-law-of-attraction-doe_b_783718

Spalding, B. T. (1964). *Life and teaching of the masters of the far east.* Marina del Rey, CA: DeVorss & Co.

Stein, B. Retrieved from Brainyquote. https://www.brainyquote.com/quotes/ben_stein_383479

Stubbs, T. (1999). *Ascension handbook.* World Tree Press.

Tanio, B. (1992). Vibrational frequency list. Retrieved from http://just-alist.blogspot.com/2008/03/vibrational-frequency-list.html

Tesla, N. Goodreads.com quote retrieved from https://www.goodreads.com/quotes/361785-if-
you-want-to-find-the-secrets-of-the-universe

Thoreau, H. D. BrainyQuote. Retrieved from https://www.brainyquote.com/quotes/henry_david_thoreau_163655

Thoreau, H.D. In Dyer. https://www.drwaynedyer.com/blog/manifesting-101-mastering-the-art-of-getting-what-you-want/

Tolstoy, L. BrainyQuote Retrieved from https://www.brainyquote.com/quotes/leo_tolstoy_105644

Troward, T. (2007). *The creative process in the individual.* New York, NY: Cosimo Books.

Voice of the I AM (1936, May, 16-17).

Voice of the I AM, (1936, May, 22-24).

Voice of the I AM, (2004, Nov. p. 41)

Wattles, (1910). *The Science of getting rich.* Firestone Books.

White, S. E. (1965). *The Betty book.* New York, NY: E. P. Dutton.

Zukav, G, & Francis, L. (2002). *The heart of the soul.* Fireside Books.